The State in Action:
Public Policy and Politics

CW00569727

1990

THE STATE IN ACTION: PUBLIC POLICY AND POLITICS

James Simmie and Roger King

Pinter Publishers, London and New York

© James Simmie and Roger King 1990

First published in Great Britain in 1990 by
Pinter Publishers Limited
25 Floral Street, London WC2E 9DS

British Library Cataloguing in Publication Data

A CIP catalogue record for this book is available from the British Library
ISBN 0 86187 748 9 (hardback)
ISBN 0 86187 749 7 (paperback)

Library of Congress Cataloging-in-Publication Data
A CIP record for this book is available from the Library of Congress

Typeset by Selectmove Limited
Printed and bound in Great Britain by Biddles Ltd.

Contents

PART V CONCLUSIONS

Tables

Preface

The inspiration for *The State in Action* arose during a series of meetings held under the auspices of a joint Political Studies Association and British Sociology Association working group on public policy and politics. Discussions at these meetings turned frequently on the question of the lack of connections between abstract theories of the state and empirical descriptions of public policies. The former were regarded as often proceding without serious regard to what various elements of the state actually did in practice. The latter frequently produced a great deal of information with little attention to theoretical understanding.

The State in Action attempts to bridge this gap in three ways. First, it sets the understanding of state actions within a brief summary of contemporary theory. Within this context dual state theory is used as a starting point, but only that, for the development of empirical questions concerning what states actually do. Second, British state institutions are used as the main empirical focus of the book. They are not examined in theoretical and empirical isolation. Where possible their development and actions are seen in the context of comparisons with other advanced Western capitalist countries. This process helps to uncover some of the similarities and differences in state actions in particular policy areas. Third, the policy areas examined are not simply described empirically. Each chapter seeks to provide a combination of empirical information and grounded or middle-range explanations of the development of recent state actions within that policy field.

This has been an ambitious and difficult task. It would not have been so worthwhile attempting had it not been so. The editors are greatly indebted to the contributors for their patient efforts to secure the objectives of the book. What has emerged, among other results, is the huge complexity of state actions in the advanced capitalist countries considered here. This shows the weakness involved both in discussions of the state as if it were a uniform monolith; and in functionalist descriptions of its actions as necessarily being in the interests of one particular group. Indeed, much state action is shown to be somewhat inadequate in achieving its specified and/or underlying objectives.

For all this, the editors hope that this volume will contribute to bridging the gap between abstract state theory and empirical descriptions of government policies. The objective of the book can therefore be summarised as an attempt to introduce comparative discussions of state action in between the levels of abstract theory and abstracted empiricism.

James Simmie
London, September 1989

The Contributors

David Banister is Senior Lecturer in Transport Policy at University College London. Since 1980 he has published one book on mobility and deprivation in rural areas, and two resource books on rural transport and planning and a complementary volume on urban transport and planning. In addition, he has jointly edited *Transport and public policy planning* and *Transport in a free market economy*. His research interests are in policy and planning issues as they relate to transport.

Roger Duclaud-Williams is Lecturer in Politics at the University of Warwick and was Visitor Institut D'Etudes Politiques (Toulouse). His publications include *The politics of housing in Britain and France* (Heinemann Educational Books, 1978) and 'Teachers unions and educational policy in France', in M. Lawn (ed.), *The politics of teacher unionism* (Croom Helm, 1985).

Wyn Grant is Reader in Politics at the University of Warwick where he teaches economic policy, comparative industrial policy, British economic performance, public administration and US politics. He has written extensively on economic and industrial policy, government–industry relations and business interest associations. His most recent books are (edited) *The political economy of corporatism* (1985); (with Jane Sargent) *Business and politics in Britain* (1987); (edited) *Business interests, organizational development and private interest government* (1987); (with William Paterson and Colin Whitston) *Government and the chemical industry: a comparative analysis of Britain and West Germany* (1988); *Government and industry: a comparison of the US, Canada and the UK* (1989). He is currently working on a co-edited internationally comparative volume on economic organisation in the Second World War, and is planning a study of the politics of adjustment in the dairy industry in major OECD dairy producers.

Malcolm Harrison is Lecturer in Social Policy at the University of Leeds. His publications include papers, reports and monographs in the fields of housing, planning and welfare state theory. He had edited *Corporatism and the welfare state* (1984) and (jointly) *Planning control* (1987). Current research includes work on the politics of property rights in the welfare state, and a project on the black-led housing associations in northern England.

R.J. Johnston is Professor of Geography at the University of Sheffield. His main teaching activities cover the recent history and philosophy of human geography, urban geography and political geography, and he has written widely on all three – including *Geography and geographers* (1979, 1983 and 1987), *On human geography* (1986), *City and society* (1984) and *Geography and the state* (1982). His main research interests at present are in the electoral geography of Britain, on which he has published *The geography of English* *politics* (1985), *Money and votes* (1987) and *A nation dividing?* (1987).

Roger King is the Director of Humberside College of Higher Education. His main publications include *Respectable rebels: middle-class campaigns in Britain* (Hodder and Stoughton, 1979), *The middle class* (Longman, 1981), *Capital and politics* (Routledge and Kegan Paul, 1983) and *The state in modern society: new directions in political sociology* (Macmillan, 1986).

John Mohan is Lecturer in Geography at Queen Mary and Westfield College, London, where he formerly held an ESRC Postdoctoral Research Fellowship. His principal research and teaching interests are in health policy, particularly privatisation and restructuring in the British health sector, and the human geography of modern Britain. He is the co-author of *Commercial medicine in London* (Greater London Council, 1985) with B. Griffith and G. Rayner, the editor of *The political geography of contemporary Britain* (Macmillan, 1989) and the author of numerous articles and book chapters on geographical aspects of health care policy in Britain.

Michael Moran teaches in the Department of Government at the Victoria University of Manchester. His chief teaching and research interests are in British politics and comparative public policy. His most recent publications include *The politics of banking* (1986) and *Politics and society in Britain* (2nd edition, 1989). He has recently completed a comparative study of the financial services revolution, and is beginning, with a colleague, a comparative study of health care policy.

James Simmie is Senior Lecturer in Sociology and City Planning at University College London. He teaches courses on urban sociology and city planning, and post-industrial society and the future of cities. His research interests include the sociology of city planning, international comparative planning in capitalist, mixed and socialist economies and the significance of new technologies for the future of systems of post-industrial cities. He has written extensively on these subjects. His main publications include *The sociology of internal migration* (Centre for Environmental Studies, 1972), 'Physical planning and social policy' in R. Raynor, and J. Haden (eds), *Cities, communities and the young* (Routledge and Kegan Paul, 1973), *Citizens in conflict: a sociology of town planning*, (Hutchinson, 1974), *Power, Property and Corporatism; the political sociology of planning* (Macmillan, 1981), 'Corporatism and planning' in W. Grant, ed. *The Political Economy of Corporatism*, London, Macmillan, 1985) and with S. French, *Corporatism, participation and planning: the case of contemporary London* (Pergamon, 1989). He is currently working on a co-edited volume on *Pluralism and decentralisation in Yugoslavia* and an international comparative study of city regional planning in the San Francisco Bay Area, London and Ljubljana.

Robert Smith lectures on housing in the Department of Town Planning at the University of Wales College of Cardiff. As a member of Cardiff's Centre for Housing Management and Development he is currently engaged in a variety of research relating to issues of policy, finance and management in the housing field.

Part I Introduction

1 Policy and process in the modern state

Roger King

The boundaries of the state

A feature of discussion on the modern Western state is the 'boundary problem', or the issue of how state institutions and processes are to be delineated from social, economic and other political phenomena. Whatever analytical distinctions we come armed with, contemporary political life is characterised by an apparently messy co-mingling of the public, private and semi-public. Not only do some individuals move with increasing ease between public and private institutions – senior civil servants, for example – but public decisional processes frequently embrace both official (governmental) and non-official groups. The question of where the state begins and ends is further complicated by theoretical positions attributing an overarching function or purpose for the state, so that any agency contributing to that purpose is deemed part of the 'state apparatus'. Thus, for example, in some views media and educational institutions may be characterised as part of the state because they are regarded as functioning on behalf of capital, the primary purpose ascribed to the state. Yet, descriptively at least, such bodies often seem far removed from the procedures and practices of state officialdom.

The boundary problem is reinforced in those societies without a tradition of 'stateness'. The idea or concept of the state lacks precision and significance in American and British experience in comparison with that of continental Europe. In the 'stateless' English-speaking societies, the view of the composite and pluralistic character of public authority, the separation and balance of different powers and interests, contrasts strongly with that of the integrated 'public power' of continental Europe, which is often defended in highly abstract and impersonal terms. In continental Europe the consciousness of institutions is developed and closely associated with the state. It stems from the period of the centralised monarchies in the sixteenth century and the rediscovery of Roman law as a means of overcoming fragmented medieval sovereignty. Roman law conferred on the continental European state the distinction between public and private (civil) affairs. A separate domain of public law, which pertained to the impersonal abstract character of the state, emerged with its own principles to guide legislation and administration and with a distinct system of administrative courts, distinguishable from the civil law which applied to relations of private individuals. This distinctive legal basis to the identification of the state was, however, absent in England.

There, a relatively cohesive political community had already developed through its feudal institutions the idea of making law through statute, while Roman law's association with autocratic government appeared incompatible with feudalism's tradition of a limited monarchy.

None the less, the notion of the modern state is associated generally with the idea of a distinctive public realm, analytically and formally separate from the rest of society, or private affairs. Its social relationships typically entail command and obedience in which individual actions are guided by a belief in the existence of a legitimate order of authority. Identifiable persons, such as political leaders and officials, maintain that order through the exercise of authority and this order endures as long as the conception of its legitimacy is shared by those who exercise authority and by those who are subject to it. In other associations, however, relations are typically based on affinities of ideas and interests. They may be based, for example, on considerations of material advantage or be prompted by a sense of familial or professional solidarity with others. In the modern state, therefore, access to positions of public authority has become, at least formally, separated from kinship ties, property interests and inherited privileges. Decision-making at the legislative, judicial and administrative levels is subject to impersonal rules and with a degree of freedom from constellations of social interests.

It is also useful to consider the relation of state power to civil society, or political economy (Gamble, 1981, p.54). This relationship stems from the apparent separation of society and the state with the development of a new market economy, particularly the new freedoms of civil society, and the growth of the liberal constitutional state. One approach, associated with the economic individualism of Adam Smith and the British School of political economy was to seek to restrict the state to a specific role: that of enforcing the general rules that govern civil society. This by no means implies a weak state, for the state may require considerable powers to enforce such rules. But it does imply a 'restrained' role which precludes detailed interference in civil society.

The legitimacy or authority of state power that derives from such conceptions finds expression in the early 'social contract' theorists and their speculation on the limits of state power. For Hobbes the limitations were more implied than explicit: individuals had a moral obligation to obey the state's commands and laws so long as the state preserved their security. For later theorists such as Locke and Montesquieu these limits were more pronounced, for they regarded the state as only one of the associations of individuals, and one without any extensive claims over them. Constitutions, it was argued, should seek to prevent accumulations of power preferably through provision for institutional checks and balances, or by a confederation of states (Macpherson, 1966). These essentially negative concepts of government complemented the view that it was civil society that was the sphere of individual liberties and that governments should limit themselves to promoting the conditions of, particularly, economic liberty. In contrast, a continental European tradition associated with Hegel and Rousseau regarded the state as a higher moral community, an end in itself, which should actively seek to counter the harmful effects of civil society (Dyson, 1980). German Hegelianism, in its concern for the spiritual life, was especially conscious of the state as a basis of community and altruistic commitment.

Although liberal constitutionalism has become broadened to include a notion of representation that was more compatible with that of democracy, liberty – the safeguarding of the private sphere from arbitrary government – has remained paramount. In its commitment to the efficacy of rationalism and science, liberalism has inevitably recoiled from the idea that the simple majoritarian principles of democracy provided 'sound' or technically informed decisions. It finds modern expression in neo-pluralist support for professionalism in the public services. The occupational organisation of professional groups in government is seen as preventing 'irrational political interference' in service provision and protecting citizens against state tyranny. As Dunleavy (1986) notes, 'The internalised controls which professional occupations seek to develop in their trainees are seen by neo-pluralists as a possible substitute for external control of administration and services by elected representatives. Indeed, they may actually prefer professional safeguards to traditional democratic accountability.' Liberalism, therefore, has tended to welcome an element of protection for the administrative process from the instabilities, inertia and irrationalities in public policy that stem from political interventions. In Britain, too, central governments, particularly Conservative, have welcomed the development of professionalism as a counter to the alleged 'excesses' of local Labour councils and as a more general balance to the dangers of localism (Laffin, 1986).

Modes of decision-making

In the modern Western polity, interest, or pressure, groups which develop alongside or within formal institutions have been seen to play an increasingly crucial representative role in democratic systems. The pluralist view of the pressure group world and its benign and open influence on democratic processes was a central component of the 'sociology of democracy' in the 1950s and 1960s. Pluralism's major exponents, such as Dahl and Polsby, regarded power as widely distributed between groups, with no particular group necessarily dominant and no group without at least potential political influence. Any group of individuals can organise and ensure that its preferences are taken into account by decision-makers if it is so determined. The number of interests and potential interest groups is in principle unlimited with no single set of interests (e.g. capital, or the state) necessarily victorious. Thus power is distributed non-cumulatively and public decisions reflect demands from the political market. In this view the state is construed as either a neutral and rather passive switchboard for contending interests, or its agencies as simply one set of interest groups among all the others.

Since the early 1970s this view has undergone serious criticism and revision, stemming from a rise in social conflict and economic recession in the advanced capitalist societies. Pluralism came to be seen as a source of the increased 'ungovernability' of Western societies as 'rising expectations' resulted in the 'overload' of the state bureaucracies. For writers such as Schmitter, P.C. (1974) 'Still the century of corporatism?' *Review of Politics*, 36, 85–131 new forms of interest group intermediation with the state provide a better basis than pluralism for securing increased social and economic coordination to add to the system's regulative capacities. Corporatism is better able to manage demands for goods of a kind (e.g. collective consumption, welfare) which pluralist systems of interest representation with their narrow, self-interested and exclusive definitions of group goals have never provided.

Middlemas (1979) reinforces the view that corporatism is a response to crises. During the First World War it was characterised first by increased state intervention in the economy and areas of social policy, and then by a change in the nature of key economic interest groups from primarily private associations to ones with regular and mutually supportive relationships with government. These developments have come to be seen as deriving from the inability of the market and liberal democratic institutions to provide both the conditions of capital accumulation and conflict resolution in modern complex and class-divided societies. Corporatist analysis therefore underlines the importance of relationships between the state and those groups corresponding to the social organisation of economic production and distribution. These relationships are characterised by exchange: the leaders of the groups help construct and even implement state policy, and in return are expected to secure agreement from their members for state policy and if necessary overcome internal dissent. Corporatism therefore seeks to generate class collaboration and the view that national goals and a united effort to secure them are more beneficial to all interests than narrow, sectional and class-divisive campaigns.

Market, bureaucratic and corporatist forms of decision-making

Cawson and Saunders (1983) have developed a theory of different modes of state action that generates an ideal typical framework for analysing resource allocation.

The market mode

This rests on the assumption of invisible and spontaneous mechanisms in the market that allow resources to be allocated independently of the exercise of political authority. The state's role is minimal and facilitative, guaranteeing only basic requirements for accumulation such as private property and the legal enforcement of contracts. 'There is no attempt to plan the allocation of investment or other economic resources; capital flows to where the rate of return can be maximised' (Cawson and Saunders, 1983, p.15).

The bureaucratic mode

In this mode resources are allocated authoritatively by state institutions. Associated with state socialism, the allocation process is governed by explicit rules and commands. The inefficiency, inflexibility and inability to take account of unforeseen consequences make it an inappropriate method for resource allocation in capitalist production.

The corporatist mode

In contrast, corporatist decisions are neither imposed by objective laws nor by a determinate political authority but reflect the outcome of a bargaining process between corporate interests and the state. The assumption is that each party is able independently to exercise some form of sanction. 'Power is thus neither pluralistically dispersed, nor concentrated, but polycentric within an overall hierarchy' (ibid., p.16). This form of state interventionism is institutionalised by ad hoc or quasi-autonomous agencies on which the major interests are directly represented and which implements policies discriminately rather than as in the bureaucratic mode through a universally applicable code of rules. Privilege is accorded to firms or sectors with high accumulation potential, for example through specifically negotiated planning agreements. In this mode the state is neither directive nor coupled to an autonomous private sphere but is intermeshed with it in a complex way which undermines the traditional distinction between public and private.

Corporatism, therefore, differs from pluralism in the amount of decisional authority a group acquires from the state and the role of interest groups as co-responsible 'partners' in governance and social guidance. Thus corporatism involves not just bargaining between the state and functional groups but also the implementation of public policy through the groups themselves. Not only do such interest groups represent or advance their members' interests but they are also prepared to enforce on their members compliance with agreements reached with the state and perhaps other groups in the 'national interest'. The state also has an interest in minimising the number of groups it has to deal with and in legitimising the more 'responsible' and representative groups. Certainly in comparison with pluralism there is an assumption in corporatism that the state more actively forms and sustains the system of interest intermediation and is deeply interested in its outcomes.

In some interpretations (Panitch, 1980) corporatism is a devise for drawing the workers into the capitalist system, forcing them to accept wages and other forms of restraint, and is a political structure designed to protect capital in periods of crisis and declining profitability. However, capitalists are often very reluctant to become involved in corporatism, as it can constrain entrepreneurial sovereignty and possibly lead to redistribution policies. Conservative and Right administrations have also tended to prefer market solutions to those of corporatism in recent years.

The issues of pluralism and corporatism clearly feature strongly in any discussion of the modern state. Many of the contributors to this volume directly examine both the claimed attractions to governments of corporatism, as well as its theoretical utility in explaining contemporary political processes. Duclaud-Williams, in his chapter on education policy in France and Britain, challenges the assumption that corporatism is necessarily beneficial for rulers. Rather, the French state has been weakened by the absence of pluralism, which is more advantageous in offering leaders the prospect of alternative solutions from different social interests. Consequently in pluralist arrangements such leaders have increased space or independence in arriving at and implementing decisive executive action. French governments, however, have experienced much greater difficulty and immobilism in seeking major change in the face of a more monolithic network of professional and political interests.

Grant, in his contribution on industrial policy-making, also questions the assumption that corporatist processes are most apparent and potent at the level of national representational aggregation. In his view firms rather than sectors have become much more influential and autonomous actors in representing interests to government. In an increasingly competitive and transnational context large businesses in particular regard interest articulation as one part of a corporate advancement strategy. The growth of a company state may signal the weakening of aggregating transectoral bodies seeking some form of representational monopoly. However, in his piece on transport policy, Banister cautions against the ability of states to deal only on a company or contractual basis. It is important to recognise planning and coordination, particularly in the area of transport, as continuing and necessary functions for modern governments whatever their political line.

The relevance of corporatist analysis for local political processes is also still being established. Cawson and Saunders (1983), for example, extended their typology of state expenditures and different modes of decision-making to the allocation of functions between central, regional and local government. This allocation to different levels of government plays a vital role in resolving the contradictory pressures on government in market societies. Cawson and Saunders's 'dual state' model locates social investment expenditures within central and regional government structures that are insulated from popular control. Corporatist arrangements reflecting the state's primary interest in securing the needs of capital accumulation are more likely to be found at this level. Politics is class-based and expressed in the hierarchy of capital and labour associations. On the other hand, social consumption expenditure is largely in the hands of local government, and here are found non-class, consumption–reproduction struggles (over education, housing, health care provision, etc.) in which other than capitalist interests are likely to prevail. However, because of the financial and institutional dependency of local government on the centre, local consumption demands and decision-making can be severely restricted.

However, in his chapter on the local state, local government and local administration Johnston casts doubt on the 'dual state' thesis. He suggests that while the theory is plausible it is empirically dubious. Aspects of the local state are also involved in the politics of production. There is a long history of local 'boosterism' in the United States while in the United Kingdom employment-promoting policies have been a growing characteristic of municipal councils. Moreover, the theory offers an insufficient account of why some services are locally administered and other are locally governed, or why places differ in the relative importance of those two aspects of the local state apparatus.

Central–local relations

Cawson and Saunders (1983) suggest that the two different types of political process found in the 'dual state', and associated with central and local levels, may be characterised in terms of four variables: organisational, function, political and ideological.

Organisational. One approach to central–local government relations is concerned with the relationship between organisations at the two levels. Rhodes (1981), for example, points to organisational power struggles between central and local government in which each organisation has at its disposal particular resources. Although this struggle generally takes place within certain rules, it is essentially a zero-sum game to change the balance of freedom and influence between the two groups. This 'power dependence' characterisation of the relationship between Whitehall and the local authorities suggests that both have resources for autonomous action but also that they are dependent on each other for resources outside their own control. For example, central departments tend to have broad-ranging and general financial control over policy, while local authorities possess ground-level operational control and expertise. Multiple conflicts of interest within local government between different tiers and political parties confound simple models of central–local relationships. However, the increasing 'nationalisation' of local politics in a number of countries and indicated in Britain, for example, by the growth of national local authority associations provides a relatively stable and homogenising influence for individual authorities.

The organisational approach has appeared particularly pertinent to analyses of British politics since the return of Conservative administrations determined to control tightly all local authority expenditure, including that which is locally raised, and which has resulted in severe turbulence in central–local relationships. A problem with the organisational approach, however, is that it tends to ignore the substance of central–local relationships and the wider social framework within which they are situated.

Function. Saunders (1984) suggests that the increased tension in recent years between central and local government is not simply a reflection of an organisational power struggle but is a product of the deeper tension between production and consumption priorities within the state. Cawson and Saunders's (1983) ideal-typical, dual state framework associates the requirements for production with policy processes at central and regional level, and those for collective consumption at the local level. Thus the attempt to control local government from the centre 'has been part and parcel of the attempt to subordinate social to economic priorities in order to restore profitability to private sector investment' (Saunders, 1984, p.28).

Political. Similarly, the central–local division may be regarded as reflecting the different modes of interest intermediation associated with the different tiers and their typical form of expenditure. In this view the investment needs of capital are maintained through largely secretive corporatist policy processes, while local struggles over collective consumption are characterised by a more open or pluralistic politics – but which is subordinated to central, corporatist and investment influence.

Ideological. Finally, the ideological principles associated with centrally-located, production-based, corporatism are founded on the market and private property, while those associated with local consumption are characterised by collectivism, civic rights and social welfare.

In this dual state thesis the typical formation of local interests is based on consumption sectors, between private house owners and council tenants, for example, rather than class divisions. Although some campaigns may draw membership predominantly from one class, they do not constitute class struggles if mobilised in terms of people's relationships to consumption issues as opposed to production. Indeed, the fragility and fragmentation of community responses to public expenditure cuts – typically localised and limited to a narrow range of concerns – is because 'local consumption-based struggles are not class struggles and cannot, therefore, simply be taken under the wing of a socialist movement whose primary concern lies in national questions of economic policy' (Saunders, 1980, p.551). This view directly challenges one version of the 'local state' thesis put forward by Cockburn (1977), Corrigan (1979) and others, which identifies the function of local government as essentially the same as that for central government, namely pursuing the interests of monopoly capital. It is assumed that local government is merely one branch of the capitalist state and that general theories of the capitalist state can be applied in virtually unmediated fashion to the 'local state'. The function of the local state is, therefore, to facilitate capital accumulation through the provision of infrastructure (e.g. communications, land clearance), helping to maintain the reproduction of labour, and keeping order and generating political legitimacy in responding to working-class demands. In the dual state view, however, the local level has a specificity, through the provision of collective consumption, that serves to distinguish it from central government.

A problem with the term 'local state' is that it is used to denote two contrary meanings: one in which it has at least relative autonomy from the central state, and the other in which it is simply a local arm of the central state. Duncan and Goodwin (1982) suggest that the local state, like the central state, is a historically-formed social relation and it is constantly being restructured in ways not always functional for capital. Local government develops as part of the conflicts and compromises between different groups and classes in which outcomes, although tending to be functional for capital, have not been guaranteed – not least because social change is not mechanical but the result of people's responses to relations and events. Thus, in Britain, the emergence of local democratic government in the nineteenth century could not be considered a more 'functional' solution for dominant classes than, for example, extending non-electoral institutions to the new industrial towns. Rather, 'the old system was breaking down socially: in many of these towns the working class was developing its own centres of local power . . . (and) the old system was differentially functional for different ruling-class groups' (Duncan and Goodwin, 1982, p.169). The result was a partial and internally contradictory response by ruling groups to changing social relations and the development of a local–central state system which has been 'a periodic battleground' between the different classes. Consequently, as Dearlove (1979) has indicated, the 'problem' of local government is that it is especially vulnerable to working-class demands. The effect of local reorganisation in Britain in the 1970s – characterised as a response to poor 'councillor calibre' and local 'inefficiency' – was to seek to reduce working-class influence by creating larger authorities and internally reorganising councils with the stamp of corporate management. However, Duncan and Goodwin, and Dearlove, although critical of 'local state' theories that posit too tight a functional fit between state and capital, offer analyses based on the centrality of class relations at that level rather than the collective consumption approach found in the dual state thesis. We should note, too, that local government reorganisations in the name of efficiency are also introduced by labour and socialist parties aware of the inaccessibility, bureaucratisation and alienating characteristic of local governments and the often unequal distributive consequences of these features for, particularly, the working class. In Britain, despite recent efforts by socialist councils to protect localities from Conservative public expenditure cuts by arguing for the 'defence of local democracy', there is a long-established suspicion of local government within the Labour Party as a potential obstacle to a reforming central state (Bassett, 1984).

The relative attractiveness of local state theories on the one hand, emphasising the functionality of local government for capital and its role as a branch of a unitary state, and, on the other, the dual state thesis which focuses on the specificity of collective consumption at the local level and the attendant dangers this poses for the central state and capital, tends to vary on the Left with whether a socialist or non-socialist party is in government at the national level. Dual state theory seems to have great explanatory potential for recent attempts by central governments in many Western economies to circumscribe the financial power of local authorities and control levels of collective consumption that threaten both the fiscal base of government and the profitability of capital. Central government has a number of strategies that it can employ for this purpose: organisationally restructuring and subordinating local government; recommodifying or privatising services previously state-provided; 'de-politicising' local decision-making by giving more powers to appointed, non-elected regional bodies; and ideologically associated attacks on local government with popular cynicism of local government bureaucracies. These strategies are not without their difficulties, as witnessed by the setbacks experienced in Britain by central government's efforts to abolish the second-tier metropolitan counties. Elected local government has an established democratic legitimacy and attacks on it can attract cross-class and cross-party opposition. On the other hand, however, the pluralistic and fragmented local politics of collective consumption makes united or coherent resistance difficult as groups are affected differently in the various consumption sectors. Nor is there much sign that the public sector unions, strategically located at the interfaces of production and consumption, and national and local politics, are able to cohere local opposition, for example, within local Labour parties.

However, the dual state thesis has its critics. As we noted previously, Dunleavy (1984) suggests that most spending is capable of multiple classification and that the characterisation of expenditure is determined by the tier of government within which it is located, rather than a particular form of spending being allocated by a particular level of government. Moreover, the fit between social consumption provision and local government varies across countries and is a relatively recent phenomenon in Britain, becoming pre-eminent only in the 1970s. Dunleavy (1984, p.76) regards as a critical difficulty with the dual state thesis its poor predictability in comparison with other models over the allocation of social insurance functions between tiers of government.

Although the realm of urban politics may have a theoretical specificity that derives from local governments' role in the provision of services, there are increased external constraints on localities. This involves the power of large business for local policy-makers, but also the increasing influence of central government and professional ideologies and interests. In comparison with corporatist modes of interest intermediation, professional groups in central and local government change policy through internal processes of ideological development. In local government, policy in particular areas often seems dominated by professional 'fashions' nationally generated, and adopted almost uniformly by authorities (Dunleavy, 1981; 1984). 'Policy communities' or 'issue networks' exist around specific issues, comprised usually of those drawn from the professions working in local government, the local authority associations and leading politicians and officials.

State theory and public administration

Recent approaches generally reject the notion of the state as a unitary instrument of rule for a particular group or class. Not only is the state divided into different sections, but these often possess conflicting interests. Moran, in his chapter on major finance markets, concludes that different state agencies are born in different historical circumstances, have different organisational cultures and are charged with different regulatory tasks. Consequently, state structures seem to be as internally competitive as financial markets, with different agencies representing different interests and forming part of a complex set of competitive coalitions that straddle the ostensible divide between state and economy.

There is increasing recognition that the state, central and local, should not be regarded as a unified or monolithic entity. Marxists, for example, have increasingly regarded the state itself as an arena for struggle from which may emerge any one of several eventualities. Other approaches emphasise the importance of intergovernmental relations and machinery in understanding policy outcomes, and the influence of departmentalism – differing government departmental interests – and quasi-governmental and intermediary bodies in decisional processes. Greenwood and Wilson (1984, p.30) have noted that while the role of governmental departments 'is theoretically to advise ministers about policy and implement ministerial decisions . . . departments, however, are not neutral in policy matters. They are part of a complex policy community, embracing client groups, media correspondents, outside 'experts', informed MPs and so forth, within which many policy attitudes are generated and developed.' Departments, therefore, tend to develop their own values, interests and loyalties, with a finely-tuned sense of defending their own 'patch'.

Over recent decades, as the state apparatus has extended and as governments have become more interventionist, consultation by departments with those affected has increased, because this is now regarded as a democratic norm and also to ensure the effective implementation of policy. This 'enables departmental officials and client groups to achieve consensus in private before submitting an "agreed policy" to ministers' (Greenwood and Wilson, 1984, p.25). The result is that conventional distinctions between the policy role of politicians and the administrative role of officials is more difficult to maintain in practice. So is the delineation between what is public and what is private, or the parameters of 'the state' and 'non-state'. Rather, 'in many key policy areas "the policy community", comprising not only officials but "businessmen, academics and spokesmen of various interests" is crucially involved in initiating or implementing a programme' (Dunsire, 1982). Consequently, governmental departments not only receive representations from pressure groups but also play such a role themselves. Pressure groups and departments, equally committed to a particular policy area, may collaborate in pursuit of resources against similar alliances in other policy areas. In the view of Richardson and Jordan (1979, pp. 35, 40) this has consequences for policy style, for a strong group system alongside a process of departmental conflict leads to incrementalism in governmental policy-making.

In all Western industrial nations the central state administration is not the only form of public sector agency. Decentralised and specific forms of service provision, revenue collection and legally-allocated authority are well-established features of modern politics, especially in the governance of localities, although the extent and type of decentralisation varies between societies. There are often two fundamental forms of public organisation apart from the central state. One form is the local authority, which is an elected body and covers a wide range of local public services, with powers to generate income through local taxation and charges for some services. The other is the quasi-governmental agency, such as housing associations, which tend to be single-issue agencies with control over only one policy area. Organised at either national, regional or local level, quasi-governmental bodies are generally non-elected, appointed by ministers, and with executive responsibilities.

Newton and Karran (1985, p.12) note that local government in the United Kingdom is distinctive in the range and amount of services it is required to provide. In unitary states comparable to Britain, such as France and Italy, there exist important regional and provincial levels of government, sharing service and financial responsibilities with central and local government. In Britain, however, local government 'has exclusive responsibility for a great many services which are provided by higher levels of government, or are shared by different levels, in other countries'. The British system of government is highly centralised, and has become more so as a consequence of recent legislation. The central level has been characterised as 'non-executant', using broad financial controls for the implementation of policy and laying down general rules for dealing with whole classes of sub-central agencies in the same way. Dunleavy and Rhodes (1983, p.112) suggest that this 'hands off', lack of 'fine grain' control results in a 'gulf between central ministers and municipal governments in terms of lack of personal contacts or administrative involvements [that] is far wider in Britain than in countries which have supposedly been more centralist, such as France'.

Central government control over local government is also supplemented in other ways. It is not hampered by the political and geographical divisions that characterise local government, and this facilitates 'divide and rule' strategies by central government (Newton and Karran, 1985, p.129; Rhodes, 1985). Unlike civil servants, local authority employees are not part of a single unified service. In Britain each council employs its own staff and, unlike the top civil servants who are usually generalists, local government officers are often specialists who 'have loyalties to their profession as well as their employing authority and this further weakens the concept of a unified service' (Greenwood and Wilson, 1984, p.137). The committee system in local government also tends to contribute against strong corporate administration, despite recent efforts to move in that direction. None the less, as earlier indicated, central government is not a monolith in its dealings with local authorities. Some government departments have sought close regulatory control over local authorities in ensuring standards of service and national policy implementation (e.g. the Home Office), while others (e.g. the Department of Education and Science) have generally followed a persuasive and promotional strategy.

The relationship between central government and quasi-governmental bodies, which have developed enormously in the last three decades or so, can also vary. Quasi-governmental bodies may be either government created or a private organisation that acquires the attributes of government. Straddling the public–private boundary, quasi-governmental bodies operate at one remove from central and local government. The Pliatsky Report (1980) delineated three distinct types in Britain –executive, advisory and tribunal – and noted that whilst normal patterns of departmental control and ministerial accountability did not apply, relationships with the parent department are infinitely variable. Dunleavy and Rhodes (1983, pp.110–11) suggest two main reasons for their creation. One is simply organisational decentralisation to allow more operational autonomy and efficiency, or perhaps to avoid too direct an implication for government in sensitive areas or potentially unpopular decisions. The other is where the administrative function is so large that it must be broken down for its exercise to become manageable. Hood (1981) argues that non-departmental bodies are too useful for politicians to abolish them readily and that government agencies are increasingly operating within an overall context of government by grants and by indirect administration rather than by the older pattern of directly hired bureaucrats at the centre.

Palmer (1985) argues that the growth of quasi-governmental bodies indicates that the boundaries of the state are flexible and not theoretically pre-determined. Their major characteristic is a relative autonomy within the state and research attention should be drawn to the conditions and the extent to which quasi-government bodies are able to sustain this. Although such agencies clearly are useful to governments, they may also pose problems, especially if they become closely oriented to their 'client group'. Rather than being somehow functional for government, quasi-governmental bodies could severely hamper its objectives. Central government may seek closer control of quasi-governmental bodies in times of financial stringency, but may come to recognise that a decrease in their institutional relative autonomy also raises problems and may help to 're-politicise' issues.

The sometimes conflicting nature of quasi-governmental/governmental relations and the course that these may take is not simply a contingency of good or efficient administration, but often reflects competing political objectives. There are a range of formal and informal mechanisms open to government in controlling quasi-governmental bodies: financial allocations, appointments, reviews and audits, directives and general political harassment. In turn quasi-governmental bodies may deploy a variety of resistance techniques. However, as non-elected bodies, quasi-governmental bodies retain an attraction even for governments ostensibly opposed to them. In Britain, as Dunleavy and Rhodes (1983, p.129) note the, Thatcher governments, despite initial hostility, 'have in practice become considerable enthusiasts for single-function quasi-governmental agencies . . . chiefly because the government has been unable to entrust local governments with key functions while maintaining a very tight squeeze on revenue spending'.

Policy communities and issue networks

We have noted that the blurring of the distinction between public and private association in modern government, alongside increased recognition of infra-governmental departmentalism and conflicts, helps give rise to the notion of 'policy community' in explanations of public decisional processes. In their study of the British Treasury, for example, Heclo and Wildavsky (1981) point out the recognition by its officials that their desires cannot prevail, unless they maintain a community to support them, because they are faced by a confederation of departments. The Treasury, like other departments, is not averse to using outside public opinion to build pressure for its policies.

Laffin (1986, pp.6–7) usefully distinguishes between 'policy communities' and 'issue networks'. For him 'policy community' refers to a relatively small group of participants with interests in a particular set of issues of concern, or potential concern, to central government. It is generally composed of politicians, officials, representatives of governmental and non-governmental agencies, and leaders of 'responsible' interest groups. Membership of a policy community is strictly controlled. Laffin notes the operation of 'stringent entry criteria, varying among issue areas, but including such criteria as possession of expert knowledge, occupancy of a senior position in a relevant organisation, what civil servants call "soundness", meaning that the person can be trusted to observe the norms of the community, and reputation "for getting things done"'. On the other hand an 'issue network' is less sharply delineated with membership more open and conflictual. A policy community may be seen as the 'core' of an issue network, and which the latter seeks to influence and its members join. Relationships between policy communities and issue networks vary among policy sectors which, as Laffin observes, raises the question of those conditions under which policy communities widen policy debates, perhaps because it requires further support or information. Participants may experience cross-pulling loyalties and obligations: government officials may have to reconcile sympathy for a client group with the requirements of government policy, and interest group leaders the need for compromise with the demands of members. The policy community itself may engender a sense of allegiance that displaces original loyalties. Policy communities tend to operate across the line demarcating central from local government and indeed are often a mechanism for bridging contrary interests, particularly through the involvement of national local authority associations. Policy communities may be the means for attracting support for local aims by nationally-oriented local government officials, and for 'selling'central objectives. The influence of policy communities in the determination of policy may vary between policy sectors and over time. The re-emergence of ideological politics in Britain in recent years (Plant, 1983) and the re-establishment of the doctrine of 'leaders know best' under Conservative administrations (Rhodes, 1983a), has meant that policy sectors have come to be dominated by political leaders and partisan objectives. Morever, some policy sectors may be endemically more open to political intervention than others. Policies may determine politics (Lowi, 1972), with some policies less amenable to non-technical or non-professional influence than others.

Rhodes (1985) has also argued that policy communities are a distinctive feature of policy-making in central–local relations, although he cautions against over-estimating the shared nature of such communities. Rather, relations within policy communities reflect different power resources and are asymmetric, with government possessing the capacity to constitute policy communities by controlling membership, access, the agenda and timing of consultation. As defined, the concept of political community has advantage over that of corporatism, avoiding connotations of hierarchy and discipline and yet recognising the limited number of actors in any policy area.

In his study of the national community of local government in the United Kingdom Rhodes (1986b) outlines how the influence of policy communities within the national government environment varied in three distinctive periods between 1970 and 1983. In the first period consultation and bargaining between the central and local government 'partners' was the norm, with policy communities especially influential. Central spending departments and their associated professions had a vested interest in increasing service expenditure, and generally overcoming Treasury objections. Between 1974 and 1979, however, a strategy of incorporation was predominant, with the Labour government seeking top-level integration in its dealings with the local authorities. The national local authority associations were recognised as peak associations and brought directly into central decision-making, particularly the planning of local expenditure within general spending plans through a newly created Consultative Council on Local Government Finance (CCLGF). Rhodes notes that the national local government associations were promoted into greater prominence than before but that the main bodies that found their influence decreased by this change were the many different policy communities promoting increased spending in the various service areas. Thus 'the CCLGF helped along a shift of influence within local government away from service-oriented councillors and officers (e.g. school education) and towards local politicians and finance directors more concerned with "corporate planning", increased efficiency and financial soundness' (p.139). The aim by central government, and especially the Treasury, was to build up a shared understanding of economic realities between itself and local authority leaders in overcoming pressures for increased spending, in return for more direct involvement in policy-making.

The associations, however, lacked the characteristics to engage in a full-blown corporatist arrangement with government. They were not in a position to regulate their members, whose membership was not compulsory, nor to claim a monopoly of representation. Moreover, there was often intense political and geographical rivalry between the different national associations. The Conservative administration that was elected in 1979, however, had little time for incorporative mechanisms and reversed earlier attempts to negotiate with local government. The privileged position of the local government associations has ebbed away, to be replaced by unilateral decision-making and close control of the expenditure decisions of individual local authorities as well as for local government as a whole. It marked a movement from incorporation to government direction and re-assertion of authority. In turn, the process of increased involvement by the national local government community in the policy communities has moved to one of disengagement.

The work by Rhodes (1986b) indicates the different organisational and other interests between the state and policy communities that can surface as conflict and constraints in policy processes. It also points to the importance of examining the relationship between organisations rather than specific institutions, and the possibility that local figures may be important national actors. However, 'the metaphors of policy networks and policy communities . . . suggest multiple networks at the centre and direct attention to the comparison of policy areas, the degree of integration within networks, and the extent of articulation between networks' (p.24). Finally, it is possible to recognise that central government may become both less unified and more centralised. The notion 'fragmented elitism' (p.18) indicates that fragmentation and dispersion are not the same as decentralisation.

Fragmentation may be a characteristic of the centre, but dispersion describes the distribution of authority between policy communities and not its redistribution away from central departments. Thus fragmentation and centralisation coexist at the centre . . . with the extension of functional differentiation there has been an extension of national policy programmes, the emergence of centrally defined services and standards and the movement of decision-making power from small to larger – i.e. central-jurisdictions' (p.19).

Professions and professionalism

A vital component of the processes described by Rhodes is the professions, whose influence varies between political communications and on different issues within a particular political community. Moreover, we noted the increasing importance of local authority non-specialist or generalist professionals, as opposed to the professional programme or service professionals, in integrating local and central government perspectives, particularly in periods of financial stringency as occurred in Britain in the latter part of the 1970s. The latter group are sometimes referred to as the 'technocrats', while the former have been described as 'topocrats'. Laffin (1986, p.22) argues that professions are found predominantly within large-scale organisations, particularly government, and that professionalism as a form of social control forms as a counterpart and as a challenge to bureaucratic control. The routinised control associated with bureaucratisation has often proved unsuitable for service provision in the modern welfare state and two types of professionalism have developed. One, associated with such public service professionals as social workers, teachers and housing managers, involves the generation of accounts oriented towards the client rather than the employing organisation, largely as a means of legitimating claims to autonomy or freedom of control from bureaucratic superiors. A second form of professionalism is the technobureaucratic which is generated by the necessity of managing and administering the large-scale organisation in which are found the public service professions. It consists of accounts legitimising the necessity for exercising organisational power over public service professionals and resisting intervention from politicians. Polytechnic directors and chief constables are two examples of groups in Britain that recently have sought less formal power over them from local elected politicians.

Although both forms of professionalism are found at both levels of government, in Britain particularly central government has sought to encourage it as a distinctive feature of local government. Laffin (1986, p.30) suggests that this represents a strong cultural preference, 'reflecting partly the view that local government falls within the realm of the "specialist", involved in the execution of policy not the making of policy, and partly the tendency of the national political and official elites to see professionalism as a countervailing force to the forces of localism'. An aspect of this form of local governmental professionalism is that the initial education and training of staff is largely the responsibility of other bodies, such as educational institutions and professional associations. Professional 'self-responsibility' and codes of conduct are also regarded by some as providing more effective safeguards for the public than is possible for elected representatives. The growth of uni-functional quangos has helped the development of professionalised work settings and sustained pluralist notions of the separation of elites and the necessary insulation of administration from 'political interference' (Dunleavy, 1982, p.187). Professionalism and decentralisation, alongside the increased organisational potential of an increasingly educated and middle-class citizenry, is seen as providing the means for both enhanced rationality and participation in public policy-making. However, Dunleavy notes that the existence of a strong professional basis in British local government can conflict with the latter's primary purpose to provide government adjusted to local needs, because it orients local administrators to a non-local occupational community and tends to nationalise processes of local policy change (Dunleavy, 1980; 1981). Moreover, the growth of professionalism is associated with increased organisational interdependence and this may give rise to problems of accountability as it becomes difficult to identify who is responsible for a decision (Jones, 1980).

Conclusion: Public and private

In policy terms the distinction between public and private, and between the state and the market, are more complicated than the simple binaries of political ideology. The recent reform of education in Britain is a case in point. Ministers have talked increasingly of the need to reduce higher education's dependence on the state for the bulk of its income. Quoting examples from the United States (perhaps misleadingly) they have argued that the attraction of private income reduces the debilitating funding dependency of institutions on the state and releases initiative and creativity. Logically this requires the deliberate restriction of public expenditure on higher education.

Yet this fairly crude distinction between public and private underestimates their interdependency in modern society. The example of health care shows that both public and private investment is higher in the rest of Europe than in Britain. The two go together and are not necessarily antithetical. Industry, commerce and the rest of the private sector are much more likely to invest in well-funded institutions generously supported by the state than those lacking public investment.

Similarly the picture which emerges from the chapters that follow indicate a recurring pattern or strategy in New Right policy-making across a range of sectors. It involves both an increase in central power and an extension of local freedom. In housing, for example (see the chapter by Smith), policy has been marked by increased central control and a corresponding diminution in the role envisaged for local authorities, along with more market choice for consumers through provisions and incentives for home ownership and more attractive conditions for private rental. In health, too, the private–public boundary has become even more blurred, with increased competition and consumer choice both within and between the sectors, as outlined by Mohan in his contribution to this volume.

The 'freeing' of educational institutions from the state throughout the 1980s in Britain also fits this overall pattern. Those on the Right, and not so Right, suspected in a range of public sectors – not just education – that an unholy corporatist alliance of producers, government officials and trade unionists had usurped the sovereign wishes of the consumer, thus leading to market distortion, ineffectiveness, costliness and an unrelatedness to the world of work and the needs of the economy. It was part of an explanation for Britain's declining industrial performance. The response, at least on the surface, was to inject accountability more directly through consumer choice and power; if you like, through markets rather than assemblies.

Thus the Education Reform Act (1988) was the most important piece of education legislation since the 1944 Act. It aimed to change the essential power relations in the education system by:

1. Increasing the powers of the Secretary of State (e.g. over the national curriculum).
2. Diminishing the functions of the local education authorities.
3. Increasing the autonomy of governing bodies.

The issue of whether the Act was a centralising or privatising measure was apparently complicated by simultaneously giving more power to the Secretary of State, and also increasing the autonomy of schools and colleges. The increased independence and responsibilities of governing bodies was based on the assumption that more autonomous institutions would be more efficient and responsive. Yet the apparent contradiction or paradox between more central power and more institutional autonomy is illusory: they are simply two sides of the same coin. One requires the other. Thus colleges and schools could only be 'set free' provided that there were clear ground rules backed up as necessary by ministerial authority. Only a strong central authority enables the release of local initiative (through provision of increased freedoms, in part largely taken from the local not central authorities).

This is exemplified at the level of the institution. For schools the provision for a national curriculum and a centrally imposed terms and conditions of service award served to restrict professional autonomy. Yet the act also sought to free heads (managers) and governors from the local education authorities. Managerialism, rather than professionalism and political bureaucracy, provides the conditions for local control backed by national authority.

Therefore, for the schools the Act delegated finance and staffing (and their management) to schools' governing bodies as a means of encouraging initiative, commitment and greater 'value for money', and reducing local administrative and political interference. Similarly, consumerism, through the provisions for open enrolment, opting out, parental choice and increased competition between schools for pupils at a time of falling rolls provides a market reinforcement to set alongside managerialism.

Finally, it remains to be seen whether central control and consumerism, in education as well as other policy sectors, have the political consequences generally predicted. Will there be a consequent reduction in collectivist forms of representation and identity and a more atomistic reliance on autonomous effort? It will be important to recognise that even the most economically individualistic are capable of responding collectively in the defence of established rights. Harrison, for example, points out in his chapter on property struggles in housing and planning that collective resistance to the diminution of the legal and infrastructural conditions for individual advancement is still a feature of aspects of consumption politics. Yet, a prime characteristic of all the following chapters is the absence of determinism and inevitability in the accounts. Whatever the country or the sector, the interplay of groups and conflicts, both within and across the public–private boundary, shapes our policies, and not some *deus ex machina* working out a mysterious logic of history.

Part II The central state and production

2 Industrial policy

Wyn Grant

This chapter on industrial policy-making will tackle five broad themes. First, it will suggest that there is a continuing debate in many Western societies, particularly those identified by the editors as the stateless, English-speaking societies, about what the state's role should be in relation to industrial policy. In other words, should the state be in action at all in this policy arena? Second, it will be suggested that when the state is an actor in the industrial policy arena, it is often a weak and constrained actor. This is partly because of the strength of countervailing forces with their own policy objectives, notably firms. It is also a reflection of the fact that in every country (even Japan) there is considerable fragmentation in government machinery for handling industrial policy questions. Third, it will be suggested that industrial policy is an area in which a variety of subnational governments become involved. Fourth, it will be argued that any analysis of industrial policy-making must have a strong sectoral component: this is an arena in which particular policy communities have well defined boundaries and highly developed networks of relationships. Fifth, it will be argued that the trend in this policy arena is away from state intervention towards greater autonomy of action for firms. Hence, instead of a 'corporate state', we are faced with what may be termed a 'company state'.

What is industrial policy?

Blais has pointed out that many works on industrial policy do not define the term at all and 'Where a definition is proposed, it is generally disposed of in a paragraph, with the author not taking care either to justify the definition or to indicate some of the problems it may contain' (Blais, 1986a, p. 3). In all fairness, there are certain difficulties in defining the term. One could adopt a wide definition which covered any government policy affecting industry, but such a definition would embrace, for example, education policy or environmental policy. There is a case for taking such a wide perspective, but the result would be a sprawling essay which would trespass on the ground of other contributors to this volume.

One central problem is that industry is most directly and deeply affected by government's conduct of its general economic policy – for example, what sort of exchange-rate policy (if any) does it have, and how successful is it; or what is the tax regime, and how does it distribute burdens and benefits between corporate and individual taxpayers? However, general economic policy is not the focus of this chapter; rather, the subject of discussion is 'the set of selective measures adopted by the state to alter industrial organisation' (Blais, 1988a, p. 4). For pragmatic reasons concerned with the organisation of this book, I will not discuss questions of tax policy or labour-market policy. Questions of trade policy will intrude for two reasons. First, it is possible to interpret the growth of 'industrial policies' as one attempt by nation-states to cope with the disappearance of tariff-based forms of protection (another response has, of course, been the erection and development of a variety of non-tariff barriers). Second, it is not possible to discuss the United States without discussing protectionist policies: the most acceptable response at the federal level to a structural industrial problem is some form of protection.

One further problem is what is meant by 'industry'. Manufacturing industry accounts for a minority of jobs in most advanced industrial states, although it is more significant in terms of the composition of trade. However, most industrial policy measures have focused on manufacturing industries. From one perspective this emphasis reflects 'structural snobbery' (Henderson, 1986), from another it reflects the importance of manufacturing both as a provider of high quality jobs and as the dynamic basis of many service industries (Cohen and Zysman, 1987). This debate cannot be pursued here; in this chapter 'industry' is used as a shorthand for all forms of profit-generating activity, although, in practice, government policies have been relatively narrowly focused on certain types of activity (particularly on 'heavy' rather than 'light' industry).

Should the state be on the ball park?

In many Western societies, a widely held view is that the state should have very limited functions in relation to industry. For example, Ronald Reagan has commented: 'Government's legitimate role is not to dictate detailed plans or solutions to problems for particular companies or industries. No, government serves us best by protecting and maintaining the marketplace, by ensuring that the rules of free and fair trade, both at home and abroad, are properly observed, and by safeguarding the freedoms of individual participants (typescript, 4 August 1983).

Viewpoints of this kind could be seen as, in part, a reflection of the absence of any properly developed concept of the state in the Anglo-American societies. In Britain (and in Canada) perhaps the nearest approach to a concept of the state accepted by those in positions of authority is the notion of the Crown; note, for example, the use of the term 'Crown corporations' to describe public enterprises in Canada. The imprecision, mysticism and inherent limitation to radicalism implied by this term is appealing to societies which prefer *ad hoc*, incremental, empirical, pragmatic solutions to any systematic use of public power in the pursuit of an *Ordnungspolitik*. (For a fuller discussion, see Dyson, 1980, pp. 36–44.)

This option is not, of course, available to the United States, despite some pseudo-monarchical undertones surrounding the office of the presidency.

(The phenomenon of the so-called 'first family' is significant in this respect: see Caroli, 1987; Kellerman, 1982.) It is not without significance that the official handbook of the US government starts with the constitution. This is not, one suspects, because government officials have to consult it in their daily work (in the sense in which EEC officials have to consult their purple-bound copies of the treaties), but because of the symbolic significance of the constitution as a source of authority. Yet what is striking about the American system of government is the *absence* of effective authority in an area like industrial policy, in the sense that any one person or institution can make a final decision on an issue and that it can actually stick. One response to this problem was the rise of the 'imperial presidency'; a more enduring response has been the resolution of questions through the judicial process. One commentator on American industrial policy has noted, 'Coordination and the reconciliation of conflicts among federal economic programs are increasingly entrusted to ninety-four federal district courts, ten appellate courts, and one Supreme Court. These institutions are ill-equipped to understand or respond to the dynamics of international competition' (Johnson, 1984, p. 15).

How far does the notion of integrated 'public power' in continental Europe focus attention not on *whether* the state should be involved in industrial policy, but *what* it should be doing and *how* it should be doing it? First, one must stress that there is no unified continental approach to these questions. Danish industrial policy, for example, has been influenced by a persistent tradition of liberalism (Sidenius, 1983; Braendgeard, *1988*). West Germany, however, is often seen as an example of a system which displays a capability for capitalist self-organisation (Dyson and Wilks, 1983). This analysis is correct in so far as, for example, German trade associations are more effectively organized than those in Britain (Grant, 1986), or in terms of the closer links between the banks and industry than in Britain – although the significance of the 'house bank' phenomenon has been sometimes overstated. Moreover, one should not exaggerate the extent to which German businessmen see the state as 'their' state (to borrow Vogel's terminology). Contradictory tendencies for public status and private autonomy are present. As Streeck observes, the German public has 'traditionally regarded the state as a natural proponent of the common good. At the same time, however, a business association that would appear to its members as an extended arm of the state would lose its internal legitimacy' (Streeck, 1983, p. 274).

Nor does the case of Japan really help us in the search for a system in which the state is seen as a fully legitimate partner in industrial policy-making. It is, of course, the case that in Japan, 'the processes of industrial development and state-building were interdependent' (Boyd, 1987, p. 67). Moreover, 'Intimate government – industry relations have the sanction of history and culture . . . and, in the absence of any serious challenge to such collaboration, extensive channels of communication have developed between the principal parties to the relationship' (p. 87). However, close relations of this kind do not necessarily conform to prevalent concepts of the modern state. As the editors note, the social relationships of the modern state 'typically entail command and obedience'. Yet intervention by the Japanese state (particularly Ministry of International Trade and Industry) is based on the notion of 'administrative guidance', which lacks any 'coercive legal effect' and relies on encouragement and persuasion as its main devices (Wakiyama, 1987, p. 211). Quite often, this persuasion has failed, as in attempts to rationalise the Japanese auto industry.

Of course, one should not pretend that the Japanese attitude to industrial policy is, say, the same as that of the Americans. A key difference is that 'Industrial policy has been accorded a very high priority through the post-war period in Japan' (Boyd, 1987, p. 87). In the American case a company-led rather than a state-led approach to industrial adjustment predominates, although in practice quite a lot of interventions are justified on 'national security' grounds and funded through the defence budget. Even so, the difference is not just one of presentation and mechanism, but also one of policy content and effectiveness.

One approach to the question of whether the state should be in action in relation to industrial policy is through an examination of how particular national state traditions define what constitutes acceptable intervention. Another is to ask general questions about what the role of the state is in relation to industry in a capitalist economy. One can ask such questions by looking at the issues from the viewpoint of the company and from the viewpoint of the state.

In principle, most companies would be happy the less they see of the state. In practice, they will often qualify that position. First, an important subset of companies in a number of industries are highly dependent on government contracts (notably the defence industries, including aerospace and shipbuilding; telecommunications; pharmaceuticals; and construction). Second, companies will look to their national governments to protect them against 'unfair competition'; more often than not, this means competition they cannot cope with. Third, companies will happily take any government investment incentives that might be around to encourage them to open a new plant or place it in a particular location (although whether such incentives actually influence their decision is less certain). Fourth, companies may be happy for governments to regulate their industries if such regulations mean assured profits (because they can charge higher prices than would be possible in the presence of greater competition), and erect barriers which are difficult for potential new competitors to scale. Fifth, a company facing serious financial difficulties may turn to the government as a 'banker of last resort' to bail them out.

Government may develop industrial policies for a number of reasons. It may be motivated by a concern about the competitiveness of its economy, or of particular parts of it. These concerns were exacerbated in the late 1960s and 1970s by the consequences of the decline of traditional tariff protection, and the impact of the two oil shocks: hence, the proliferation of industrial policies over this period. Government may also be concerned about the absence of competition within the domestic economy, although (with the exception of the United States) competition policies do not generally amount to very much. Companies have strong incentives to ensure that competition is limited, and governments may be more interested in building up 'national champions' in particular sectors than in enhancing competition. Governments may be concerned about the regional distribution of employment, and may seek to promote industrial growth in areas of high unemployment. They may be concerned about inefficiencies in capital markets which make it difficult for particular types of enterprise or project to attract funding. Above all, governments may be concerned about the collapse of a major firm, particularly if it is the dominant employer in a politically sensitive area.

A variety of short-run political considerations and compromises may influence the way in which industrial policy develops. However, the whole issue of industrial policy is underpinned by a more general debate about the efficacy of the market mechanism. As Atkinson comments:

At the core of the debate on industrial policy is the question of market allocation. Can we trust or expect the market to allocate resources in a manner that will ensure economic growth and political stability? Those who see near perfect markets operating in most spheres of economic activity are inclined to respond in the affirmative and proceed to outline those rare occasions on which the market might conceivably fail. Those less sanguine about markets either see market failure as a widespread phenomenon, or argue that market outcomes, no matter how efficient, are by no means compatible with important political goals. (Atkinson, 1988, p. 259)

It may well be the case that 'the market failure justification for industrial policy and government intervention in general has been used to excess – that is, applied to situations in which it is simply not valid' (McFetridge, 1985, p. 5). However, it is not possible to resolve that debate here, so let us assume for the purposes of argument, that market failures are not infrequent. It does not follow that these failures can be cured by government intervention. Indeed, government intervention may exacerbate the original problem, or introduce new problems.

At the risk of some exaggeration and over generalisation, industrial policy in most Western societies is a mess. Large sums of public money have been spent, often to very little effect, in achieving policy goals (which are not always clearly specified). This may be because industrial policy has been insufficiently coherent and systematic. The Canadian 'picture of a company-led model of industrial adaptation influenced by numerous, if uncoordinated, governmental industrial policies' (Schultz and Alexandroff, 1985, p. 124) could be replicated elsewhere, not just in Anglo-American countries but even in countries such as France which have been seen as models of state-led adjustment. Policies have often had the effect of postponing adjustment, making the industrial structure of the country concerned even less competitive. In Britain selective assistance schemes appear to have been 'directed at modernising capacity in sectors which turned out to be facing decline' (National Audit Office, 1987, p. 3). This might be thought to be desirable if it eases the burden imposed on those groups of workers most affected by industrial change, but in fact there are good reasons for believing that they are not particularly likely to benefit from industrial interventions. Trebilcock argues that political forces tend to produce policies 'that first favour trade protection to preserve output and employment, then favour subsidies to firms to maintain output and employment, and finally favour subsidies to labour to facilitate mobility' (Trebilcock, 1986, p. 336).

Against this background it is not surprising that organisations such as the OECD (which both reflects and amplifies policy trends in its member states) have placed an increasing emphasis on a more liberal approach to problems of industrial adjustment. The OECD has developed (and its member states have endorsed) the concept of 'positive adjustment policies', arguing that the achievement of macroeconomic policy goals may be jeopardised if governments allow industrial and other microeconomic policies to conserve 'inefficient economic structures, thus undermining the market forces on which the success of macro-economic policy greatly depends' (OECD, 1983, p. 115). However, even the UK government recognises a role for an industrial policy 'to help remedy perceived defects in the operation of market forces' (National Audit Office, 1987b, p. 10). It may therefore be argued that the challenge facing policy-makers is one 'of finding the form of state participation which is most productive in each situation' (McFetridge, 1985, p. 6). This in turn raises the question of the competence of the state (in practice, its bureaucrats) to deal with industrial policy problems, an issue considered in the next section.

The state as an industrial policy actor

In a major comparative study of the steel industry Mény and Wright and their collaborators set out to investigate the political and administrative constraints on the capacity of states to manage industrial crises. They concluded that the steel crisis led to the emergence or strengthening of the state as the major actor in the steel industry, 'But it was a restrained and constrained state: it was omnipresent, but not omniscient. It was certainly not omnipotent' (Mény and Wright, 1987b, p. 95). Among the constraints on state action identified were the legal and institutional context, the internal cohesion and competence of the state itself, and the resources available to countervailing forces. The state was, perhaps, more than one actor among many, but even if it had a leading role, it could act effectively only in conjunction with others. Mény and Wright comment (p. 93) that 'the steel crisis and its management reveals both the power of the individual nation-state and the limits to its power', an observation that had applicability across the whole range of industrial policy.

Mény and Wright argue (p. 45) that it was not so much policy principles or conceptions of the legitimacy of state action that acted as constraints, but rather the 'inefficacy of its machinery for dealing with the crisis'. A recurrent problem in the making of industrial policy is that information resources which are essential for effective decision-making are concentrated in the companies. As Atkinson observes (1986, p. 262), 'Much industrial policy is *not routine* and *requires specialised, technical knowledge.* . . . Sophisticated information systems and flexible, discriminating responses are necessary even for the most routine programs of selective financial assistance to industry.' However, one also has to place any information that is gathered into some kind of framework of understanding if it is to be used sensibly and coherently. The difficulty here is that 'industrial intervention has lacked a clear theoretical foundation to guide it (unlike other areas of microeconomic policy such as monopoly policy and environmental protection)' (Grant, R., 1982, p. 389). Grant suggests that, within a market model, the only appropriate starting point is that of the sources of market failure, but this takes us back to difficulties referred to before and which there is not space to tackle here (see Grant, 1989, for a discussion).

Mény and Wright note (1987b, p. 45) that 'Another striking feature of the steel crisis is the extent to which it reveals the multiplicity of decision points within, and the fragmentation and compartmentalisation of, the State apparatus which is involved in industrial policy-making.' This fragmentation and compartmentalisation is a general phenomenon, albeit more marked in some countries than in others. It is, for example, much more a feature of the industrial policy-making process in France than has been acknowledged until recently. The difficult question is, of course, whether the fragmentation of decision-making is a cause or effect of the incoherence of policy. The most likely explanation is that they tend to amplify one another.

Three general points can usefully be made about the machinery available in different countries for dealing with industrial policy. First, central finance ministries tend to be strong, and industry ministries weak. Second, a considerable number of government departments are usually involved in industrial policy, leading to repeated demands for greater coordination at the centre, demands which usually have very little effect. Third, although there are variations in the degree of fragmentation from one country to another, these variations should not be exaggerated.

The influence of the British Treasury on economic policy-making in Britain is well documented and is a frequent source of complaint. However, the Treasury is by no means unique; indeed, if anything, it is typical of a more general pattern. This should not surprise if we recall that the success or otherwise of industrial policy depends to a considerable extent on general economic 'climate-setting' measures which are usually the responsibility of the central finance ministry. In addition, industrial policy often requires quite substantial public expenditure, the approval of which is generally a task of the central finance ministry.

Thus, for example, in France 'The Ministry of Finance plays a distinctive and important role in industrial policy' (Cawson, Holmes and Stevens, 1987, p. 13). Even in Japan the Ministry of Finance is, 'in a sense, the most important government agent involved in industrial policy, since the principal instruments of industrial policy are direct budget and revenue items over which MOF has final approval' (Boyd, 1987, p. 71). The general ideological outlook of ministries of finance is well summarised in a comment on the Canadian Department of Finance: The 'ideological' bias of the department is non-interventionist and market-oriented; it is intellectually sceptical about state-led adjustment and about picking winners and losers. It favours reliance on the market rather than the state as the agent of change and, if necessary, opts for industry-neutral assistance as opposed to more sector-specific intervention (Chandler, 1986, p. 203).

The strength and ideological certainty is matched by the weakness and confusion about goals often shown by industry ministries. Thus in Sweden there was 'no explicit policy and no adequate administrative apparatus within the Ministry of Industry to cope with industrial crises' (Lundmark,

1983, p. 241). In West Germany the Research and Technology Ministry (the nearest equivalent to an industry ministry) became a base for Left-oriented ministers during the era of SPD rule, building external bases of support by concentrating its funds on a few large firms such as Siemens. However, the Ministry's distinctive political identity did not, of course, survive the end of SPD rule, whilst its policy of concentrating funding on a few firms became the object of criticism. In France 'The Minister of Industry is seen as a low status minister, and his or her access to the President may be less than that of the heads of major firms' (Cawson, Holmes and Stevens, 1987, p. 14). In Britain strengthening the Department of Trade and Industry as a counterweight to the Treasury has been a favourite nostrum of reformers but the Treasury has continued to exert a substantial influence on industrial policy-making, not least when an active industrial strategy is being pursued (see Grant, 1982).

It might be objected that Japan provides an exception to this general pattern. However, as Hill has pointed out, the 'Japan Inc.' version of Japanese economic success has 'tended to emphasise the power of MITI and to ignore the position of both the Ministry of Finance and the intermediation of the banking system in that success' (Hill, 1983, p. 77). Industrial policy reformers in the West are understandably inclined to exaggerate the importance of MITI, and to underplay the importance of such factors as the high savings ratio in Japan. As Boyd notes (1987, p. 70), 'There has been too great a willingness to construe the Japanese economic system in terms of an economic Leviathan with MITI as the grey matter. MITI is, of course, important but its precise weight within the state apparatus is difficult to determine and has changed over time.'

In any case one cannot discuss industrial policy formation simply in terms of a finance ministry and an industry ministry. Many other ministries are involved in the formation of industrial policy. Thus, even in Japan, 'MITI does not enjoy exclusive responsbility' (Boyd, 1987, p. 81). Shipbuilding is the responsibility of the Ministry of Transport; agriculture, forestry and fisheries are dealt with by an influential Ministry of Agriculture (not an unusual feature in many countries); there is a strong Ministry of Construction, and a rather weaker Ministry of Posts and Telecommunications.

The precise division of responsibility for particular industries differs from one country to another; indeed, one of the features of industrial policy-making is the frequent reallocation of responsibilities, usually not in the pursuit of administrative coherence but to reflect changes in the political influence of particular ministers. However, most countries have some kind of transport ministry. All have an agricultural ministry, which is usually responsible for what is often one of the largest industries in most countries, food processing (see Pestoff, 1987). The first oil shock led many countries to establish energy ministries. In Britain the Ministry of Fuel and Power, victim to a fashion for larger departments, was resurrected as the Department of Energy; however, it has always been seen as a rather peripheral department (the assignment of Tony Benn and Peter Walker to it was something of a political punishment), and once the task of electricity privatisation has been accomplished it seems likely to disappear. Indeed, the West Germans have managed without an energy ministry at all. In many countries (although not in Britain) there is a posts and telecommunications ministry, whilst in Britain the key pharmaceutical industry is the responsibility of the health ministry. Last but not least, in many countries the Ministry of Defence is responsible for the defence industries. Indeed, in the United States one could reasonably claim that the Pentagon is the most active industrial-policy department, given the defence-driven character of American industrial interventions.

In addition, most countries have a number of quasi-governmental agencies involved in industrial policy. In the Republic of Ireland, the Industrial Development Agency is the main mechanism for the development and delivery of an industrial strategy. In the absence of an effective state bureaucracy, or coherent political direction, the Italian state holding companies acquired responsibility, first for modernising the Italian economy, and then for rationalising it and giving it a greater exposure to market forces. Even if non-ministerial bodies do not have the breadth of responsibility assigned to them in the Irish Republic or in Italy, they may have responsibility for important areas of policy. Thus, in many countries, there is an effort to protect competition policy from direct political influences: note the responsibilities of the Office of Fair Trading and the Monopolies and Mergers Commission in Britain, the Federal Cartels Office in West Germany, or the Fair Trade Commission in Japan.

Given this proliferation of departments and agencies with an interest in industrial policy, the problem of policy coordination is a recurrent theme in discussions about improving the quality of industrial policy formation. In systems such as Britain, where 'departmentalism' is rife, interdepartmental committees have a key role, at least in the minimal sense of sorting out turf fights. It has been claimed that, in the French case, interministerial committees have been a reasonable success (Green, 1983) although there are grounds for some caution about what has actually been achieved (Hayward, 1986). A recurrent theme in Britain is the demand for a Cabinet-level committee to coordinate industrial policy.

The problem is, of course, what does coordination mean? Does it mean finding out what other departments are doing, so that one does not duplicate or contradict their initiatives? Or does it mean developing and implementing some industrial 'grand design'? Even in the former, minimal sense of coordination, little has been achieved in most countries. A comment made by Atkinson about Canada applies to many other countries: 'no department or agency has emerged to coordinate industrial policy in the manner that the Department of Finance conducts macroeconomic policy' (Atkinson, 1986, p. 276). The more general lesson to be drawn here in relation to the wider concerns of this book is that one is not confronted with a monolithic, purposive state in the field of industrial policy, but rather with a fragmented state, uncertain of what its objectives are or how to attain them.

Having said that, clearly there are differences in the coherence of policy-making mechanisms from one country to another. Apart from Canada (which has special problems to be discussed in the next section), the award for the least coordinated set of mechanisms must go to the United States. One objection that might be made immediately is that the United States does not have an industrial policy. This is undoubtedly the case (unless one adopts a very elastic definition of what constitutes an industrial policy), but the United States does claim to have, and has some political interest in developing, a trade policy. The President's Commission on Industrial Competitiveness (1985, p. 38) found that decisions on trade policy were split 'between at least twenty-five executive branch agencies and nineteen congressional subcommittees'. It was noted (p. 39) that 'This fragmented approach to US trade policymaking causes trade policy officials to spend much time coordinating trade policy, rather than designing and implementing it. Fragmented trade policy responsibility in the United States seriously limits our ability to respond to the growing volume and complexity of international trade.'

The underlying problem here is, of course, the whole nature of the American system of government. If one looks at the various actors involved in decisions that might affect industry, at least four sets are involved. First, there is the Congress which, apart from its well-known committee system, has its own agencies serving it (e.g. the Office of Technology Assessment). Second, there is the White House, and the special advisers and agencies attached to it (such as the Office of the US Trade Representative). Third, there are the various executive departments located away from the excitements of 1600 Pennsylvania Avenue: old stagers such as the Department of Commerce, and newer ones such as the Department of Energy. Last and not least, there is the judicial branch: whereas Japan has one lawyer per ten thousand people, the United States employs twenty (Johnson, 1984, p. 15); indeed, 'The federal judiciary has attracted growing criticism from Congress and the public for intruding too deeply into social policy making' (Brickman, Jasonoff and Ilgen, 1985, p. 127).

Although it has been emphasised that one must not place too much stress on the role of MITI, Japan is characterised by the survival of an industrial policy imperative, and 'close government–industry collaboration in the management of the economy' (Boyd, 1987, p. 85). This is clearly a very different policy-making environment from that found in the United States. However, too much emphasis should not be placed on the role of different state forms in producing this outcome. Many other factors are at work: the dominance of the *keiretsu* in the Japanese economy; the absence there of a significant defence industry; the centralised nature of the Japanese education system; the role of the dominant Liberal Democratic Party; the practice of *amakudari* ('descent from heaven') as a facilitator of industry–government–party contacts; the group orientation of the Japanese, and a variety of other cultural factors. What should be clear (but is not always to politicians) is that creating a 'British MITI' would not create the conditions for industrial success on Japanese lines.

Conflict between different levels of the state

As King notes in his introduction, a characteristic of the modern extended state apparatus is the conflict between different levels of the state. This conflict is seen in its most acute form in the federal state, although it is certainly not absent elsewhere. It is worth considering the case of Canada as an example of the problems of industrial policy-making in a federal system. Canada has been chosen because 'the reality throughout most of the twentieth century – and at no time more than the present – has been a situation in which the central government exercises less power, and the provincial governments exercise more power, than in any other developed country' (Stevenson, 1982, p. 65).

As has been pointed out, industrial policy-making in all states is made more difficult by the problem of functional coordination between different departments with a stake in different aspects of policy. In a federal system this difficulty is confounded by the problems of federal–provincial coordination (not to mention interprovincial coordination). Not surprisingly, 'When to the diffusion of focus within the federal government is added the diffusion of responsibility in the industrial policy field between the federal and provincial governments, which often diffuse responsibility within their own structures, government policy-making almost necessarily becomes *ad hoc*, reactive, and inconsistent' (Trebilcock, 1986, p. 346).

In order to understand the problem of industrial policy-making in Canada, four general comments need to be made, three of which have applicability (in a general analytical sense) to other federal systems. The one that does not is the question of Canadian national identity. Given the complexity of this issue, it will not be possible to explore it in any depth here. It should be noted, however, that one may have a state apparatus without a sufficiently well-developed sense of national identity to sustain the actions of the state. Even allowing for the improvement in relations between Quebec and the Federal Government, it is open to question whether the sense of Canadian identity is sufficiently strong to underpin the development of a coherent and effective federal industrial policy.

Two other issues which arise in the Canadian case are of more general applicability in the consideration of federal systems. One is that a political game is going on between the federal and provincial levels. An easy let-out for provincial politicians in a federal system is to 'blame Ottawa' (or Canberra, or wherever). Equally, federal governments can and do play provinces off against each other. Manoeuvres of this kind can produce short-run political advantages, but they do not contribute to the quality of policy-making.

One also has to consider the underlying political economy of the particular country. In other words, where are the concentrations of economic and political power? In Canada the answer has been clear: in Quebec and in Ontario, where manufacturing industry and population is concentrated. Ontario, in particular, is the most populated province and 'the home of more than 50 per cent of Canada's manufacturing capacity' (Tupper, 1986, pp. 354–5). The maritime provinces have been relatively poor, and have required substantial federal government assistance. The resource-based economies to the west (oil in Alberta, forestry in British Columbia) have a more independent economic base, but are vulnerable to downturns in the price or demand for their commodities.

A fourth consideration is the calibre of decision-makers at the provincial level, particularly in the smaller and poorer provinces. This is, of course, a contentious issue. How does one measure calibre? In one sense, anyone endorsed by the democratic process is good enough to govern. The fact that federal systems have thrown up some rather unusual premiers could be seen as simply an unfair value judgement by a metropolitan outsider (but perhaps not entirely unfair: see Starr, 1987). There is a problem, even if most Canadian writers would not use such colourful language as Stevenson when he refers to what he terms the 'lumpen-separatism of used-car dealers in Alberta' (1982, p. 235). It would be unfair to categorise provincial governments in federal systems as the last refuge of the lumpen bourgeoisie, but questions may legitimately be raised about the horizons and vision of provincial politicians who cannot hope to aspire to federal office.

Political scientists usually take a relatively benign view of federalism. (A useful corrective is Scharpf's analysis of the 'joint decision trap' in German federalism which he sees as leading to suboptimal policy outcomes: Scharpf, 1988.) In general, however, it is vaguely seen (particularly by non-specialists on the subject) as a 'good thing' which disperses power, provides enhanced opportunities for participation, etc. However, as the Canadian case shows, it poses serious problems for the quality of industrial policy-making. There is no doubt, for example, that it leads to bidding against each other by subnational governments for desirable projects, a process from which the company concerned is often the main beneficiary. 'Even when the enterprises attracted were legitimate and successful, the effect of ten different industrial strategies has been to fragment even further an industrial sector which is already too fragmented for the size of the Canadian market' (Stevenson, 1982, p. 113). There is a growing trend towards unilateralism, rather than a search for interdependence: 'while governments seldom pursue industrial policies that are clearly contradictory, there remains a lack of policy coordination between the federal and provincial governments and between provincial governments themselves. In most major areas of industrial policy, each government pursues its ends with scant reference to the goals of the other actors' (Tupper, 1986, p. 347).

It might be thought that problems of this kind do not arise in Britain. However, the United Kingdom, to use Rokkan and Urwin's (1983) terminology, should be thought of as a 'union' rather than a 'unitary' state. Industrial policy-making in Scotland (and to a lesser extent, Wales and, in a different way, Northern Ireland) is separated from industrial policy-making in England. It is often forgotten that the Department of Trade and Industry is responsible for industrial policy in England, not the whole United Kingdom. The interest of the Scottish Office in industrial policy (including the existence of distinctive Scottish nationalised industries) gives bureaucratic representatives of Scotland a seat on any interdepartmental committee dealing with industrial issues. This is a useful resource, particularly combined with the political veto which the Secretary of State for Scotland is sometimes able to exercise, as in the case of the threatened closure of the Ravenscraig steel works. The poor performance of the Conservatives in Scotland in the 1987 election is likely to make them even more susceptible to Scottish sensibilities.

Even so, one must not exaggerate the autonomy of the Scottish Office: it is a secondary actor in a complex policy-making network, rather than an independent power base (although the Scottish Development Agency does enjoy a real autonomy of action). 'Despite the inevitable parallels between policy measures in Scotland and in the UK, there is some scope for initiative at Scottish level in connection, for instance, with the promotion of inward investment, stimulating small-firm growth, encouraging the involvement of indigenous companies in subcontracting, assisting the advertising of Scottish products, industrial rationalisation and so forth' (Hood and Young, 1984, p. 44). However, 'the impact of industrial policy is very constrained by the fact that the proportion of total identifiable public expenditure in Scotland in this area is so small' (p. 400).

Local authorities are also becoming increasingly active in developing and implementing industrial policies in Britain, in large part in response to problems of the decline of long-established industries, and increased unemployment, within their boundaries. With the limited resources at their disposal, the scale of the problems that many of them face, and the location of corporate headquarters in London or abroad, the extent to which they are able to make an impact on local industrial structures is often limited. A further difficulty is that the extent to which local authorities should be involved in work of this kind has been a contentious issue in central–local relations: for example, the efforts of the former Greater London Council to develop a systematic industrial strategy for London did not meet with favour in government circles. The least contentious form of local authority activity – advertising in the press or on television to persuade firms to come to Telford, or Scunthorpe, or Milton Keynes – is probably the least useful. Local enterprise boards have been most successful where they have pursued realistic strategies, based on an assessment of particular local needs not met by existing provisions, for example, the emphasis of the West Midlands Enterprise Board on medium-sized companies, an important element in the regional economy.

Policy communities

Government–industry relations is highly differentiated sectorally, with a series of policy communities made up of different actors processing different issues in different ways. Deubner has argued (1984, p. 501) that '"sectors" have a highly interesting role in explaining politics' (ibid.). In particular, he maintains (p. 517) that 'Not all industrial sectors . . . enjoy the same degree of attention at the political level.' Deubner points out that employers' associations and unions in a particular sector may unite to protect and promote sector specific interests (although one might add that such coalitions are more likely in West Germany than in the UK). Bargaining between employers and labour can create and accentuate differences between sectors over time.

Deubner makes a convincing case for sectoral analysis, but his argument that 'highly concentrated sectors have a clear advantage in influencing government decisions' (ibid.) is open to question. Farmers are generally relatively small-scale producers, yet one phenomenon which may be observed across Western societies is the influence enjoyed by farming interests which generally have a symbiotic relationship with agricultural ministries. In an interesting analysis of the British situation, Cox, Lowe and Winter, (1987a, p. 16) argue that the policy community for rural conservation can be 'characterised as large, diverse and pluralistic; that for agriculture, as small, tightly-knit and corporatist'. Agricultural interests have been able to preserve 'the autonomy of the Ministry [of Agriculture] and of the farming community in the administration and implementation of agriculture policy; and . . . the autonomy of the farmer in making production and land use decisions' (Cox, Lowe and Winter, 1987b, p. 186). The fact that no one farmer is large enough to be politically influential on his own has encouraged the formation of effective farming organisations which have benefited from a partnership relationship with the state.

Sectoral differences in patterns of government–industry relations may be illustrated by considering the contrasting cases of the chemicals and dairy processing industries. A number of differences between these two sectors may be enumerated as follows:

1.   The chemicals industry largely produces intermediate goods for other industries rather than for the final consumer, whereas the diary processing industry is more concerned with producing finished products (for domestic consumers and the catering industry).
2.   The chemicals industry is highly internationalised in terms of patterns of trade and the dominance of international companies. Although there is international trade in dairy products, liquid milk is largely produced for a national market, and national differences in taste still influence patterns of demand for other products. Although there are multinationals in the industry, national producers (particularly cooperatives) remain significant.
3.   Government intervention in the chemicals industry has largely been confined to such areas as competition policy and environmental and health and safety regulations. Although there is some state ownership in the industry, governments (apart from countries such as Italy) have not generally used state-owned companies as instruments of industrial policy (an abstinence partly explained by the fact that the industry is capital intensive and hence not a large employer). In the dairy industry there is significant state intervention in all Western countries (including the United States) to try and secure conditions for the orderly marketing of products.

These differences have a number of consequences both for policy networks in the two industries, and the way in which problems are handled. Although the chemical industry has highly effective industry associations, the dairy industry has a much denser network of institutions handling a wider range of tasks. Consider, for example, the dairy industry in Canada (limiting the analysis to federal institutions and the province of Ontario). At the provincial level on the industry side there is a Milk Marketing Board and a Cream Producers Marketing Board, as well as an Ontario Dairy Council (for processors) and an Ontario Milk Transport Association. There is a complex network of industry advisory committees, as well as an Ontario Dairy Herd Improvement Corporation. The main institutions on the provincial government side are the Milk Commission of Ontario, and the Dairy Inspection Branch of the Ontario Ministry of Agriculture and Food. At the federal level organisations include the National Dairy Council and the Dairy Farmers of Canada, as well as a Dairy Bureau of Canada (a producer market expansion agency). The Canadian Dairy Commission is responsible for an industrial milk subsidy, and there is also a Canadian Milk Supply Management Committee and a Canadian Milk Recording Board. Although the arrangements in Canada are particularly complex because of the federal–provincial dimension, a similar dense network of specialised institutions could be found in all OECD member states. In the chemical industry there are far fewer industry institutions; in particular, quasi-governmental agencies confined to the industry are far less common.

Institutional differences are of relatively little significance if they do not make any difference to the way in which issues have been handled. However, problems facing the chemical industry have been tackled in a different way from those facing the dairy industry. Both the dairy industry (farmers as well as processors) and the petrochemicals industry have faced problems of overcapacity. In the dairy industry government agencies have been closely involved in most countries in trying to tackle the underlying problems through a variety of measures, for example by offering farmers financial incentives to leave dairy farming, adjusting price support levels for dairy products, or imposing a variety of quota arrangements. Other than in the European Community, these measures have been introduced at a national level. In the chemical industry the task of sorting out the overcapacity problem has been left to the firms themselves, through a variety of bilateral arrangements involving capacity swaps or the formation of joint companies to facilitate rationalisation. These measures have often involved cross-national collaboration, e.g. the formation of a joint company between ICI and ENI to rationalise PVC production. In so far as governmental authorities have been involved, one of the principal actors has been the European Commission which has had to sanction the arrangements under Community competition law.

What 'the state' means in each sector is clearly different. In the case of the dairy industry, the distinction between the state and the non-state, between the private and the public, has clearly become blurred. A number of institutions, for instance marketing boards, cross the boundary between the two. The relationship between the state and the industry has many of the hallmarks of mesocorporatism. In the chemical industry the distinction between the state and the industry is more clearly maintained (although it is obviously somewhat less clear in countries which have state-owned chemical companies). 'The state' for an internationalised industry like chemicals may mean the European Community (or the OECD or UN agencies which draw up a number of regulations affecting the industry) rather than national governments. Many of the activities of industry associations resemble conventional forms of pressure politics, involving long drawn-out consultation exercises on, say, proposed new environmental regulations. One cannot understand 'the state in action' in industrial policy without examining sectoral variations which often persist – as in the case of the dairy industry – in the face of different national traditions of government–industry relations.

Corporate state or company state?

Other than in relation to the dairy industry, relatively little mention has been made of corporatist theories in this analysis. This omission is deliberate. It is contended that corporatist theories are less useful in explaining patterns of government–industry relations in the late 1980s than appeared possible in the 1970s. There are exceptions to this general picture, not just in particular sectors such as the dairy industry. For example, industrial adjustment in a number of smaller West European democracies continues to display marked neo-corporatist traits (see Katzenstein, 1985). Corporatist theories may also be of some value in attempting to explain developments in East European countries such as Hungary where the Chamber of Commerce has been officially given the task of intermediating between its business members and the authorities.

A more helpful, and more generally applicable, approach might be to revive the concept of the 'company state' (Willis and Grant, 1987). In 1977, when most analysts were searching the skies for harbingers of the coming corporatism, Ganz concluded an examination of government–industry relations in Britain by suggesting that 'the most interesting factor to emerge from this analysis is the opposite of corporatism, the company state' (1977, p. 97). Ganz commented:

Government assistance to industry raises the basic problem of using private bodies for public purposes. The Company or the Contract State is the result. It represents the reverse side of the Corporate State, in that it shows the difficulty of making private bodies publicly accountable for the public money they receive and of using private law mechanisms for public ends. (p. 106)

Placed on a broader canvass, the notion of the company state implies that the purpose of the state, as an economic actor, is to facilitate the operations of companies. Such a context can lead to a variety of cooperative business–government activities which may prove mutually beneficial for government and industry, if not for wider publics or the long-term health of an industry. An interesting example can be drawn from the history of the forest industry in Canada, which has involved at different times a 'corporate-political game to gain access under secure tenure arrangements to new timber supplies in return for substantial increases in the revenues paid to provincial governments' (Gillis and Roach, 1986, p. 248). The downside is that Canadian public policy has failed to deal adequately with 'forestry and forest conservation. . . . Canadian governments have too often settled for the minimum acceptable solution, rather than enact effective measures that would go beyond the exploitive ethic' (p. 253).

It must be emphasised that the company state is not a minimal state. The company state takes a variety of measures to promote industry and, in certain respects, to control it. It does involve an increasing emphasis on direct company–government interactions, leading to an increasing use of government relations divisions rather than industry associations. This last feature is particularly marked in the Anglo-American countries, and it may be objected that what has been described does not apply to countries with a longer *dirigiste* tradition such as France. In fact, the French state has been penetrated by companies, so that it is often their servant, rather than their partner or their master. It is 'widely acknowledged inside and outside the state system that the Industry Ministry is the lobby for business within the government.' (Cawson, Holmes and Stevens, 1987, p. 14). In discussing the case of the actions of Thomson, Cawson and his colleagues (p. 28) point out that it has 'captured' the Industry Ministry, effectively becoming 'Thomson's lobbyist and spokesman within the administration'. However, Thomson has also been able to go straight to presidential level, bypassing the Industry Ministry. Similar access to the highest levels of government is available to leading British firms.

The general picture that emerges from this survey is of the state as a rather constrained and ineffective actor in the sphere of industrial policy. The policies pursued are often poorly coordinated and ineffective, and government institutions may often be acting as the agents of companies, rather than systematically influencing company decision-making (although central finance ministries are generally above pressures of this kind). Of course, the question of what the state should be doing, if anything, in this policy area remains an open and controversial one, although in some countries state involvement in industry is seen as more legitimate than in others. However, privatisation of state assets is under way in a number of Western countries, and the general mood of the times is in favour of a retreat of the state from industry. This retreat is unlikely to be total, because of persisting concerns about competitiveness in a number of countries, and the newer political pressures for more stringent environmental controls. 'The one thing that is clear is that no matter how the economy is to be guided, the process must relate more to international competitive conditions than to internal political preferences' (Crookell, 1985, p. 73). The problem is how to achieve that objective in a democratic system of government.

Guide to further reading

Wilks and Wright (eds) (1987) offer a number of readings on recent conceptual and empirical work in the area of government–industry relations, covering Japan, the United States and West European countries. Mény and Wright (eds) (1987) is one of the most impressive collections of essays on a particular industrial sector (steel) covering a number of Western countries and raising a number of fundamental issues about the role of the state in the industrial policy arena. Rather different sectors are covered in Grant (ed.) (1987) (food processing) and Grant, Paterson and Whitston (1988) (chemicals). Some fundamental issues about the role of sectors in industrial politics are tackled in Deubner (1984).

Atkinson's (1986) essay provides one of the best available treatments of the role of bureaucracy in relation to industrial policy. Hayward (1986) covers some important issues about the roles of the market and the state in the context of a discussion of France. The debate about industrial policy is extensively reviewed in some of the seventy-two volumes of research studies published by the Royal Commission on the Economic Union and Development Prospects for Canada, notably Blais (1986a and 1986b). The essays contained in Dyson and Wilks (eds) (1983) are still worth reading, particularly in terms of the characterisation of national industrial policy styles. A more recent assessment of national policy approaches is to be found in Duchêne and Shepherd (eds) (1987). Zysman (1983) includes a useful typology of alternative adjustment strategies. Hall (1986) cogently sets out the case for an institutional analysis of the politics of state intervention, as well as providing a valuable comparative analysis of British and French experience. Grant (1989) examines the character of government–industry relations in three countries with a market-oriented approach to industrial policy (Canada, the United Kingdom and the United States).

The usual concentration on larger countries is redressed in two scholarly studies of smaller European countries, particularly Austria and Switzerland (Katzenstein, 1984, 1985). There is a growing literature on the newly industrialising countries (Deyo (ed.), 1987; Harris, 1986; Saunders (ed.), 1981).

3 Financial markets

Michael Moran

Introduction

In this chapter we will examine one of the most neglected of all aspects of state intervention in the modern economy. The study of financial markets is highly developed, but for the most part that study has largely been by economists. The result is that the characteristic concerns of political scientists have been neglected. In particular, little attention has been paid to *the state in action in financial markets*: in other words, to the ways different kinds of state institution typically try to intervene in markets, and to the way these interventions combine with the actions of the firms in the marketplace. The purpose of this chapter is to provide an overview of these matters, and the material is organised with this introductory purpose in mind. The range of examples is limited to the relationship between the state and the financial markets in the most important capitalist economies. In particular, we shall concentrate our examples on the United States, the United Kingdom and Japan. This is because, as we shall shortly see, it is the financial centres of these countries that really matter in the world financial marketplace, and it is the domestic and the international actions of these three states that are by far the most significant in illuminating the modern relationship between states and financial markets.

In providing an overview of state action in financial markets, we begin at the most obvious starting point, with a sketch of the nature of those markets. We then show why states intervene. This is followed by an exploration of the institutional structures in which state intervention is organised. The next section shows that there are similar cross-national patterns in the recent evolution of these structures, and explains why this is so. The final part of the chapter briefly picks out the key features of state action illuminated by the particular cases examined in these pages.

The nature of financial markets

The activities that take place in financial markets are highly varied and complex, but the essential nature of the financial marketplace can be simply and succinctly summarised: *a financial marketplace is a social arena where a financial service or a financial instrument is traded or exchanged.* From this simple definition follows important consequences. The chief of these is that the range of instruments and services traded is highly diverse. The financial marketplace is often equated with the hectic trading that goes on in the dealing rooms of the large corporations that buy and sell foreign exchange. Thus Strange writes:

The Western financial system is rapidly coming to resemble nothing so much as a vast casino. Every day games are played in this casino that involve sums of money so large that they cannot be imagined. At night the games go on at the other side of the world. In the towering office blocks that dominate all the great cities of the world, rooms are full of chain-smoking young men all playing these games. Their eyes are fixed on the computer screens flickering with changing prices. They play by intercontinental telephone or by tapping electronic machines. They are just like the gamblers in casinos watching the clicking spin of a silver ball on a roulette wheel and putting their chips on red or black, odd numbers or even ones. (Strange, 1986, p. 1)

This 'casino like' atmosphere is indeed an important aspect of some of the most important financial markets. Nevertheless, the range of dealings goes well beyond speculative dealings in foreign exchanges or the shares of corporations. It encompasses the great mass of exchanges that are transacted daily in national banking systems, down to the most trivial cheque cashed by the smallest depositor. It extends also to some of the most important lifetime economic transactions made by private individuals – for instance the act of investing in an insurance policy in order to produce a pension for retirement, or the contracting of a mortgage for the purposes of house purchase. In short, while the hectic dealing rooms conventionally summoned up to represent the financial marketplace are indeed important, financial markets in totality are mass markets involving virtually every member of the community. This fact, as we shall soon see, has an important bearing on the nature and purposes of state intervention.

The diversity of the financial marketplace extends not only to the range of financial instruments with which it deals: the range of services traded is equally wide and two are particularly important. The first is information and intelligence. Some of the most important firms are involved in selling up-to-the-minute information about prices and trading conditions, much of it supplied electronically through telecommunications networks. More generally, there is a large market in economic intelligence packaged in a wide variety of formats. Most of the largest financial services firms have substantial research departments that gather and analyse data about market conditions and prospects, and these data are sold as economic intelligence to customers. A second major service can be labelled commercial expertise. Among the most important retailers of this expertise are the biggest law firms, the largest multinational accounting firms (there are eight dominant in world markets), the largest insurance companies and the biggest banks. The range of these commercial services is highly varied: it includes, among other things, accounting and auditing, the management of investments and the provision of legal services in respect of contracts (Ingham, 1984, pp. 40–78).

This list should demonstrate a point that is often neglected: 'financial markets' encompass a major, and diverse, part of any modern economy.

Financial services are part of the wider 'services sector'. Like that wider sector, they are growing – in range, in numbers employed and in the geographical scale of operations (OECD, 1987). To put it simply, the financial marketplace is a marketplace like anywhere else: in it, goods (financial instruments) and services (information and intelligence, commercial expertise) are traded for a price. From this follow a number of consequences which impinge in important ways on the behaviour of the state. Three are especially noteworthy.

First, like any other marketplace the financial market is an arena where competitive struggles take place – between firms, between interest groups representing collections of firms and between states and parts of states. Second, the outcomes of these competitive struggles are unequal: there are winners and losers. One of the most important roles of state agencies, we will see, is to try to influence who wins and loses, and to manage the results when the fate of losers threaten the wider stability of markets. Third, like most competitive struggles in advanced market economies the struggles in the financial marketplace are increasingly being organised on a global scale.

In this global organisation three states, and their associated financial centres, are especially important. The first is the United States: the richest financial markets lie in the United States; the American currency, the dollar, is the single most important currency in which financial instruments are traded globally; and for most of the years since the Second World War the largest private financial institutions were American (Gilpin, 1987; Strange, 1988, pp. 88–114).

The second key state is Japan. In the 1980s Japanese firms displaced their American rivals from the leading position in a wide range of markets, and Japan became the leading creditor in world markets. The third major state is the United Kingdom. British firms, and domestic financial markets in Britain, are comparatively unimportant in the wider world system, but London is one of the three great world financial centres, alongside Tokyo and New York. As Table 3.1 shows, it is actually the leading centre for the international banking markets.

Table 3.1: Comparative size of international banking centres, by nation (per cent share of total lending)

	1985	1987
United Kingdom	24.5	21.6
Japan	10.4	18.3
United States	12.8	9.6

Source: *Bank of England Quarterly Bulletin*, May 1988, p. 217

The aims of state action

Financial markets are diverse and complicated social institutions; this diversity and complexity produces corresponding features in the range and purposes of state action. In summary the objects of state intervention can be described under four headings: maintaining the confidence and trust needed for financial exchanges to take place; shaping the identity of winners and losers in competitive struggles; acting as a customer and as a supplier in the markets, and safeguarding the interests of individual consumers of financial services. We can briefly discuss each of these in turn.

The creation of the conditions under which economic exchange can take place in an atmosphere of confidence is a general function of any state in a market economy. It is a particularly central function in the case of financial exchanges, however, because willingness to make an exchange depends in large part on a sense of assurance about future conditions. We contract many insurance policies in the expectation of future gain, and that expectation rests on confidence that the insurance company will continue to be run in an honest and prudent way. Likewise, we place our savings with a bank or building society only when we are sure that they will not unexpectedly collapse. The whole structure of financial exchange rests on this largely unthinking foundation of trust – and that foundation, in turn, has been laid by long traditions of state intervention designed to ensure that financial institutions are run prudently and to ensure, in the event of collapse, that depositors and savers do not lose (Wilson, 1980, pp. 288–300). Some of the earliest cases of state intervention in financial markets were shaped by the need to create confidence and trust in the financial system. This is especially true of banking markets. 'Central banking' – the use of the state to guarantee the stability of the banking system – was virtually invented in the United Kingdom during the later decades of the nineteenth century. The Bank of England, although nominally a privately owned institution, in this period guaranteed the resources of the banking system whenever a crisis of confidence in a particular bank threatened confidence in the wider community of banks (Hirsch, 1977; Kindleberger, 1978). In the United States after the Wall Street crash of 1929, when almost half the nation's banks went out of business, the state was compelled to create a system of 'deposit insurance' to protect the savings of bank customers, and to pass elaborate legislation governing the rules under which banks operated (Burns, 1974). In virtually every modern state there now exists a publicly controlled central bank, or some equivalent state agency, whose responsibility is to guarantee the stability of the banking system and thus to create the sense of trust essential for the functioning of the wider financial system.

The state's function as a fundamental guarantor is long established. Rather more recent is the interest of state agencies in influencing the identity of winners and losers in competitive struggles. It is, however, a natural outgrowth of features that we noticed in the last section – the growing importance of financial institutions in the 'service' sector of modern economies, and the growing extent to which competition in financial services is taking place on a global scale. Some of the most important changes in financial markets in recent years have been the result of interventions by states anxious to influence the outcome of competitive struggles. The actions of states are guided by a variety of considerations. In some cases they intervene as the 'sponsors' or defenders of the interests of their own national firms against foreign competitors. Thus extensive reforms in Japanese financial markets since the mid-1980s were in part the outcome of pressure from the US Treasury Department, which was anxious to have Japanese markets opened up to large American banks and securities houses (Frankel, 1984, pp. 1–5). In other cases they have intervened in their own markets to favour one group of interests at the expense of another. In the United States in the mid-1970s, for instance, state agencies compelled the New York Stock Exchange to introduce price competition among its members, a demand that was supported by big institutional investors and giant financial services firms (Seligman, 1982, pp. 439–534). In yet other instances, again, states intervene to influence the struggle for business between different world financial centres. In Britain after 1983, for example, the Bank of England and the Department of Trade and Industry obliged the City of London to reform its trading practices, in the belief that only by these changes could London's position as a world financial centre be assured against the challenge of other locations (Reid, 1988).

It will be obvious that the state intervenes in financial markets in many guises. The complexity of these interventions is made greater because states are never merely outside agents guaranteeing the stability of markets or regulating competitive conditions: they are also active players in the markets, both as customers and as suppliers of services. The most striking single instance of the state as customer is the almost universal practice of entering financial markets to fund state debt. In some important cases the state's role as an indebted customer has greatly increased in recent years, and has played an important part in guiding regulatory policy. Thus in the 1980s the American Federal Government became massively indebted in the markets, and a substantial proportion of that debt was lent by Japanese institutions (Gilpin, 1987, pp. 330–3). In Japan also the state has been a significant customer in the market for credit (Feldman, 1986, pp. 5–8). In the Japanese case the state's need to raise debt in the late 1970s was the single most important reason why, in that period, government-led reforms of trading practices began to be implemented.

The state's role is further complicated by its position as a supplier of services. Every financial system in the capitalist world has institutions, owned or controlled by the state, that provide banking or other financial services, often in direct competition with privately owned firms. One of the most striking instances is provided by the Japanese Post Office. The Post Office in Japan, contrary to the image suggested by its name, is anything but a mere retailer of stamps. It is one of the most successful institutions in the banking system. Its aggressive business practices have contributed significantly to financial change in Japan; conversely, its determination to defend its privileges as a state body have been a major feature of the struggles for financial reform in that country (Suzuki, 1987).

As the central position of the Post Office in the Japanese system emphasises, modern financial markets are mass markets, and this feature lies behind the fourth influence guiding state intervention: customer protection. Of course the state's historical role in guaranteeing the honesty and prudence of banks was itself an important kind of customer protection. The growing range and diversity of financial instruments and financial institutions has, however, pushed the state's responsibilities in this respect well beyond the conventional banking system. The most striking instance is provided by Britain. Since 1986 we have had a Financial Services Act which unifies a wide range of provisions for customer protection into a common statute and under common institutions. The Act obliges investment businesses to obtain a licence as a condition of doing business, designates a range of so-called 'self-regulatory organisations' to administer this system and creates a Securities and Investments Board to oversee the workings of these self-regulatory organisations and their member firms (Berrill, 1986).

The purposes of state intervention are thus highly varied: to create the trust needed for financial transactions to take place; to influence the outcomes of competitive struggles in markets; to act as both a customer and supplier in those markets; and to provide customer protection. The structures through which the state acts show similar variety; but beneath this variety are some striking common features. To these matters we now turn.

The Structures of state action

The forms and channels through which states act to shape financial markets are almost inexhaustible: anything from the general legal framework for the enforcement of contracts, to the most minute details of taxation policy, can and do mould the competitive conditions under which financial instruments and services are traded. In the narrower field of overt state intervention in the financial marketplace the range of instruments used by the state is also highly varied. The most important include legal ownership of financial institutions (widespread in the banking industries of many economies); the issuing of directives to individual firms (commonly used to influence credit allocation); the insistence that entry to a particular market be dependent on obtaining a licence from the competent authority (the basis of control in both the banking and securities markets in the United Kingdom); and the regular inspection of the internal structures and balance sheets of firms (common in banking regulation).

Beneath the variety suggested by ownership, direction, licensing and inspection, however, some recurrent features stand out. The most important is that state intervention in financial markets is institutionally complex and differentiated. It is a useful shorthand to write of 'the state' in action in financial services, but it is no more than a convenient shorthand. Everywhere, state intervention is governed by a complex administrative division of labour and by jealousies and rivalries between the various state agencies at work.

Not only is it impossible to find an instance where an integrated state acts towards the financial markets in a unified manner; even individual state agencies are often riddled with internal rivalries. The extremes of fragmentation are illustrated in the case of the United States. It has been estimated that there are at least ten Federal agencies, and over fifty agencies of individual states, concerned with the control of American financial markets (United States Congress, 1986, p. 298). These include central departments of state (like the Treasury), the central bank (the Federal Reserve Board), the Securities and Exchange Commission (which oversees, among other things, the stock exchanges) and the Commodity Futures Trading Commission (which oversees many of the newer financial markets in the United States).

This formal institutional fragmentation is, however, only a part of the story. There exists a division of functions between the many agencies, but it is an unclear division. There are constant battles for regulatory jurisdiction between agencies. Individual institutions, because they are created at different times and in different circumstances, have different organisational 'cultures', a factor which intensifies the conflicts arising out of battles for regulatory jurisdiction. Thus, not only is there no unitary 'state in action' in American financial markets; it sometimes seems that many agencies devote more energy to frustrating each other's ambitions than to controlling the financial markets.

America is only an extreme example of a common pattern. The Japanese state, for instance, has often been viewed by Western observers as uniquely well organised to act according to a coherent, strategic plan; but in the area of financial services regulation it is deeply divided internally. The superficial institutional structure does indeed suggest remarkable coherence. A single central agency, the Ministry of Finance, carries out a range of key functions – for instance, licensing and inspection of financial institutions, management of government debt – that elsewhere are divided between different agencies. This picture of unity and coherence is, however, misleading. The Ministry of Finance is, despite its comparatively comprehensive responsibilities, still forced to compete with other agencies in the state structure. The most important example of this is the long history of conflict between the Finance Ministry and the Ministry of Posts and Telecommunications: the latter, as the title suggests, is responsible for the Post Office, and is thus a defender of Post Office interests and privileges in any arguments over regulatory reform (Horne, 1985, pp.118–41). A more serious obstacle still to the unity and coherence of the state actually lies within the Ministry of Finance itself. By virtue of the scope of its jurisdiction, the Ministry contains a range of conflicting interests. It is organised into a number of separate bureaus divided, roughly, by their functional responsibilities: thus there exist separate banking and securities bureaus. The history of the Ministry is, however, in part a history of the struggle between these bureaus, both for control over regulatory authority and on behalf of competing economic interests in the marketplace (Horne, 1985).

It might be imagined that the United Kingdom had escaped this pattern of fragmentation, both because the City of London is a uniquely cohesive financial community and because one institution, the Bank of England, has dominated public intervention in the financial markets of the City.

This picture of cohesion was, however, always misleading and is becoming more so with the passage of time. Many important financial markets – for example, life and general insurance, and the market in housing mortgage finance – are organised outside the City of London, and have been under the regulatory umbrella of central government in Whitehall. Even in respect of City markets there is a long history of tensions between the claims of the Bank of England and the central institutions of economic management, like the Treasury (Moran, 1981). At the end of the 1980s several years of radical change to the system have left the regulatory structure even more differentiated. Among those with a say are the Bank of England, central departments (such as the Treasury and the Department of Trade and Industry) freestanding regulatory agencies (such as the Office of Fair Trading) and a wide range of bodies having a mixed public/private status, set up under the Financial Services Act of 1986 (the Securities and Investments Board and its subordinate self-regulatory organisations).

These examples show that, whatever the advantages of brevity in writing of 'the state' in financial services, the benefits of brevity are purchased at the expense of significant over-simplification. The distinguishing feature of states is that they are riddled internally with institutional jealousies and rivalries.

If it is inaccurate to speak of the state as if it were a unitary actor, it is equally inaccurate to assume that state agencies and the markets they regulate are marked by clear lines of administrative or legal separation. Not only are states fragmented into numerous quarrelling parts; there typically exists no clear separation between those institutions nominally in the 'public' and those nominally in the 'private', sector.

The practice of fusing the public and the private in the regulation of financial markets has its roots in the distant past. Many markets have historically been organised as self-governing institutions. The most striking illustrations are provided by the case of exchanges, whether formed to trade company stock or other forms of financial instruments. The historical origins of banking regulation also lie in the practice of privately owned institutions performing regulatory duties. The modern idea of a 'central bank' as the guarantor of the stability of the whole banking system was pioneered in the nineteenth century by the Bank of England, then a privately owned body. Indeed, the Bank was only taken into public ownership in 1946, after it had already assumed a dominant position in financial regulation. In the United States the central bank, though established by statute in 1913, had a constitution which for the first two decades of its life put it closely under the control of private banking interests (Wooley, 1984,pp. 30–47).

The existence of deep rooted historical traditions of self-regulation helps explain why, when modern states intervene in financial markets, they commonly do so through a wide range of representative associations and formally constituted self-regulatory organisations. In Japan both the stock exchanges and the associations of firms in the securities industry are licensed by the state to carry out regulatory functions (Oda and Grice (eds), 1988). The United States has arranged matters in an even more explicit and formal fashion. The Securities and Exchange Commission has for over half a century overseen a range of self-regulatory organisations (principally the stock exchanges) that possess a state licence to regulate their own affairs. Britain is the clearest case of all. Until the 1980s the most important financial markets in the City of London were governed by largely independent corporate bodies (such as the Stock Exchange) and trade associations given an informal licence to police their particular markets by the Bank of England. The 1986 Financial Services Act has extended and formalised this system, replacing a self-regulatory structure that had grown up in a haphazard fashion with a consciously constructed set of institutions endowed with statutory powers and responsibilites, but funded by the markets and incorporated as private companies (Reid, 1988,pp. 203–60).

The line between the state and private interests is further blurred by a final feature of the structure of state action. Not only are states fragmented and internally divided; these fragments are in turn often connected to particular groups of private interests in the struggles that take place over policy. States are deeply penetrated by private interests, and in turn deeply penetrate those interests. The most important lines of division over policy, therefore, do not separate 'the state' from 'the market': they divide coalitions of institutions drawn from the public and the private sector, opposed by other coalitions made up in the same way. In both Japan and the United States, for instance, the most contentious issue in financial market policy is the proper division of function between banks and firms operating in securities markets. In both countries there exist legal prohibitions forbidding banks entering securities markets. In both systems large banks are anxious to break this regulatory prohibition. The lines of battle, however, are not between banks and state regulators: they are between, on the one hand, banks and their allies in bank regulatory agencies; and on the other, securities firms and their allies in the state regulatory structure (Whitener, 1988a).

The state is a powerful presence in financial markets, but it is far from being a unified or independent presence. The institutions of the state are fragmented into quarrelling parts; there is a long tradition of allowing markets to regulate their own affairs; there has grown up a network of semi-private self-regulatory bodies; and parts of the state are typically united in coalitions with private interests against other state institutions.

It should not be imagined, however, that the structure of state action is unchanging. On the contrary: the single most striking feature of the chief world financial centres is the altered role of the state in recent years. This we now examine.

The changing structure of state action

The most important world financial centres have in recent years experienced a common financial services revolution. This revolution has usually been described with the label 'deregulation'. In New York, London and Tokyo a wave of reform has swept away many barriers to competition. At the beginning of the 1970s a wide range of restrictive practices in British banking was abolished; between 1975 and 1980 numerous restrictions on price competition were dismantled in American banking and securities markets; in London after 1983 new and freer competitive rules were introduced to the Stock Exchange; and since 1984 there has been a powerful movement to remove barriers to competition in Japanese markets.

These 'deregulation' movements obviously have significant implications for the role of the state. It is tempting to interpret the events of recent years as a retreat by states. In some areas this is indeed what has happened. Since the early 1970s there has been rising competition in financial markets. This competitive pressure has spurred the pace of innovation and has encouraged firms to search for ways of circumventing regulatory restrictions. This process has been further assisted by technology: the most important markets increasingly communicate by globally organised electronic networks that recognise no national boundaries (*Heertje*, 1988). In Strange's words: 'the markets are predominantly global, while the authorities are predominantly national' (1988, p.89).

Faced with these conditions, states have often retreated in the face of markets. Thus the British banking reforms of the early 1970s amounted to an admission by the state that it could not direct in detail the way banks allocated credit in a sophisticated economy (Moran, 1986,pp. 29–54). After 1980 the American state began to phase out a generation of legal controls over interest rates, in part because innovation in the markets was already making the control meaningless. At almost the same moment the Japanese and the British states were abolishing restrictions on the export of capital, in recognition of the fact that financial markets were making such restrictions ineffective. The domestic reforms in Japan have also involved the abolition of many administrative restrictions on competition previously imposed by the state.

The financial services revolution has, therefore, involved some striking instances of retreat by states in the face of competitive struggles and innovations in markets. Yet any general picture of state agencies as institutions in retreat would be seriously misleading. While the state has withdrawn from some areas of control, it has advanced in others. In particular states, the totality of state control may well have increased rather than diminished. The most dramatic case is that of Britain where, after almost two decades of 'deregulation', the state is a more pervasive presence than ever in the financial markets. In recent years, many financial markets in Britain have for the first time been subjected to regulation backed by the power of the statute book. In banking, legislation enacted in 1979 created a formal system for the recognition of banks, equipped the regulator (the Bank of England) with extensive power of supervision and created a distinct category of bank regulators. This legislation was strengthened after a banking collapse in the mid-1980s. The Financial Services Act of 1986 is – as we have already seen – an even more remarkable expansion of legal controls. It ends the long tradition of largely autonomous City regulation; creates a unified and comprehensive system of licencing for financial institutions; and establishes formally constituted regulatory bodies deriving their power and authority from statute (Berrill, 1986).

In the United States a similar, though less dramatic, trend is noticeable.

Legislation passed in 1975 considerably increased the powers of the Securities and Exchange Commission and of its subordinate self-regulatory organisations (Miller, 1985). Since the late 1970s there has existed – under the umbrella of a federal agency, the Commodity Futures Trading Commission – a whole new system of controls over markets that had previously largely escaped public regulation. During the 1980s there also occurred in the United States a major extension of public regulation over 'insider trading' (dealing in markets using privileged information acquired in a position of trust). This campaign included legislation (passed in 1984) and highly publicised enforcement campaigns which resulted in the apprehension and jailing of prominent financiers. The campaign has also influenced the Japanese system: in 1988, in an unprecedented move, the Japanese Ministry of Finance introduced new prohibitions on insider trading, sparking off a wider series of regulatory reforms in the industry designed to curb that practice (Whitener, 1988b).

The changing pattern of state action in financial markets cannot therefore be adequately summed up in the language of 'deregulation'. In some instances states have indeed abolished controls; in other areas rules have become more elaborate, have been newly embodied in law and are being implemented by agencies endowed with statutory authority. In some states, of which Britain is the most convincing example, the total effect may well be to expand the range of state action.

The explanation for this expansion of control lies in the competitive struggles taking place in markets, in the impact of crisis and scandal on systems of regulation and in the tendency for the leading world financial centres, as they become more integrated with each other, to develop similar systems of regulation. Each of these is considered here in turn.

We noticed earlier that competition and innovation in markets had undermined some regulatory barriers and had led to their dismantling. But the competitive struggles and the process of innovation have not taken place independently of state agencies, let alone against their wishes. Precisely because individual agencies are parts of coalitions with particular interests in markets, they have been major pro-active agents in financial change. The financial services revolution that took place in Britain after 1983 happened because state institutions, like the Bank of England and the Department of Trade and Industry, wanted the revolution to happen. Many individual state agencies actively encourage aggressive competition. In the United States, for instance, the revolution in banking practices has been in part the work of banking regulators anxious to ensure the expansion and profitability of their regulatory 'clients' at the expense of other groups in financial services. A regulatory agency has a direct interest in the competitiveness of the firms it regulates, since its institutional prestige and resources are closely bound up with the prosperity of the markets that it oversees.

The involvement of state agencies in the process of financial change was considerably deepened in the 1980s by the growing intensity of international competition in financial services. As financial services industries became major arenas of world competitive struggle, states were embroiled in that struggle in the hunt to secure advantages for their own national firms agains foreign rivals. There began, in Cooper's phrase, a 'financial services trade war', in which states used their control over regulation to bargain with other states on behalf of their own client firms (Cooper, 1987). The story of financial change in Japan in recent years is a story of such bargaining. The American, British, West German and other states have threatened to exclude Japanese firms from their own markets in order to lever open the Japanese system to foreign competition.

The single most important reason why the financial services revolution has so often involved a widening in the scope of state action, therefore, is that state agencies have themselves been key agents in making that revolution. Furthermore, as competitive struggles in financial services have been increasingly organised on a global scale state agencies have acquired a central role in sponsoring and defending the interests of some national firms against foreign rivals.

If the part played by state agencies in competitive struggles is the most important reason why state action has expanded in scope, the most immediate reasons have been scandal and regulatory failure. Thus the considerable strengthening of legal controls in the American system in 1975 was the result of a series of collapses of firms in the securities industry in the late 1960s (Seligman,1982,pp. 450–66). The 1979 Banking Act in Britain, a landmark in the growth of state regulation, was the direct result of a great crisis in the banking system that in the mid-1970s led numerous banking institutions into insolvency (Reid, 1982). The origins of the 1986 Financial Services Act in Britain lie in scandals caused by the collapse of firms involved in investment management (Gower, 1982, 1984). The strengthening of legal controls over insider dealing in the United States, Britain and Japan was throughout the 1980s accompanied by successive scandals (Whitener,1988b).

The intensification of legal controls over insider trading in the world's greatest financial centres connects to the third force for change identified above: the extent to which the increasing international integration of financial markets is creating pressure for common standards guiding state intervention. Until the beginning of the 1980s it was possible to say that, while the state was an important actor in all the world's important financial centres, the style of state intervention varied significantly. The agencies of the American state operated according to a unique American regulatory style (Vogel,1986). They were bound by a huge and complex body of statute and case law; their relations with firms were often highly acrimonious; and the actions of the state were open to a great deal of public scrutiny. By contrast, in Britain the law was comparatively unimportant; the markets were highly autonomous; the most important regulatory agency, the Bank of England, stood at one remove from the central machinery of government in Whitehall; and there was little public scrutiny of the activity of financial regulation. In Japan, by contrast, the most important public agency was a Ministry headed by a Cabinet Minister (the Minister of Finance), and the system largely worked through the unique Japanese method of 'administrative guidance': this involved issuing 'guidance' which, while not having the force of legal compulsion, was nevertheless characteristically adhered to by financial institutions.

By the end of the 1980s some of this distinctiveness remained, but it had considerably diminished in the intervening years. There occurred, in summary, a marked shift in both the British and Japanese cases towards the American model. In some instances, notably Britain's 1986 Financial Services Act, there was a conscious attempt to replicate many of the features of the American regulatory structure (Berrill,1986). In others – notably the world-wide campaigns against insider trading – American pressure was partly instrumental in transmitting American styles and American standards. In the emerging global markets American voices are predominant because the American state remains the most experienced of financial regulators, because America's wider world power is still great and because American financial markets remain the largest and most valuable.

Conclusion: the state in action in financial markets

States are powerful and pervasive forces in financial markets. Without the social stability and the legal framework guaranteed by state power, exchanges in financial markets would not take place. In more immediate ways states are also key actors: they prescribe competitive conditions, seek to influence winners and losers in competitive struggles, try to manage financial systems when crisis and collapse threaten, and play major roles as both customers and suppliers. In all the varying forms taken by the state, however, certain recurrent features are apparent.

First, *states are not unitary actors*. Governments are complex systems of institutions organised according to equally complex, and often unclear, divisions of labour. Different state agencies are born in different historical circumstances, have different organisational cultures and are charged with different regulatory tasks. One of the recurrent features of the state in action in financial markets is the existence of struggle and competition within the state structure. In financial markets, where rapid change is constantly altering the nature of firms and the boundaries between markets, the natural stresses between state agencies are intensified by the problems of staking out the bounds of agency jurisdiction in a constantly shifting environment.

Second, *states are not independent actors*. The agencies of the state do not operate as forces external to financial markets. In all the major world financial centres there exist coalitions of conflicting interests struggling with each other over the terms of competition in markets. State agencies are integral parts of these coalitions, helping to mobilise interests against rival coalitions that also enjoy the support of different state institutions.

Third, *states are international actors*. This dimension of state activity has become increasingly important with the growing internationalisation of the financial services sectors. The most prestigious and important state agencies concerned with financial markets – for instance, finance ministries and central banks – have become involved in the competitive struggle at the global level. Understanding state action thus now demands more than an analysis of domestic state structures and domestic interests in financial markets; it requires an understanding of the international networks of which state agencies are a part. As competitive struggles rise to a global scale, so the alliances taken on by state institutions acquire a correspondingly transnational character. State agencies remain, at the beginning of the 1990s, key actors in financial markets; but their importance rests on their participation in coalitions of interests that cross the traditional boundaries of the nation-state.

Guide to further reading.

The most important background to the state's changing role in financial markets is provided by the developing context of the international economy, especially of the international financial system. The essential starting point is Strange (1988). The whole work should be read to understand the full range of her arguments, but chapter 5 is especially important. Strange (1986) is less convincing and more polemical, but is nevertheless enlightening. Gilpin (1987), notably chapter 8, offers an estimate of the financial power of the American state which is directly at odds with Strange's arguments. He is especially revealing on the Japanese/American connection in the financial services revolution.

From these general considerations the student can proceed to the analysis of particular countries. Ingham (1984) is not only historically comprehensive on Britain, but reviews much of the existing literature about the City of London, the state and the British economy. Moran (1986) describes the politics of banking regulation while Reid (1988) is up-to-date on the 'City revolution'. On the United States Seligman (1982) is a massive and authoritative study of Wall Street and its regulation. Wooley's (1984) study of the Federal Reserve is one of the few examinations by a political scientist. The rise of Japan has produced a number of illuminating studies. The passages in Gilpin (1987) already referred to make a good beginning. Horne (1985) is a thorough study of regulatory policy, emphasising the fragmented nature of the state structure. The early pages of Frankel (1984) are revealing about pressure from the American state for Japanese financial reform. Feldman (1986) though technically complex in parts is also worth reading with an eye to its political implications.

It is often remarked, rightly, that financial markets, and the state's roles in them, are changing rapidly. The student should bear this in mind: books and articles date quickly. Any undergraduate wanting up-to-date information (for instance for a project or long essay) should use the excellent 'trade press'. Three publications regularly produce accessible, well-researched articles: *The Banker, Institutional Investor* and the *International Financial Law Review*. Two 'official' periodicals – the *Bank of England Quarterly Bulletin* and the *Federal Reserve Bulletin* – frequently contain up-to-date wide-ranging comparative articles. The *Japan Economic Journal*, which should be available in good economics and business libraries, is a weekly which is a mine of up-to-date information about Japanese regulation. Finally, the *Financial Times* (daily) has regular, authoritative summary discussions of financial markets worldwide.

Part III   Changing central, intermediate and local state responsibilities

4 Local state, local government and local administration

R.J. Johnston

The last decade has seen a great flowering not only of empirical studies of the state but also of theoretical attempts to understand its nature. (Excellent contemporary reviews of the latter include Alford and Friedland, 1985, and Dunleavy and O'Leary, 1987.) As part of this enterprise there has also been a growing interest in what has become known as the *local state*. Whether there can be such an institution as a local state is the focus of debate, since the concept of a state implies, to some, an autonomous, sovereign body and they find it difficult to accept the apparent notion of one sovereign body containing within itself a set of subordinate such bodies. The issue is one of local autonomy (Clark, 1984): if the local state is not autonomous, is it a local state?

If one treats the term local state as synonymous with either or both of local government and local administration, then its empirical existence as part of the state apparatus (Clark and Dear, 1984) is unquestionable. Virtually all contemporary states, capitalist and socialist, have complex systems of local administration, and many have local governments too. *Local administration* is defined here as a territorially decentralised arm of the central state; *local government* is a territorial unit governed by representatives elected separately from those who run the central state. There is, then, almost invariably a local apparatus as part of the state: it is understanding the nature of that apparatus – whether it is administration or government, and why – that is the focus here.

The chapter has two main concerns. First, it seeks to appreciate whether a local state apparatus is necessary. This is done by placing the study of the local state in the context of the state itself, and appreciating why the latter requires local organisations and institutions in order to operate. Second, the chapter explores the differences between local government and local administration, as alternative modes of implementing the local state apparatus. This is done by way of a comparative study of the local state in the United States and the United Kingdom, again set in the context of an understanding of the state as a whole. Those case studies are insufficient for broad generalisations about the nature and form of the local state, but they provide both insights to the issues raised here and a framework for further investigation.

The state as a territorial institution

In order to appreciate the nature of the local state apparatus it is necessary to look briefly at the nature of the state itself. It is widely accepted in analyses of capitalist societies that the state – or some institution performing the functions currently played by the state – is a necessity: without a state, the conflicts and crises inherent to capitalism could not be managed and contained for long, and the mode of production would rapidly self-destruct. As Mann (1984) puts it

The only stateless societies have been primitive. There are no complex, civilized societies without any centre of binding rule-making authority, however limited in scope . . . societies with states have superior survival value to those without them. We have no examples of stateless societies long enduring past a primitive level of development, and many examples of state societies absorbing or eliminating stateless ones. (p. 195)

Mann does not refer specifically to contemporary socialist societies, but his use of the term 'complex, civilized societies' can be interpreted as embracing them.

Although the state as an institution is a necessity, as the embodiment of force in society (Mann points out that the only alternatives to force in sustaining a social order – exchange and custom – lack long-term viability) the particular nature of the state is not, even within a single mode of production. Nor is the number of states a necessity, though experience suggests that small states are increasingly vulnerable in the global capitalist world-economy and that without fewer, larger states control of that system, and of the environment, may decline. (On a related point, see Laver, 1984, 1986.) It is necessary to have a state to perform certain functions – for an argument of what they are see Clark and Dear (1984, pp. 42–3) – but the way in which those functions are performed is a consequence of local decision-making, set in its historical and cultural context and reflecting immediate contingent conditions.

There is, however, one feature of the state that Mann argues is necessary to its ability to undertake its role – it is, and must be, an institution that has sovereignty over a territorially demarcated area: this is one of the major criteria distinguishing state power from other sources of power. Thus he claims 'that the state *is* merely and essentially an arena, a *place*, and yet *this* is the very source of its autonomy' (1984, p. 187) and 'The state is, indeed, a *place* – both a central place and a unified territorial reach' (p. 198). He does not develop the foundations for this case very fully, but parallel recent work by Sack (1986) provides the necessary insights into the importance of *territoriality* to the exercise of power. Sack shows that territoriality ('A human strategy to affect, influence, and control' p. 2) provides 'a form of classification by area, a form of communication by boundary, and a form of enforcement or control' (p. 28).

These characteristics are readily appreciated: by defining the state territorially the people and land subject to its sovereignty are readily identified, the boundaries of its power are readily indicated to (outsider) others, and within them its power is uniformly applicable. Other characteristics follow. Territoriality reifies power, by linking it to the 'things' in the container; it displaces attention from inter-personal to impersonal control (not 'I say you can't do that' but 'It is the law of the land that you can't do that'); and it provides a focus for the development of a state ideology, a commitment to a territory rather than to economic, social and political systems.

In looking at the exercise of state power, Mann draws attention to two separate ways in which state elites (those with ultimate power over the state apparatus) might exercise it. The first he terms *despotic power*, defined as 'the range of actions which the elite is empowered to undertake without routine, institutionalised negotiation with civil society groups' (1984, p. 188). Such power may be allocated to the elite – through an electoral process, for example; it may be operated by the elite and with at least passive acceptance from the civil society; or it may be taken to itself by the elite and imposed, by force if necessary, on the subject groups. It involves the exercise of autonomy – the state elite is empowered (or empowers itself) to rule. The second type is *infrastructural power*, defined as 'the capacity of the state actually to penetrate civil society, and to implement logistically political decisions throughout the realm' (p. 189). It involves widespread penetration by the state of virtually all aspects of everyday life: such penetration may be despotic or it may be with the (implicit) consensus agreement of the members of civil society.

Mann uses this categorisation of two types of state power to produce a four-fold typology of types of state, according to whether they rate high or low on their use of each. Thus feudal states are low on both; they penetrate civil society only weakly and the state elite exercises little despotic power (working through local subsidiaries). Imperial states share the low infrastructural power of the feudal but are high on despotic; their monarchs exercise substantial control. Of those that are high on infrastructural power, authoritarian states are high on despotic too, whereas those characterised as bureaucratic are low on that scale – in them the state elite penetrates civil society by consensus rather than by force.

Why should state elites exercise these two types of power? The case for despotic power lies very largely in sources of power other than the economic, which Mann claims lies at the heart of 'complex, civilized societies'. These are ideological (the power over minds, as with religion), political (the power to influence behaviour), and military (the power to subjugate and control physically): the three may be linked (and one or more may be linked with economic power, as in modern capitalist states) but they are conceptually separate. (For more detail, see Mann, 1986.) Elites may wish to impose themselves and their beliefs on others: others may willingly accept such imposition. With regard to infrastructural power, the case – at least in the economic sphere (the sphere of production) – is that without the penetration that it involves then complexly organised societies (whether capitalist or socialist) would collapse. Thus, in O'Connor's (1972) well-known trilogy, it is necessary for the state to exercise infrastructural power in order to: secure social consensus (an ideological and a policing function); secure conditions of production (by promoting accumulation strategies in capitalism, production strategies in socialism); and secure social integration (ensuring a basic standard of welfare for all).

It is not the purpose of this chapter, given its title and focus, to develop further these ideas about the nature of the state. This discussion has provided a necessary introduction to what follows however, since to examine the nature of the local state apparatus without some appreciation of the state itself is akin to trying to understand the nature of a carburettor while knowing nothing of the internal combustion engine or the nature of the pancreas without appreciating its role in human physiology. Hence we turn now from considering the necessity and nature of the state to the necessity and nature of the local state apparatus.

The need for a local state apparatus

Mann's case for the state necessarily being a territorially-defined institution is that only in that way can it exercise power, because the territoriality strategy provides it with its separate characterisation, and hence base for autonomy. Its despotic power (and all states exercise despotic power, some more than others) extends to the limits of its territorial reach; all people within that reach are the subjects of the state elite and all other phenomena therein are potentially under its control. Similarly, its infrastructural power – its ability to obtain and store information and to tax, for example – extends over all those who reside within its territory, and the environment is under its regulation, if not control. In all but feudal states, as he argues, those powers are widely and heavily used. The contention here is that such exercise of powers necessitates a local state apparatus in all but the tiniest of states.

Despotic power involves control over aspects of the existence of others. It may involve the exercise of ideological power, moulding opinion in certain ways and monitoring activities to ensure that they are consistent with the ideology. Such activities involve close contact with the individuals concerned if the strategy is to be successful, and the elite are to be sure both that people are socialised into a particular ideological set and that no deviations occur. Thus churches, as Sack (1986) clearly demonstrates, have hierarchical spatial organisations and have long been structured territorially in order that the ideology of the elite can be sustained among the masses. (One of the problems of all such organisations, especially the largest, is the degree of local variability that will be allowed in religious practices without them being characterised as deviant.) As a developing school of thought in human geography stresses, places matter (Johnston, 1985) because they are separate local cultural contexts in which people learn the use of their human characteristics and thereby exercise their constrained 'free will'. Armies, too, are organised on strict hierarchical lines according to a well-defined 'span of control' theory (Sack, 1983), though that hierarchy need not be territorially delimited. (It usually is, especially on the field of battle.)

With regard to the exercise of despotic power by states, the case for local administration clearly follows. If acceptance of, and subservience to, the state ideology is necessary to its existence, then controls must be put in place. These will involve local arms of the state, acting for it and with it. Those local arms may be low-key, non-interventionist, even virtually invisible; they may, on the other hand, involve extensive displays of power and control.

Infrastructural power penetrates all aspects of civil society – the sphere of reproduction every bit as much as the sphere of production. In any large and complex society, this involves not only a many-faceted state apparatus (Clark and Dear, 1984, identify eleven separate, yet major, components of the capitalist state apparatus) but also a major organisation structure. To take just one simple example: the operation of a capitalist economy requires a uniform system of weights and measures, without which contracts cannot be agreed. Not only must an agreed system be created and taught, it must also be overseen: all balances should register the same when a standard weight is placed upon them; all petrol pumps must deliver the same quantity of gasoline when a gallon is asked for; all rules used to measure the length of a piece of cloth must conform precisely to the norm. Thus there is a need for a 'weights and measures inspectorate' that ensures that the system is maintained. It need not be organised territorially, but it is difficult to conceive of a more efficient way.

The immense range and variety of functions undertaken by the modern state as part of its exercise of infrastructural power means that it needs many equivalents of the 'weights and measures inspectorate'. These are largely administrative functions, putting centrally agreed decisions into operation: the locality in which they are applied is an administrative convenience, and little more. With such functions, spatial uniformity is imposed: all places must use the same system.

Spatial uniformity is not the dominant characteristic of civil society, however: as already stressed, places differ. Capitalism is, necessarily, an economic system characterised by uneven spatial development (Harvey, 1982; Smith, 1984), producing a map of places that differ not only in their productive characteristics (what is done where) but often also in how production is organised (the pattern of local social relations: Johnston, 1986a) and how social life (local culture) is structured. The characteristics of that map are crucial influences on how it changes under processes of economic restructuring as the pattern of uneven spatial development is reorganised (Massey, 1984; Peet, 1987). Thus local circumstances vary, and with them the needs for state activity (both qualitatively and quantitatively). This is widely illustrated in the empirical literature on differences between local governments in both their spending on public services (Sharpe and Newton, 1984) and their attempts to influence the economic processes (Boddy and Fudge (eds), 1984). Again, it can be argued that a system of local administration is by far the most efficient way of responding to these differences. What is of great interest, and taken up in the next section, is the degree of autonomy that should be given to such local administrations.

Local government or local administration?

Having argued that a system of local territories is the most efficient way of operating both despotic and infrastructural state power, though not that such a local state apparatus is a necessity, we turn now to considering the nature of that system – how it is operated. This consideration is set in the context of two ideal types of organisation: local administration, in which the local territories are run by employees of the central state (i.e. the system is essentially bureaucratic); and local government, in which day-to-day control is exercised by politicians and/or bureaucrats elected by the residents of the territory, or some enfranchised group among them (i.e. there is a political element to the operation). These ideal types can be represented as abstract, polar extremes; the empirical situation is that in most systems, especially those low on despotic power, there are elements of both. Our concern is to understand why there are variations, essentially variations between countries, in the relative importance of the administration and government modes.

Local government in the USA and the UK

That such variations exist empirically is beyond doubt, and can be illustrated by comparing the situation in the United Kingdom (essentially England and Wales) with that in the United States. (For further detail, see Johnston, 1984a.) The latter case is characterised by a plethora of local governments; in the former there is a substantial, and increasing, local administration element.

Decentralised local government has a long tradition in the United States, especially in those parts of the country where the ideologies of individualism and community have prevailed. (These are what Elazar, 1984, terms the individualistic and moralistic cultures, each of which has its own cultural hearth on the north-east seaboard. The third such culture – the traditionalist, or paternal – is characteristic of the south, where the elitist attitudes have been less disposed to widespread local democracy on the scale found elsewhere in the country.) This is reflected in the very large numbers of local governments; in 1977 there were almost 70,000, including 18,862 municipalities, 15,174 school districts, 25,962 special districts, 4,031 townships and 3,042 counties. Each of these is a creation of the relevant State government, and its powers are thereby limited by State constitutions, most of which conform to what is termed Dillon's (1911) Rule:

a municipal corporation possesses and can exercise the following powers and no others: First, those granted in express words; second, those necessarily or fairly implied in or incident to the powers expressly granted; third, those essential to the accomplishment of the declared objects and purposes of the corporations – not simply convenient, but indispensable. Any fair, reasonable, substantial doubt concerning the existence of power is resolved by the courts against the corporation, and the power is denied.

Strictly interpreted, Dillon's Rule means that local governments only have freedom of action within clearly specified State constitutional constraints.

Most States have modified Dillon, however, to allow a greater degree of 'home rule', which, as in Colorado, gives local governments full power over local activities with State intervention allowed only in matters of statewide concern. However, State governments have increasingly been claiming that local activities have wider implications, claims that have in many cases been upheld by the Courts (see Johnston, 1986b), so that the autonomy implicit in those home rule charters is more apparent than real (Clark, 1985). (Similarly, the Federal government has increasingly claimed that countrywide issues are raised by many State government actions, thereby allowing Federal jurisdiction: see Clark, 1981, on Supreme Court interpretations of the Commerce Clause and the consequent erosion of States' rights. Reagan, 1972, claimed that the only State right remaining is the right to be a State!)

Despite those constraints, little has been done to reduce the number of local government units, with the sole exception of school districts which were reduced from 108,579 in 1942 to 15,174 in 1977 – most of the amalgamations took place in rural areas where depopulation had eroded the viability of many of the districts with few pupils. Indeed, in metropolitan areas the number of governments has been growing, for two main reasons. First, more suburban municipalities have been incorporated, and annexations have increasingly been resisted (Teaford, 1979) as residents and other landowners reap the fiscal and environmental benefits of separateness (Miller, 1981): benefits which have very largely been sustained by the courts, with a few exceptions where deliberate racial discrimination has been proven (Johnston, 1984b). Second, where problems have been encountered, as with limits to borrowing money to finance developments, a common solution has been to create new, single-purpose special districts that are fiscally independent (Stetzer, 1975). Thus the Detroit Standard Metropolitan Statistual Area – SMSA (population 4.4 million in 1980) contained 107 separate municipalities in 1977, overlapping 108 school districts, 26 special districts and 108 other local government units. Even so, its 349 separate local governments paled into insignificance alongside the 744 in Pittsburgh, 864 in Philadelphia, and 1,214 in Chicago.

This situation contrasts very strongly with that in England and Wales, in three ways. First, the British equivalent of Dillon's Rule – *ultra vires* – is much more precise: local governments can only operate functions specifically allocated to them by legislation, much of which is written to give close central oversight to the exercise of those powers (Johnston, 1983). Second, whereas most American States have relatively liberal incorporation and annexation laws that allow local people to determine the boundaries of local State territories, in the United Kingdom the definition and delimitation of comparable areas has been by the fiat of central government (though prior to 1974 it was possible for town councils to petition for municipal borough and county borough status). Thus, although there was extensive consultation with local politicians, the major reform of local government in the early 1970s was very much a central state activity, and much of the outcome reflected the operation of central political concerns rather than local issues (Johnston, 1979; Dunleavy, 1980). Third, there is a long tradition of central government taking important functions away from local governments and reallocating them to local administrations, created by and answerable to Parliament rather than to a local electorate.

Why should such major differences exist? In part they reflect the major constitutional difference between the federal state in the United States and the unitary state in the United Kingdom. But there is much more to it than that, as the following paragraphs explore.

Theories of local democracy

In both countries the systems of local government are lauded by the state elite as vibrant examples of democracy, of government of the people, for the people, and by the people (as in some of the relevant US Supreme Court judgments: see Johnston, 1984b). Local government, as opposed to local administration, is promoted because it constitutes a check to centralised state power, and provides an effective and efficient response mechanism for dealing with the geographical variations in need that result from uneven spatial development (Johnston, 1982).

In the United States, this pro-local democracy stance has been bolstered by an economic theory which presents an ideological underpinning for the fragmented system of home rule. According to this theory (Tiebout, 1956) the primary purpose of a local government is to provide the services that the residents require, for which they pay through property and other taxes. If an area, especially an urban area, had but a single local government, then the package of services provided and the tax burden needed for it would have to reflect a consensus agreement: it would represent the views of the median voter (as described in Downs, 1957, classic economic theory of democracy) and could be considered unsatisfactory by many, perhaps a majority, of the constituent electorate. If, on the other hand, there was a large number of independent local governments, each offering a different service/tax package, then people could choose that which most suited their requirements. There would, in effect, be a market in local governments, with the unattractive packages having to be modified in order that the local governments offering them could be sustained.

The empirical reality does not fit this theory, because its assumptions regarding information and mobility are not valid and because of the way the local government system has been used by the relatively powerful to promote their interests: both their fiscal interests (minimising their tax bills, particularly with regard to subsidising services used by others who pay more taxes) and their environmental interests (promoting exclusive residential areas on both socio-economic and racial grounds, for example). Thus both industrialists and affluent home-owners have used the zoning powers of municipalities to produce tax/service/environment packages that are highly beneficial to themselves and, in consequence, prejudicial to those excluded from their territories. (For examples see the essays in Tabb and Sawers (eds), 1984, and also Johnston, 1984b.)

Britain has no comparable theory to sustain local democracy, though a great deal of rhetoric is produced by the political parties to support the supposed independence of local governments (see Duncan and Goodwin, 1982a). Two attempts at developing general theories are relevant here, however. The first is Pahl's (1975) notion of urban managers, gatekeepers (including public sector bureaucrats) who control access to scarce resources, such as public housing. This implies that local governments are really local administrations, in that the managers work to professional norms (see Knox and Cullen, 1981) rather than to local political direction. There are indeed examples where this is so, where the professionals have been the agenda-setters and, to all intents and purposes, determiners of major aspects of public policy. There are many counter-examples, however, and increasingly local politicians (especially those employed by Labour-run city councils known as the 'New Urban Left: Gyford, 1986) are becoming more professional themselves and taking more direct roles in both determining policy and ensuring that it is implemented. Pahl's theory is thus closer to local administration than to local democracy, and is less relevant to the contemporary situation in some places than it was even just a decade ago.

The second of the theories is that which Saunders (1986) calls the 'dual politics thesis'. This treats the two spheres of production and consumption (or reproduction) separately. Each is a focus of political conflict, but the nature of the conflict can differ in four ways: (a) according to the interest groups that are mobilised in the conflict – whether they are economic classes, for example, or what Dunleavy (1979) calls consumption sectors; (b) according to the mode of mobilisation – whether in the traditional electoral arena of party politics, for example, or the corporatist situation where pressure groups lobby and influence governments and parties outside the arena; (c) according to the level of the state system at which mobilisation occurs – central or local, for example; and (d) according to the ideology that informs state action – managerial professionalism or pragmatic pluralism, for example. The 'dual politics' come about, in Saunder's schema, because of differences between the politics of production and the politics of consumption, on all four dimensions.

The politics of production – conflict over the processes of capitalist accumulation – involve class interests, in which the dominant ideology is that of private property rights. These interests are promoted through corporatist means – by trade unions and producer groups seeking to influence government policy, for example – at the level of the central state. On the other hand, the politics of consumption – conflict over the provision of services necessary to reproduction and social life – takes place more at the local state level, with the different interest groups competing to advance what they define as their citizenship rights. Thus what Saunders (1979) terms urban politics involves local democratic struggles over public sector goods and services and the local state apparatus exists to resolve those struggles.

Saunders's theory, while attractive, is based on a simple dichotomy that is unfounded empirically; elements of the local state apparatus are involved in the politics of production, too, with a long history of local 'boosterism' in the United States, for example, and a growing interest in the United Kingdom in 'local economic policies' designed to promote employment in particular places (Mawson and Miller, 1986). Of course, central governments, including State governments in the United States, set the critical parameters of such policies (they have exclusive control over the money supply, for example, and can limit what taxes are raised locally, and how they are spent) but do not preclude local boosterism. (On what is done in the United Kingdom, see Mills and Young, 1986; Hodge and Staeheli, 1990, illustrate how conflicts over production and consumption issues produce separate voting patterns in the Seattle urban area.)

Saunders implies that the two spheres of activity are autonomous, but this cannot be so, according to his critics, because for the long-term health of capitalism issues of production must take precedence over those of consumption. Thus, as Dunleavy and O'Leary (1987) express it, according to Saunders's model:

local government structures, and perhaps some politically visible sections of the national state apparatus, are entrusted with responsibility for social consumption spending. Policy-making in this area is deliberately pluralist, mopping up political energies, providing a reassuring appearance of controversy and popular influence, and sustaining a needs-oriented ideology which seems to indicate the social neutrality of state policy. In practice, local governments or elected regional governments are rigidly controlled by the centre to prevent them adopting policies hostile to capital interests, and their decisions are extensively determined by prior central state commitments of resources. (p. 252)

The degrees of freedom of local governments over welfare spending are thus curtailed, for example, to fit the fiscal ideology of the central government in certain situations, as with the Reagan and Thatcher projects of the 1980s.

These various theories all provide insights to the nature of the local state apparatus. They are insufficient, however, either to provide explanatory accounts of why some services are locally administered and others are locally governed, or of why places differ in the relative importance of those two aspects of the local state apparatus.

The price of democracy

This discussion of the where and when of local democracy is set in the context of an argument about democracy at the level of the state. A map of the countries where democracy is currently practised (see Johnston, 1986c) shows that it is concentrated in the countries around the North Atlantic basin; the largest outlier is India. This suggests a correlation between the level of economic development (or socio-economic modernisation) and the presence or absence of democracy; such a correlation has been adduced by Coulter (1975; for a critique see Taylor, 1985).

From that correlation it is possible to make the relatively simplistic deduction (as Coulter, 1975, does) that democracy follows modernisation, so that as economic development proceeds democracy follows; what are recognised as basic human rights by the United Nations (Johnston, 1986c) can only be made available when a certain stage in the expansion of capitalism (à la Rostow, 1960) is reached. This is what Taylor (1988) terms the 'myth of developmentalism'. The proposition fails to note that where democracy is present it has invariably only been yielded to the people by a state elite after decades of struggle. Further, the proposition over-simplifies the situation by basing its case on cross-sectional rather than time-series data. Most of the countries that currently practice liberal democracy (to be clearly distinguished from the people's democracy practised in Eastern Europe: Johnston, 1986c) have done so for several decades; they experience peaceful transfers of power after elections and rarely, if ever, have irregular transfers. A considerable number of other countries – most of them in South America, Africa and Asia – currently do not have liberal democratic regimes, but have had on at least one occasion in recent decades.

It could be argued that those countries that have had some experience of democracy in recent decades, but where no permanent liberal democratic regime has yet been established, are close to that crucial point in Rostow's stage model where the transition to democracy occurs; they are currently undertaking experiments but have yet to find a successful *modus operandi*. This is outwardly plausible, but fails to account for the many residuals – both countries that are economically relatively developed and have not experienced democracy and those which have established liberal democratic regimes but do not rank highly on most economic development scales (see Taylor, 1985, on Coulter's, 1975, identification of such residuals). An alternative case, based in world-systems analysis, sets democracy more firmly in the context of class struggle in a world characterised by uneven spatial development.

Liberal democracy can be interpreted as a concession to the population of a country, or that segment of it which is enfranchised. It gives them some influence and power, to control capitalism and to win further concessions for themselves. It is yielded as part of the legitimation process; and popular participation is lauded in the ideology of individual freedom that is characteristic of liberal democracies. Such 'buying' of legitimation can be afforded, it is contended, because the pro-capitalist elite is rich enough to do so since it can exploit the population of other states, according to the classic core-periphery model of uneven spatial development. (The exploitation need not be of the population of another country. Democracy could be yielded to one group within a country, to sustain their support on the basis of exploitation of other, non-enfranchised, groups there: South Africa provides an obvious example.)

What then, of the countries which have had what appear to be temporary flirtations with democracy? Presumably they are not in the situation where democracy can be afforded for long; then why offer it at all? In the periphery and semi-periphery of the world-economy, states face two sets of forces. First, there are those of global capitalism, that are seeking sites for production as part of the restructuring processes taking place under the 'new industrial division of labour' (Frobel, Heinrichs and Kreye, 1980); countries are competing with others to attract investment that will serve international as well as local markets. Second, they face class conflict within their territories, as part of struggle over the returns from such investment. To obtain the investment, they have to provide an image of stability, with a disciplined labour force, no threat that investments and profits will be expropriated, and so on. Democracy does not always conform to such an image: it can give the impression of uncertainty, and will frighten investors away (even in advanced countries: see Finer (ed.), 1975); yet if it isn't yielded, popular unrest may create another form of instability. As a consequence, what has occurred in a number of countries over recent decades has been a sequence of alternating periods of democratic and non-democratic rule, with irregular transfers of power (usually military coups) ending the democratic periods on the argument that the country needs a period of stability in order to restructure: such coups are often followed by increases in aid from the major capitalist nations (Johnston and Taylor, 1987). Thus democratic instability in the periphery of the world-economy is a consequence of the inability of the local (partly comprador) elite to afford it.

There are exceptions to this model, of three types. The first are those countries where no democratic experiments have been conducted, and where despotic power remains high: most have either very low levels of economic development or very unequal distributions of wealth. The second are those with relatively permanent democracies despite low levels of development, such as India: in those, party systems survive by seeking new bases of electoral support every few years after failing to deliver on earlier promises – what Osei–Kwame and Taylor, 1984, call the 'politics of failure' (see also Taylor, 1986; Johnston, 1987). Finally, there are the socialist states where people's democracy is practised. Here, too, despotic power is high and is justified by the need to sustain the discipline required to achieve rapid economic development in those countries without the inequalities and crises inherent in capitalist processes of development.

The price of local democracy

This argument cannot be translated directly to analyses of the situation in the United Kingdom and the United States (though see Johnston, 1984c, on the de-democratisation of British politics). It does, however, provide a useful background for studying the differing experiences of local democracy in the two countries.

A straightforward deduction from the theory outlined above would suggest that as countries experience substantial and long-lived economic problems then those holding economic power may press – covertly rather than overtly, unless the crisis was very deep – for reductions in democratic power. It can be argued that this is exactly the case in Britain at present. At the national scale, the growing importance of the corporatist element, according to Saunders's dual politics model, and the commitment of all major political parties to the promotion of accumulation strategies point to a retreat from the pluralist ideology that underpins liberal democracy. But it is at the level of the local state apparatus that the withdrawal from liberal democracy is most apparent, as local government is increasingly being replaced by local administration.

That process of replacement is not entirely new, of course, for British central governments have been removing powers from the local state apparatus for much of the present century – as in the operation of certain social services and the health services, as well as with the delivery of public utilities: appointed boards, perhaps with some local government nominees, now operate what were formerly the provinces of elected councillors. In the 1980s this removal has been further advanced, not so much by taking functions away as by tightening the constraints on local government freedom (as in the operation of public housing, especially its sale, and of the schools service: higher education is being entirely removed from local government control) and by insisting on the privatisation of service delivery. All this has been done as part of a major programme of state support for economic restructuring which involves substantially reducing public expenditure so as to release investment: a major feature of this has been the introduction of rate-capping legislation, which determines how much each local government can spend and substantially penalises those which spend more.

The substantial reduction in local government, and either its replacement by local administration or its decline to little more than an elected local administration, can be interpreted as comparable to the de-democratisation policies in the peripheral states of the world-economy discussed above. It is reducing the scope of the politics of consumption, and thereby reducing the liberal democratic, pluralistic element in British society: the politics of production, dominated by the corporatist mode, is becoming increasingly important, as more goods and services are 'recommodified' from the public to the private sector. (The ideology of pluralist liberal democracy remains, of course, and there has been no call for its removal.)

From this one case study it would be possible (if not sensible) to derive a simple cyclical model that associated local government with periods of relative prosperity and its replacement by local administration in periods of major economic restructuring. But this would assume that the contemporary contingent circumstances in Britain are characteristic of other places and other times. The US experience suggests otherwise.

Why is it that while local government in the United Kingdom is under substantial attack, the system in the United States is apparently sound and under no threat? Why are the Americans apparently sustaining local democracy while the British are eroding it? The answer lies in the different approaches to local government in the two countries, which can be summed up in a single statement: in Britain, local democracy is characterised by partisan politics whereas in the United States the main feature is pragmatic business.

The party system in the United States is not as dominant as in the United Kingdom, even at the national level: members of the legislature have much more freedom from party whips in the United States. At the local level, the differences are even greater. The parties do operate in some US local governments, especially in the largest, old cities, but they are not committed to ideological positions in the same way that parties are in British local government. Instead, they are pragmatic and are built on local coalitions of interest groups rather than national electoral cleavages; many are (and even more have been) built around individual politicians and the power of patronage that they have exercised – corruptly in more than a few cases. In a lot of situations, this means that the actions of US local governments are as well described by the corporatist model as by the pluralist. (See, on a related issue, Smith's 1987, characterisation of ethnic politics as nationally organised in Britain but organised by neighbourhoods in US cities, where again the parallel with corporatism is strong.)

A more important feature of the American local government system, however, is the degree to which party politics (even of the type described above) are avoided and the operations are very akin to those of businesses. This characterisation owes much to the Reform movement of the early years of the present century, which saw the need to replace the corrupt local politics by a different managerial style. Reform led to most of the States introducing legislative provisions that allowed municipalities to adopt one of a number of organisational modes, several of which involved only small elected councils and a great deal of power being allocated to appointed managers. In some States these municipal charters include provisions: banning political parties from electoral participation; eliminating elections by territorial units (wards) that allow minorities to win representation; limiting spending powers – without electoral approval – and thereby controlling the potential growth of big government (with the fragmented system of special districts as a result – see above); and allowing popular initiatives so that resident participation (direct democracy) is advanced. Basic to this movement was a belief that politics is essentially evil. As Judd (1979) expresses it:

the municipal reformers sought a system free of political conflict. . . . They assumed that their own conceptions of the public interest were objectively true and beyond challenge. The answer to class tensions was not a redistribution of political and economic power. It was, rather, a brand of social reform which would perpetuate social economic and governmental institutions but *make them more efficient and therefore beneficial* to all classes . . . . Reformers . . . saved the pool from themselves. (p. 116)

The widespread adoption of the Reform package (57 per cent of municipalities by 1929) means that many American local governments are indeed little more than local administrations, and the fragmented system encourages different groups to promote their interests in an essentially free-market situation (Miller, 1981). In this way most US local governments conform to the national political ideology; the exceptions are some of the big cities, with their concentration of social problems, and there fiscal crises are forcing adoption of 'realistic market policies' (see David and Kantor, 1979, on the New York fiscal crisis, and Graz, 1986, on the revitalisation of Boston). By contrast, the process of 'nationalisation' of local politics in Britain in recent decades means that the pluralist model operating there is in conflict with the corporatist model at the centre. This has been most apparent in recent years, as Labour councils characterised as 'New Urban Left' have come into conflict with the policies of economic restructuring, based on a reduction of the private sector, promoted by Conservative governments from 1979 on (see Boddy and Fudge (eds), 1984). The contingent circumstances are very different, and have led to the attack on local democracy in Britain (that has included the abolition of certain authorities: O'Leary, 1987).

In summary

This chapter has argued that the state is a necessary body to the capitalist (and probably the socialist) mode of production, and that it is necessarily a territorially defined body: without a spatially defined, and defended, status, the state elite cannot fully exercise the despotic and infrastructural power that are central to their operations. Second, it has shown that a local state apparatus may not be a necessity, but that it is hard to see how a modern state could exercise either form of power without such an organisational structure.

Having established the requirement for a local state apparatus, attention turned then to its mode of operation – local government or local administration. By way of a comparative study of the United States and the United Kingdom, it was shown that the choice of one or the other was a function not only of structural requirements but also the particular contingent circumstances and their interpretation in the local cultural and historical context. The outcome is that we can appreciate why we have local governments and local administrations and as a consequence have a framework for analysing the role of democracy in the running of the local state apparatus.

Guide to further reading

For introductions to the various theories of the state, see either:
R. Alford and R. Friedland (1985) or P. Dunleavy and B. O'Leary (1987).
    There is no standard text on the local state: see, however, G.L. Clark and M.J. Dear (1984) and S.S. Duncan and M. Goodwin (1988).
On territoriality, see R.D. Sack (1986).

5 Health care policy and the state in 'austerity capitalism':

John Mohan

Introduction

State intervention in health care delivery is an established feature of advanced capitalist societies, but the reasons for it and the character of state intervention vary considerably. In this chapter I shall attempt to analyse the nature of and reasons for state intervention in the health sector, concentrating on two states often thought to represent almost polar opposites – the United States and Britain.

One immediate difficulty is exactly how to define health policy. A range of policies could be regarded as being concerned with health in its widest sense – housing legislation, pollution controls, and provision of sanitation are some of the more obvious ones, but others might include regulation of the food, alcohol and tobacco industries (P. Taylor, 1984), road safety legislation, and town planning regulations. These all affect health in one way or another, and state policies in one sphere can contradict those in another. Note, for instance, the recent criticisms in Britain of the government's limited increases in cigarette taxation (Public Accounts Committee, 1989), and in particular the view that decisions made by other government departments 'profoundly influence' the underlying causes of heart disease.

On a narrower definition, health policy includes, as well as health care, several measures designed directly to promote health, whether focused on individuals (advocacy of 'healthier' lifestyles through the exercise of individual choice), on workplace and environmental hazards, or on social class influences. Since the definition of and the explanations adopted for health inequalities very much reflect political ideology (Carr-Hill, 1988) it is not surprising that major differences of approach are evident between states, as has been shown via a comparison of Britain, Italy and the United States (R. Taylor, 1984). In Britain debate has been polarised between materialist versus individualist explanations, with the Conservative government sternly rejecting the Black Report (Townsend and Davidson, 1982) on inequalities in health, because of the expense of the programme of collective action it required, and favouring instead an individualist approach. But while people do make choices about their lifestyles, they do so in a context heavily structured by government decisions (Smith and Jacobson, 1988).

In order to narrow the scope of this chapter, I concentrate on health *care* policy, that is, on efforts to guarantee access to health services rather than on policies to improve and promote better health. Discussion is organised around the following themes. First, I briefly present comparative statistics on health care in various OECD states, and I discuss the problems inherent in comparing health care delivery systems, since this influences judgements about state intervention in health care. I also note the problems of assessing the results of delivering health care, in terms of the adequacy and equity of the system.

Second, I discuss the various explanations for state intervention in health care. Health care is a complex area of public policy, which highlights some key explanatory problems, especially functionalism, associated with analyses of the state, particularly from a Marxist standpoint. Explanation of health care policy cannot rely on single factors, general trends or universal principles, but must be related to historical and geographical specificities, and to class and non-class forces.

I then analyse state health care policy in Britain and the United States over the past decade, focusing on the efforts of right-wing governments to promote the 'restructuring' of the welfare state. There are three key issues here: efforts to promote cost containment; attempts to achieve internal reorganisations of health care delivery via deregulation and privatisation; and the changing balance between central and local tiers of the state, with an accompanying localism in health care policy. Arguably, the state is taking a more proactive stance, promoting a specific vision of state responsibility, but its scope for doing so may still be constrained, raising questions about the limitations to such strategies.

Finally, I consider future health care policies in Britain and the United States against the background of the views of those theorists postulating the 'end of organised capitalism' (Lash and Urry, 1987; Offe, 1985). I speculate on whether these developments indicate a novel role for the state as a coordinator, facilitator, and provider (possibly of last resort) in a decentralised, pluralist system of health care provision. However, this development should not simply be 'read off' from the postulated development of 'disorganised capitalism': it should be understood as a consequence of particular conjunctures of political forces.

Comparing health care delivery systems

Differences in health care expenditures may have very little to do with the extent of state intervention, and much more to do with demographic and economic factors. Countries at apparently similar stages of economic development can differ with regard to demographic factors and patterns of illness, which in turn influence need for health care; these can create problems of measurement and interpretation. Demographic factors might include differences in age structure, population density and distribution, birth and death rates and morbidity, economic factors could include industrial and occupational structure, public and private insurance coverage, reimbursement structures, provision of health-related social services, and so on.

Table 5.1 presents some basic data on health care expenditures in twelve OECD countries. The first columns illustrate the proportion of GNP accounted for by health care expenditures, looking first at public health care expenditures and then at total expenditure. There are very obvious differences with the United States, for instance, spending 4.4 per cent of GNP on public health care, but in total spending 10.7 per cent of GNP on health care; conversely, Sweden spends 8.6 per cent on public health care and 9.4 per cent in total. Another way of looking at this is to examine public health care expenditures as a percentage of total health care expenditures and to look at trends over time. Columns 6 and 7 demonstrate how this ratio has grown from an OECD mean of 61 per cent in 1960 to 78 per cent in 1984; countries in which growth had been especially rapid include Australia, Canada and the United States, with expansion in the latter case being due to the growth of expenditures on Medicare and Medicaid, the key public programmes introduced in the early 1960s. The OECD states seem to be approaching saturation in terms of the proportion of public health expenditures on health care, which might be taken as evidence of a trend towards increased state intervention in health care in OECD nations.

These comparisons tell us little about the outcomes of the expenditures on health care. The relations between health care provision and health status are not clear. Agreed comparative measures of health status, such as infant mortality rates and life expectancy at birth, are easily available, but no obvious correlation can be shown between expenditure and outcomes. While most West European states have among the lowest infant mortality rates and highest life expectancies, it is not obvious that increased expenditures lead to better health. Thus the United States, with the highest expenditure in the world on health care, is far from being the healthiest; indeed its infant mortality rate is bettered by fifteen OECD states; Japan and Norway, spending 6.6 per cent and 6.3 per cent of their GNP respectively on health care, achieve infant mortality rates well below those of the United States. Conversely, state intervention does not guarantee improved health, since most East European states have what are in effect nationalised health systems but they also have relatively poor health standards.

The distributional consequences of intervention also need to be examined, not least because a primary rationale, at least in ideological terms, for state intervention has been the need to redress social and spatial inequalities in access to health care. While most OECD states are approaching 100 per cent in terms of public coverage for health care, the United States is a glaring exception. Despite the availability of Medicare and Medicaid, the 'working poor' (those on low incomes and in temporary or part-time work) have very limited or no health insurance, so that the United States has been characterised as the 'land of the free, the home of the uninsured' (Cohodes, 1986), and there remain significant problems of access to care (Aday, Anderson and Fleming, 1980). In Britain there are major inequalities in access to primary care especially for the urban working class (Acheson, 1981) and, even in an ostensibly more egalitarian system, the middle classes consistently benefit more from the NHS than the working class (Le Grand, 1982). Finally, there is the question of the efficiency with which resources

Table 5.1: Comparative Indicators of Health and of Health Care Spending in Selected OECD States

	Public Health exp. as % of GDP [1]	Total Health exp. as % of GDP [1]	Male Infant mortality Rate [2]	Life expectancy at birth	Ratio of public health exp. to total health exp.		Public coverage for hospital care	
					1960	1987	1960	1980
Australia	6.6	7.8	10.5	72.2	47.6	84.5	77	100
Canada	6.2	8.4	10.4	72.0	43.1	74.4	68	100
France	6.5	9.1	11.2	70.9	57.8	71.2	85	100
Germany	6.4	8.1	10.6	71.3	67.5	78.2	86	95
Greece	3.6	4.6	16.4	73.6	57.9	79.3	30	98
Italy	6.1	7.2	17.1	71.0	83.1	84.1	87	100
Japan	4.8	6.6	6.6	74.8	60.4	72.1	–	100
Norway	5.6	6.3	8.7	72.8	77.8	88.8	100	100
Portugal	3.9	5.5	22.1	69.1	–	71.1	18	100
Sweden	8.6	9.4	7.1	73.5	72.6	91.4	100	100
UK	5.3	5.9	12.2	71.3	85.2	88.9	100	100
USA	4.4	10.7	12.8	70.9	24.7	41.4	22	40
OECD Average	5.6	7.2	11.6	71.0	61.0	78.7	75.3	95.3

Notes:
1. 1984.
2. Deaths per 1,000 live births.
Source: OECD, 1987

are used. Hospitalisation rates, and the rates at which common surgical procedures are carried out, vary greatly but are in general highest in market-based systems – with no discernible improvements in health status (see Ham, 1985).

So any comparison of health care delivery systems is a somewhat fraught business, and must consider the outcomes, equity and efficiency of the health care delivery system. In addition, any analysis of state involvement in the health arena should bear in mind that the state can intervene in health care provision in three main ways: provision, subsidy and regulation (Le Grand and Robinson, 1984). High levels of state provision, as in the United Kingdom, may be atypical for most West European states have a substantial private health care sector, to which access is guaranteed via membership of national health insurance schemes (see Maynard, 1974). Furthermore, what the state actually does varies between levels of government. Perhaps the most complex system is the United States's, where the *Federal* government's most important role is as a financer of health care; it accounts for some 30 per cent of total expenditure on health care in the United States, mainly through its programmes for the elderly and the poor. The Federal government's regulatory functions include setting standards and policing the food and pharmaceutical industries, while its role as provider is confined to Veterans Administration hospitals and (to a limited degree) medical education. The *States* share a responsibility as third-party payers for the Medicaid programme, they exercise substantial regulatory powers (e.g. the supervision of nursing homes, and the licensing of medical practitioners), and they are also providers of care, mainly via mental health institutions and some acute hospitals. The state is principally involved as a provider at the local government level where it operates public hospitals, neighbourhood health centres and performs public health functions. Regulation is limited to activities related to sanitation, such as licensing restaurants and enforcing minimum housing standards, while local governments are involved as third-party payers only in those areas that purchase health care for the medically indigent. This diffuse system of public involvement in health care delivery is reflected in a complex network of relations between government and the health industry and of course in a considerable amount of interaction between levels of government (Schmandt and Wendel, 1983, p.222). Even in relatively simple organisations such as Britain there are problems of fragmentation of responsibility; while the NHS is primarily responsible for curative health services local government also has an important role to play, especially with regard to community-based care of the mentally and chronically ill and there is at present poor coordination between the services (House of Commons, 1985).

The extent and character of state intervention has varied over time. Initially the regulatory role of the state was most important, especially with regard to supervising qualifications for entry into the medical profession in both Britain and the United States (see Starr, 1982). Subsidy and state provision came much later, with most Western capitalist states seeking to expand access to health care in the early post-war years; policy-makers focused on construction and modernisation of hospitals, the promotion of biomedical research, and expanding access to services (de Kervasdoné and Rodwin, 1984, p.5). Differences among nations existed in the post-war years, for instance in terms of systems of physician remuneration, the balance between public and private health care and so on, but there was general agreement on the need to extend the benefits of biomedical research as widely as possible, a goal which it seemed possible to achieve given rapid economic growth.

Prior to the 1980s, then, state intervention in health care was motivated by considerable faith in the capacity of the biomedical model of health to produce 'cures' for society's ills, and was facilitated by rapid economic growth. Neither condition held during the 1980s. Attention switched to inequalities in health and the social production of ill-health (Townsend and Davidson, 1982), and to the critiques of the effectiveness of modern medicine. These helped to undermine confidence in the provision of curative health services, but on their own do not account for the reduced rates of growth of health expenditures in the 1980s. More important have been the accessions to power of governments elected on a tax-welfare backlash, committed to cost-containment and, where possible, limiting the role of the state.

In summary, there is evidence of a convergence of national health care systems, in the broad direction of greater state involvement and intervention, but there are also great differences in the way health care is organised. The most obvious contrast is between Britain, where action by the state has been concerted, deliberate and top-down, and the United States, where the state has intervened essentially in order to seal gaps left by the largely market-based system.

Explanations for state intervention in health care

A number of different explanations have been put forward for state intervention in the health sector, with varying degrees of success. Here I compare and contrast these, focusing in particular on the key explanatory problems that beset many Marxist analyses.

R. Taylor (1984) contrasts some general models of the 'structural roots of variation in the development of welfare states in capitalist societies'. One of these focuses mainly on ideas and attitudes and explains health policy in terms of a convergence in these across different states (p.91). A second approach relies on cross-sectional data to test statistically the relationships between welfare expenditures and rates and levels of economic development, concentrating on the process of 'modernisation' and linking stages of economic development and political modernisation to the development of welfare states (Flora and Alber, 1981). Thus developments in welfare provision are related to three sets of variables: levels of socio-economic development, especially industrialisation and urbanisation; political mobilisation of the working class; and 'constitutional development', measured in terms of the degree of enfranchisement of the population and the extent of parliamentarism. Ringen (1987, p.30) breaks down the notion of 'modernisation' into several component factors: the increasing complexity of society, its democratisation, the growth of new interest groups (producers and consumers of welfare), economic growth, demographic change, and what he terms 'dramatic events' such as wars. However, such accounts rely heavily on cross-national data (with all the problems of comparability that implies) as well as on evolutionary, developmentalist theories of how societies work. The latter tendency is evident in Flora and Heidenheimer's claim that because non-democratic and non-capitalist societies have established very similar institutions, the welfare state 'seems to be a far more general version of modernisation, not exclusively tied to its "democratic–capitalist" version' (Flora and Heidenheimer, 1981, p.23). Such analyses can identify important general tendencies across states, but the interesting features of individual nation-states are thus subsumed under broad categories; 'general deductions based on national values' cannot provide a satisfactory explanation of the development of social policy in any one country (Weir, Orloff and Skocpol, 1988).

Pluralist accounts stress that political power is widely distributed, and that no one group is dominant; consequently, each can exercise some influence. There is no systematic bias to the exercise of power and therefore what is important to pluralists is the minutiae of negotiating processes. The strength of such an approach is its emphasis on detailed description of the actions of key individuals and interest groups in shaping health care policy; good examples would be Pater (1981) on the process of policy formulation prior to the setting up of the NHS and Rivett (1986) on the London hospital system. However, pluralists tend to downplay wider social and political influences and constraints on state intervention, concentrating on details of policy formulation and seeing the state as some kind of independent and benevolent arbitrator. One obvious difficulty is that not all groups can enter the health policy arena with equal confidence, since the medical monopoly of knowledge is itself a source of power. Hence, community and consumer groups, and their interests, have limited likelihood of being addressed. The systematic exclusion of community groups from the health policy agenda is a feature of Alford's (1975) analysis of health care politics in New York; in Alford's terms the interests of such groups are 'repressed'. More generally, the state can effectively dictate and shape the policy agenda by its own decisions on who shall and shall not be incorporated into the policy process, a good example being the attack on trade union and local authority representation on health authorities in Britain. In such circumstances the pluralist claims of equal access to and participation in the policy process ring rather hollow.

Marxists have persistently criticised such approaches, arguing that health care policy is primarily determined by the nature and outcomes of class struggles (Navarro, 1978, 1986), and eschewing general theories of welfare state evolution, in favour of 'specific historical accounts of state responses to the political articulation of class interests' (R. Taylor, 1984, p.98). They have also highlighted the structural constraints on state intervention. Following Offe (1984) the argument has been that there are 'selection mechanisms' which a priori exclude anti-capitalist health care policies (Renaud, 1975). While the capitalist state can intervene to try and regulate health care provision, limit or prevent disease, and control the social production of ill health, it 'cannot reorganise the economy so that less illness is produced' (Renaud, 1975, p.565). The fact that the state is capitalist by definition limits

its capacity to intervene in or solve social problems. This usefully reminds us of the general limits to state intervention, but is not helpful with regard to what is or is not legitimate in individual capitalist states.

The more general problem with Marxist accounts is their reliance on functionalist explanations which attribute events either to the needs of capital, the demands of the working class, or a combination of both. For instance, for Navarro (1978) events in the British health sector are usually 'determined', on the one hand, by working-class demands (by the degree of militancy of organised labour), and on the other hand by capital's requirements, notably for the reproduction of a healthy workforce. The problem is that we are never really sure which is dominant or determinant. Thus growing state intervention in health care is related by Navarro to increases in working-class militancy, but most of the measures to which he refers were usually implemented some years after this militancy peaked. Navarro fails to show the precise links between the demands formulated by the working class and the articulation of these demands in policy formation. This illustrates two principal theoretical problems: the functionalism inherent in attributing these role to the state (see Urry, 1981, pp. 116–21; Hindess, 1987); and the teleology of explaining welfare policy developments – indeed all developments in state policy – in relation to the 'balance of class forces' prevailing at any given time (Harris, 1980).

The problem with accounts like Navarro's, which stress political class struggle, is that, first, there is no automatic guarantee that the existence of a working class will lead to the articulation of demands for welfare, or that class struggle will lead to such demands, because 'the factors relevant in the structuring of interests as against capital are not necessarily those relevant in the structuring of interests with reference to state welfare' (Wetherly, 1988, p. 31). Sectionalism within the working class can impede the development of pressure for welfare services; Starr (1982, p. 245) cites the American Federation of Labour's opposition to national health insurance, which they felt would undermine their own role in providing insurance for their members (see also Stevens, 1988), and Davis (1984) notes that American unions have tended to bargain for 'strong welfare states in single unions' rather than for national, comprehensive welfare provision. Secondly, Weir, Orloff and Skocpol (1988, pp. 15–16) argue that an emphasis on political class struggle would neglect a number of interests not structured on class lines: 'the distinctive dynamics of American social policies have been rooted in shifting political coalitions which include, but necessarily go beyond, business and labour.'

This latter point also hints at the importance of producer and professional interest groups in the health care policy arena. The medical profession is the most obvious example here, and Cawson (1982, p. 91) claims that 'the postwar history of the NHS can be persuasively analysed as an unfolding interplay between professional and managerial elements'. Similarly, Alford (1975) has interpreted health care policy in the United States in terms of a conflict of interests between 'professional monopolists', seeking to protect their control over teaching, research and care, and the 'corporate rationalisers', seeking to extend bureaucratic and managerial control. Moreover, the autonomy of the

American medical profession has at times been almost absolute, if its effective veto of national health insurance schemes is anything to go by.

A final point identified by Weir et al. is the need to understand the process of state formation: 'political struggles and outcomes are jointly conditioned by the institutional arrangements of the state and by class and other social relations.' Hence the United States's development as a federal constitutional republic, its early mass democratisation, and its relatively late development of bureaucracy, has produced an exceptionally fragmented polity, in which neither capital or labour have found it easy to operate as unified political forces. The key political division, they claim, has been between a mass two-party democracy in the east, north and west, and a one-party racial oligarchy in the south. This has been an innate force for conservatism in US politics, effectively inhibiting policies for reform and 'setting parameters to welfare policies'. Furthermore, the federal state structure, with its decentralised and non-programmatic political parties, has offered greater leverage to interests that could associate across many local political districts and this has been exploited to the full by the AMA to block proposals for national health insurance. Consequently, rather than develop in the incremental manner of European welfare states, many progressive measures have been dashed on the rocks of these conservative forces. Policy breakthroughs have been clustered – the New Deal in the 1930s, the Great Society in the 1960s – and were implemented by coalitions that emerged during nationally-perceived crises that were widely understood to call for positive government action (Weir et al., 1988, pp. 16–25).

The approaches reviewed are thus of varying validity in accounting for the involvement of the state in health care. Cross-sectional studies usefully direct attention to general trends, but are weak on explaining events in individual states; pluralist accounts give much greater attention to detail and have supplied fascinating historical material. But neither really pay attention to the wider social and political context and to the articulation of class and non-class forces and their influence on welfare policies. It is this that strengthens the case for a political economy of health as developed by numerous Marxist theorists, though this is still achieved at the expense of functionalist explanations. Finally, it is important to stress the process of state formation: without an awareness of how political structures developed, analyses of political conflicts and class struggles are somewhat limited.

The entrepreneurial welfare state? Health care policy under Reagan and Thatcher

In their encounter with economic crises since the mid-1970s, states have had to develop new tactical approaches to welfare provision. Gough (1979) postulated that, in such circumstances, we would find 'not so much cuts or a dismantling of the welfare state, but its *restructuring*', and that the state, 'acting in the interests of its national capital, will seek to alter and adapt social policies to suit the perceived needs of that capital' (p. 138; emphasis in original). There is no automatic correspondence between capital's 'needs' and state policies: the ground for these policies has to be established politically. The importance of the Reagan and Thatcher regimes is not just that they are among the first governments explicitly to attempt to check the growth of state expenditures on health services, but also that they have attempted to take a proactive stance in reshaping the health care policy agenda, in ways that were perhaps unanticipated by analysts of welfare state restructuring. Thus Conlan (1988, p. 2) argues that government in the United States 'has ceased to be the passive instrument of external social and political forces and has become an active, autonomous originator of change'. Likewise in Britain the state has been actively promoting a novel, entrepreneurial role for health authorities within a more business-oriented NHS. I first discuss the wider political strategies adopted by these governments and then consider the implications for health care policy in relation to three areas: state moves towards deregulation and privatisation; attempts to gain control of health care costs, which has involved the state in conflict with the medical profession; and the changing relationships between central and local tiers of the state in the two countries. I preface these comments with a brief summary of the overall tactics of these governments.

Managing decline: deintegrative politics and welfare

The Reagan and Thatcher governments have used what Krieger (1987) terms their increased 'decisional autonomy' to pursue novel policies which he (1986) terms 'deintegrative' strategies: these have 'arrested, and indeed partly reversed, the historic tendency for citizenship rights to expand from *civil* rights to *political* rights to *social* rights'. In outline there are important similarities between the policies of these governments. Both were elected on a manifesto relating to rolling back the state; both were elected via a coalition-building process which ensured a majority if they placated certain groups of the electorate. Moreover, both were conscious of the limitations of the post-war 'Fordist' regime of accumulation which had funded rapid growth in welfare programmes for some thirty years, but was beginning to break down with the onset of 'austerity capitalism' (Bodenheimer, 1989). The political problem that would emerge was therefore how to manage decline and how to displace the costs of change onto certain marginal groups and constituencies. In Britain the solution adopted was a 'two-nation' politics (Jessop et al., 1984), a socially and spatially selective strategy to prioritise those groups and areas likely to deliver a Conservative majority. In the United States, Davis (1984) charts the rise of an unlikely alliance between 'corporate capital and the new middle strata in a strategy of cost displacement towards the working or unwaged poor'. Bodenheimer (1989) borders on the extremes of functionalism, arguing that in the era of prosperity capitalism health expenditures could increase the productivity and longevity of all workers and have a countercyclical effect, in the Keynesian sense, on demand. These conditions no longer hold, since an economy based on the exploitation of low-paid service sector workers finds it easier to 'replace' rather than 'repair' the sick; hence the economy can continue to function with 'good health care for those who deserve to be repaired, minimal services for those who can be junked' (p. 534). This vision of cost displacement was coupled to Reagan's version of a 'new Federalism': the basic problem of government was the size of government; as far as possible, therefore, responsibilities should be decentralised to state and local governments.

⟨ On this apparently radical programme one might have expected radical initiatives: a move towards insurance-based health care in Britain, perhaps, or much greater competition and deregulation in the United States. In practice the efforts of both regimes to 'roll back the state' have been limited and partial. One great difficulty has been the 'embarrassing secret'of the welfare state (Offe, 1984), which is that the Right has yet to demonstrate that advanced capitalism without the welfare state would be viable. Certainly, in Britain public support for the NHS has been such that the government have been swift to avow their support for the service. The airing of radical alternatives for public debate has been achieved through a loose association of right-wing 'think tanks' (the Centre for Policy Studies, Adam Smith Institute, etc.) operating at arm's length from government but whose members have close interpersonal connections with it. (The US equivalent would be organisations such as the Heritage Foundation.) This secretive section of the 'policy community' undoubtedly had a great deal of influence on the NHS review, but because the government were able to disown ideas emanating from it, some of its wilder flights of fancy obtained a hearing without besmirching the government's reputation.⟩

A second reason why rhetoric has not matched reality is the practicalities of implementing major reforms in both states. In the United States the system of government is 'uniquely designed to make quick and radical policy shifts difficult to carry out' (Morris, 1987, p.83), notably in terms of the ability of Congress to check Presidential power. Thus Reagan was not always able to guarantee Congressional support for his policies and so the principal effects of his policies have therefore (to date) been a slowdown in the rates of growth of health expenditures (Palmer and Sawhill (eds), 1984). In Britain there has also been the question of timetabling major legislative changes and the relationship of policies on the welfare state to the rest of the government's domestic agenda. The first terms of Conservative government concentrated heavily on neutralising some of their principal opponents such as the major industrial unions and left-wing local authorities, as well as on policies designed to revive the economy. Major social policy reforms were left until the government had achieved some successes on the economic front and had consolidated its position at the polls. Thus Reagan did not succeed in returning social policy to its pre-New Deal days; nor has Thatcher yet reversed the tide of collectivism.

Deregulation and privatisation

What is perhaps surprising about these governments is the relatively limited steps they have taken to introduce fully-blown competitive health care systems. Thus the Thatcher government's initial term of office was characterised by policies which, some felt (Klein, 1984) marked a retreat from ideology in the face of considerations of practical politics. Yet this is debatable. It is true that few steps were taken to privatise the entire service, challenge vested interests, and/or reduce funding; but in light of other battles the government was fighting, on the economic and foreign fronts, this is hardly surprising. More revealing was the set of policies imposed, in some haste, after the 1983 election, involving expenditure cuts, staff reductions, competitive tendering for ancillary services, and management reforms. Furthermore, admittedly with the benefit of hindsight, there is a thread of continuity between policies put forward as early as 1981 and those being proposed in both the 1987 Health and Medicines Bill and the 1989 NHS White Paper, namely the emphasis on welfare pluralism and the blurring of the boundaries between public and private sectors (Mohan, 1989; Davies, 1987). Kenneth Clarke admitted as much in arguing that the NHS White Paper represented 'a change of pace, not a change of direction' (*Hansard*), an indication that the government has not just responded to political exigencies but has had a strategic vision of the future NHS. Although the government has not sought to replace the NHS, it has steadily increased the scope for private funding and provision of services: direct steps taken include relaxations of controls on the size and location of private hospitals, allowing NHS consultants to undertake more private practice without loss of NHS salary, encouraging private – public sector collaboration, and (since 1980) providing state funds for long-stay care: the blank cheque written for the nursing home industry, amounting to around a billion pounds annually by 1988, is hardly marginal. Moves to a mixed economy of welfare are well underway.

There is also evidence of an ideological strategy designed to wean the electorate gradually from the view that only the state can provide, and designed to break down barriers between public and private sectors. This has taken the form of ministerial rhetoric emphasising the valuable contribution the private sector can make in supplementing the state's limited resources, and the importance of individuals providing for themselves and their families. This has been accompanied by the encouragement of less 'formal' sources of care via the promotion of an ideology of 'active citizenship' and the stress on the 'community' as the first port of call. In practical terms these statements have been allied to subtle efforts to shift some of the burden of financing away from the state: the endorsement of the income-generating activities of health authorities, the inexorable rises in prescription charges, and the imposition of charges for optical checkups, are but three. If this is not a minimal state, it is certainly a more restricted state.

But possibly the most far-reaching development has been the introduction of a managerial strategy aimed at a major internal reorganisation of the way the NHS operates. The emphasis here has been on higher levels of 'performance', concentrating on quantitative measures of inputs and resource use, rather than on the outcomes of treatment or on health status. This fuelled criticisms that performance measurement was a 'blunt tool', aimed at subjecting to market criteria 'those parts of the public sector which could not be privatised or subjected to the sanitising discipline of the trusty market' (Pollitt, 1986). In organisational terms the notion of 'administration' has been replaced by 'management', which is intended to improve accountability by identifying individuals who can be held responsible for achieving narrowly and centrally-defined objectives (Petchey, 1986). The intention and effect has been to shape the policy agenda in the Conservatives' desired image; coupled with systematic replacement of non-Tory members of health authorities, this has stifled opposition by both presenting a substantially revised policy agenda and restricting the capacity of oppositional elements to debate that agenda. It has been claimed that these developments betoken the increased ability of the state to dictate and shape the policy agenda (Haywood and Ranade, 1989), a point which echoes Krieger's comments about the 'decisional autonomy' of the Thatcher and Reagan administrations. The state is to be a more managerial, decisive state.

Privatisation would be a less appropriate way to describe the tactics of the Reagan administrations, and some commentators have questioned whether some of their key policies (like the Diagnosis-Related Groups (DRG) system of prospective, fixed-rate reimbursement for Medicare and Medicaid patients) represent a competitive or regulatory strategy (Luft, 1985). The sole Federal-sponsored efforts at planning, the Health Systems Agencies (HSAs, introduced in 1974) have been abandoned, since they are regarded as barriers to competition; hence new hospital finance will depend not at all on any criteria of 'need' and rather more on access to capital finance. This is perhaps not as significant as it appears, for States had limited directive powers; influencing hospital system development depended largely on cooperation with hospital providers and there were no formal powers to direct new hospital investment where it was most needed. Even so, eleven States have repealed their Certificate of Need programmes and only forty (out of 142) HSAs remain in existence, their funding having been picked up by States.

Federal attacks on Medicaid funding, and on federal health programmes, perhaps represent an implicit form of privatisation, for they throw much greater responsibility for financing health care for the poor onto individual States, and they have forced health facilities into a de facto competitive strategy. Thus Reagan's 1981 Omnibus Budget Reconciliation Act (OBRA) replaced categorical funding for various health care programmes by a block grant system, in which individual States were given the opportunity to make their own decisions on priorities for health care spending, within an overall budget cut by 21 per cent. The effect on mental health services has been that many community mental health centres have become far more 'entrepreneurial' and access to them has been denied to more groups of patients (Brown, 1988, pp.68–70). The only exception to the block grant system was the primary health care programme, which was funded separately as an individual block grant after considerable resistance in Congress to Reagan's proposals (Sardell, 1988). Ginzberg (1986) argues that there has been a 'destabilisation' of health care, notably by attacks on the ability of the system to provide for the poor by cross-subsidising; the scope of providers to fund such care has been removed by competition.

Finally, Kinzer (1988, p.114) suggests a number of limits to the competition-based strategy. These include the mounting evidence of electoral support for a national health programme, and the strength of public support for local hospitals, even to the extent of voting for greater local taxation in order to keep them open. Kinzer also points to the ways in which the national rates for the DRG system have been varied and qualified with allowances for a number of factors and, in a echo of a 'market failure' argument for State action, shows the number of ways competition is restricting access to health care for the poor and therefore claims that regulation is necessary to ensure that they get it. Finally, there have been 'thoroughgoing political interventions' in States known for their 'freewheeling, competitive systems': for instance, Florida has passed a law to tax the net profits of hospitals in order to enrich its Medicaid programmes.

Thus neither state has been able to implement a full competitive strategy, although both have introduced substantial innovation and partial privatisation. But the achievement of the Thatcher government has been to recast the character of management and service delivery in the NHS, and to instal value for money at the heart of public sector management more generally (Hall, 1985). Finally, there is evidence from the United States that a strategy of 'rolling back the State' may require greater State regulation and some form of intervention to guarantee the provision of services for the poor. As public awareness of the gap between the quality of public and private services grows, this may act as a stumbling-block to further deregulation and competition.

Confronting professional autonomy: the medical profession and the state

The extent to which any state is able to confront, cooperate with or defeat organised special interest groups is a key index of the state's autonomy. In health policy the state's interests are often in conflict with one of the best-organised and well-connected interest groups, namely the medical profession. For many years the situation in many states was a compromise which, tacitly or otherwise, accorded considerable autonomy to the medical profession. Bevan's famous remark that he ensured medical support for the NHS by 'stuffing the doctors' mouths with gold' reminds us that this lobby was not only bought off but that several bargains were struck (freedom to practice privately; substantial professional representation in management) which in effect branded the NHS a curative, hospital-based service. Even within the NHS, the scope given to the medical profession was such that, while total spending was determined by the state, doctors were the final arbiters of resource allocation by virtue of their clinical decisions. Furthermore, economic growth and expansion in NHS resources shielded doctors from pressures for cost containment, but as the expansion of the capabilities of medicine began to hit the ceiling of cost containment from the mid-1970s onwards, the issue of medical autonomy came to the fore.

In the United States, the lobbying power of the American Medical Association virtually enabled them to veto federal proposals for a national health system. Even when a Congress with a substantial Democrat majority was able to push through proposals for insurance programmes for the elderly and the poor, the AMA bargained for and won 'fair and reasonable' reimbursement rates, guaranteeing (at first) that they would profit from the programmes. As the US health care system has been increasingly plagued by cost containment problems in face of galloping inflation, the 'most significant battle now emerging is that between practising physicians and management' (Fuchs, 1986, p.302). However that battle is more likely to be joined at the State level than at the Federal level.

This is not so in Britain. What has for long been a relatively cosy relationship between the medical profession and the state has been ruptured by a confrontationalist government, bent on imposing its will on the NHS. Three key challenges to medical autonomy have emerged: the Griffiths report on NHS Management, the negotiations over the terms of GP contracts, and the NHS White Paper. For the government, the common theme of these proposals is that, despite the enormous sums of money poured into the NHS, major variations remain in the effectiveness and efficiency of the service, which must be ironed out through determined managerial action. Elston's (1988) analysis is drawn on here, to sketch the contours of the growing conflict between the medical profession and the state.

Perhaps ironically, the Conservatives' first term of office included concessions to the medical profession in the form of greater opportunities to practise privately, but within a few years the use and abuse of these opportunities was the subject of media and political criticism. In the face of a steady assault on their expenditure record the government had to find a scapegoat and, as the principal allocators of resources in the NHS, it was perhaps inevitable that an accusing finger would eventually be pointed at the medical profession. The attack has taken the form of criticisms of 'inefficiencies' and of variations in 'performance'; the medical profession were excluded from the NHS review in 1988, an indication of the government's non-corporatist style of policy-making; and Kenneth Clarke's pejorative dismissal of the British Medical Association as a 'trade union' is only the latest in a series of diatribes. Taken together these all amount to 'a confrontation with the medical profession (Davies, 1987) by a government determined to use its decisional autonomy to impose its new managerial vision on the NHS. The irony is that a less aggressive approach might have achieved the government's ends. Techniques of clinical audit are gradually gaining acceptance, as is the principle of peer review, but what is really important is on whose terms clinical audits are to be introduced (Elston, 1988). However, the imposition of the GP's contract, and the introduction of the NHS reviews, without trial schemes, are viewed as evidence of a totalitarian approach to the exercise of power by a government which clearly believes that its enormous Parliamentary majority gives it the scope to offer fundamental challenges to vested interests.

There seems no such danger in the United States. Indeed, the various levels of government are only one among a number of players at the policy table and they by no means hold all the aces: 'everywhere there are signs of constriction on traditional professional prerogatives' (Stevens, 1986, p.75). The most important Federal initiative has been the imposition of a prospective payment system for Medicare and Medicaid patients. Since the Federal government accounts for nearly 40 per cent of all health care spending through its contribution to these programmes, this would be expected to have a major impact on physician autonomy by forcing hospitals to cut costs. It has certainly helped shift the locus of decision-making from physicians to administrators but this is not just due to state action; general commercial pressures and the oversupply of physicians have forced the doctors' hand (Stevens, 1986).

One consequence is that individual States have taken a firm line with the medical profession but they have done so largely through alliances with business interests. Bergthold (1984; 1987) argues that in certain circumstances the 'purchasers [of health care] can overwhelm even the substantial power of providers to block regulation and planning', citing the example of California where business and the State succeeded in introducing a greater measure of price competition among doctors and hospitals, following a crisis provoked in part by a 3 per cent cut in Federal support for California's generous Medicaid programme. The defensive response of the physicians and hospitals even alienated some of their traditional Republican supporters, and in the end the 'physicians found themselves out of favour, out of power and at each other's throats'; the producer interests were 'crowded off the board' by pressures from the budget, business coalitions and insurance companies (Bergthold, 1984, p.211).

Thus professional autonomy is being challenged in both Britain and the United States. In Britain the government is sufficiently confident to confront professional groups which had hitherto enjoyed considerable freedom, while in the United States the Federal government is taking similar steps though partly motivated by its desire to cut health expenditures for the poor. The British government's confrontation with the medical profession may eventually prove counterproductive because public support for the NHS, and public esteem for doctors remain high. In the United States this seems much less likely, because the state is not alone in wanting to contain costs; business pressures, allied to physician oversupply, are serving to weaken the autonomy of doctors without the state needing to step in; as Kinzer (1988, p.116) remarks, 'in an era when the talk is all about less government and more free enterprise, most doctors feel less free than ever'.

Localism, centralism and autonomy

In some respects state involvement in health care in Britain and the United States lies at two ends of a continuum: a highly decentralised patchwork of services in the United States, compared to what is a very centralised system in Britain; considerable autonomy in the United States, compared to limited local autonomy in Britain. There are elements of convergence and divergence between the two systems.

To some extent the localism of the American system can be related to a distrust of central government and an ideological predisposition towards a limited view of obligation towards the poor and sick, combined with an idealised version of 'community'. Thus Morris (1987, p.97) argues that 'these limited views of obligation conform well to an American history of an open frontier, a belief that anyone can make their way if they try; a society where, until this century, most people lived within coherent communities of association'. Leaving aside the apparent idealism of this statement, it does suggest the importance of local, community initiative. This is a 'cultural force of great latent and often unconscious power in American civic attitudes', and Reagan has harked back to such attitudes in the 'New Federalist' policies.

Essentially, the 'new Federalism' calls for a decentralisation of responsibilities from central to State and local governments. Reagan has rarely favoured national over subnational governments in the social policy arena, and the primary aim of the new federalism has been to reduce the power, influence and morale of bureaucracies, rather than improve intergovernmental management and effectiveness (Conlan, 1988). Two key elements of Reagan's programme were therefore to cap the Federal government's contribution to Medicaid (a 5 per cent limit on growth in Medicaid support to the States was proposed in 1982), thus shifting some of the costs of insurance to the States; and the selective enhancement of State discretion. This latter has been achieved by the 'block grant' mechanism, replacing what were (previously) formally separate programmes with a centralised allocation for States to spend as they wished; only some programmes (e.g. primary health care) were spared. Thompson (1987) implies that these developments are beginning to call into question the ability of States to develop and provide their own health care services, suggesting some limitations to the strategy of localism. It could also force States into a competitive, downward spiral in which they are competing to attract economic activity via offering attractive tax packages which, in Davis's apocalyptic phrase, could lead to 'Bantustan-like conditions of social reproduction' in the 'sunbelt' (low tax) States of the American south (1984).

A further consequence of the fragmented polity of the United States and the role of individual states in health care delivery is that the policy formulation process is considerably more open to a variety of interest groups than is the case in Britain, and there is considerable diversity in the character of State intervention between individual States (and even within them, with some local government organisations, such as New York City, through its Health and Hospitals Corporation, being major providers of health care). This finds expression in two ways: variations between States in the extent of regulation, with States in the north and east being generally seen as regulatory while those in the south favour competition; and variations in the extent of coverage for the poor. For instance, some States virtually exclude the poor from participation in Medicaid by setting income thresholds, above which individuals do not qualify for the programme, at very low levels (Cohodes, 1986).

Whereas in Britain business protests about taxation are somewhat unusual, except through representative organisations such as the CBI, in the United States much more taxation is organised locally and there is much more evidence of visible pressure from business groups on issues like cost containment. Nationally this has been coordinated through organisations such as the Washington Business Group on Health, which has been operating for a number of years to lobby for efforts to contain health costs; as these are mainly paid for by employers they have come to account for substantial proportions of business costs. More locally, business organisations do exert substantial pressure on individual States, but one problem that can then arise is the need to confront provider groups such as hospital and health insurance organisations. Bergthold (1984; 1988) shows how coalitions of business and State interests have formed to promote cost-saving measures, against stiff opposition from provider organisations. For instance, in Massachusetts, both the public and private sectors were facing rapid rises in health care costs, but resistance by provider monopolies was frustrating attempts to contain these costs. The State took a proactive stance 'to precipitate the political participation of business' (Bergthold, 1988, p.429) by involving business interests in the informal discussions of its Rate Setting Commission (a body charged with determining rates of reimbursement for hospitals). The Commission excluded physicians from the policy process, and business 'became a dominant change agent'; the State allowed business interests to direct and even make policy, and the State legislative process 'ratified decisions made by business and its private coalition' (p.448). This was termed a form of 'mesocorporatism', referring to four elements: significant state presence in the policy process; a two-way implementation process, whereby battle over policy and its implementation devolves to powerful interest organisations; these groups create and organise their own constituencies; and the results of bargaining among 'peak associations' become informally binding.

There is much greater local variation in the American service than in Britain, where local political influence has been relatively limited. There have been numerous reorganisations in attempts to combine ministerial accountability with local autonomy, but no stable solution has emerged. The emphasis in recent years has superficially been on devolution of decision-making and responsibility, but associated with this has been a centralisation of authority. Government policy statements have stressed the need for decisions to be taken as close as possible to those delivering patient care. Administrative reforms have abolished tiers of administration and sought, as far as possible, to streamline the decision-making process. However, there is ample evidence to support Gamble's claim (1988, p.231) that the 'Thatcher government's own diagnosis of the crisis of state authority constantly impelled it towards intervention'. This evidence includes ministerial interference in decisions about privatisation of services, hospital closures and staff reductions (Mohan, 1989). Central control of the 'performance' of local health authorities is now much more rigorously enforced, via annual reviews of RHAs, DHAs, units and individual managers.

Local political influence over the NHS, never very strong anyway, is being steadily reduced. Even the few local authority and trade union representatives on District Health Authorities (DHAs) will now be replaced, under the White Paper, by people nominated for the skills they can bring as individuals to management. This is partly an attack on special interests, and it is partly done to facilitate the managerial agenda for the NHS. It remains to be seen whether local 'business elites' will gain the upper hand in policy-making and what effect this will have on the character of service delivery.

In addition, the emphasis is heavily on the necessity for managers to 'deliver' within the constraints of their existing budgets; if they do not, this is generally attributed by government to failures of management. Paradoxically, despite reducing direct local influence on DHAs, their scope for local initiative has been expanded. They have been permitted to engage in income generation schemes, encouraged to collaborate with the private health sector (Griffith et al., 1987), and generally exhorted to mobilise any relevant local resources rather than limit their role to that of a provider. The vision seems to be one in which the state, in the form of DHA comes to play an 'entrepreneurial, coordinative role' (Davies, 1987). The White Paper confirms this trend for it not only envisages an internal market operating within the NHS, so that health authorities will buy patient care from hospitals irrespective of ownership, it also allows for the creation of quasi-independent NHS Hospital Trusts, accountable only to the Secretary of State for Health; in principle the rationale for this is to build on and strengthen the links between hospitals and their local communities. In practice such institutions will operate as commercial organisations in all but name, and any coordinated planning with the remaining NHS hospitals and other statutory services will hardly be facilitated. The role of the state implied, far from being a quasi-monopoly provider, is a more limited, though entrepreneurial one; it seems likely to lead in the direction of greater diversity, but also greater inequality.

The end of organised capitalism and the end of collectivism?

Considerable attention has recently been given in social theory to the major social and political transformations associated with the transition from 'organised' to 'disorganised' capitalism (Lash and Urry, 1987). This raises the question of what effect such transformations might have on the provision of welfare services and on the involvement of the state in those services. For as de Swaan (1988) concludes, 'there is no historical necessity for the collectivising process to proceed at a global level'. Put another way, the welfare states which expanded, on the back of unprecedented economic growth, in much of the Western capitalist world in the post-war years, are far from being an 'irreversible' phenomenon (Therborn and Roebroek, 1986). Arguably large-scale state intervention in health care is a relatively recent phenomenon, confined largely to West European states in the post-war period; in the United States it is even more recent, far from comprehensive, and much more subject to reactionary forces than European welfare systems.

The post-war expansion of welfare states was built on a fragile and favourable political and economic conjuncture, which no longer obtains, and the problem for capitalist states since the oil shocks has been how to break with at least some of the commitments taken on in that period. Both the Thatcher and Reagan regimes have attempted that break, and their policies suggest further changes in the character of state intervention in health care delivery. Far from being an 'inactive' state, as these governments and their ideologues might have wished in their wilder flights of fancy, the evidence here suggests that the state will continue to be very active but in several different ways.

First, it suggests a reduction in the state's role as a provider of health services. Even if this is largely a British anomaly, there is no question that it is going to be reduced. The NHS White Paper sees the state, via local health authorities, mainly as a provider of funds for health care seeking the best deal for patients in a competitive market. Within this new role for the state is a heightened managerial and entrepreneurial capacity, in the Thatcher government's vision, and this novelty in the character of state intervention is a key feature of the policies of her governments. The Reagan administration has sought to reduce the Federal role as a financer but this has simply thrown more of the burden of services for the poor and elderly onto the States. In an increasingly competitive environment this has led States to take what has been termed a more 'proactive' stance on issues such as cost-containment.

Second, the state's regulatory role may have to increase in the interests of maintaining standards. As Britain has moved towards a mixed economy of welfare, the necessity for greater regulation of a growing range of providers will become apparent, raising the question of quality control. It is not clear how the revised, business-oriented membership of DHAs will respond to this challenge given their primary remit of cost control. In the United States the commercialisation of health care is squeezing services for the poor and this has led some States to intervene to regulate costs in order to sustain the resources needed to provide for those with limited or no insurance. The State has always been involved in regulation, but this role seems certain to expand.

Third, the trend is towards greater localism, autonomy and decentralisation, with an emphasis on local efforts to supply services, and on perhaps nebulous notions of 'community'. This would seem to support Lash and Urry's contention (1987, p.231) that as capitalism moves from an organised to a disorganised phase, it will replace centralised, bureaucratic modes of service delivery with localised, variegated modes of provision; a 'mixed economy' of welfare. One obvious point is that generalisations like this run the risk of falling into the same trap as the proponents of the developmentalist theories reviewed earlier. Lash and Urry's point may have descriptive validity, but it does not automatically follow that changing patterns of health service organisation can be read off from the development of 'disorganised capitalism'. If health care delivery systems such as Britain's move towards greater commercialisation and decentralisation, with an expansion of the charitable, voluntary and private sectors, this will be because of specific conjunctions of political forces. The point of the comparative section of this chapter has been to show that, especially in Britain but also the United States, the state has actively steered the health care system in new directions, even in the face of considerable opposition.

However, there may be limits to such strategies in two senses: the widening cracks that are evident in the quantity and quality of service provision, and the broader impact of untrammelled economic growth on the environment and on health. Evidence for the former point includes: rapidly-increasing NHS waiting lists; the fiasco of community care in Britain and deinstitutionalisation in the United States; the 'limits of deregulation' in the United States (Kinzer, 1988). Evidence for the latter includes the re-emergence of the health patterns of 'peripheral nations' in American cities (Bodenheimer, 1989; Hiatt, 1987) and of old public health hazards (notably pollution, water quality and food hygiene). The latter point highlights once again that state policies in one area impact on others, and points towards the need to coordinate a range of policies that all affect health – precisely the opposite direction to that in which state policies in Britain and the United States are leading.

Acknowledgement: the author gratefully acknowledges the support of an ESRC Postdoctoral Fellowship (grant no. A23320036) from 1986–9.

Guide to further reading

The best single introduction to health policy issues in Britain is C. Ham's *Health policy in Britain* (London: Macmillan 1985 2nd edition); R. Klein's *The politics of the National Health Service* is a comprehensive treatment of political debates about the NHS since its inception. Navarro (1978) provides a provocative discussion of similar issues to Klein from a Marxist viewpoint. He has also published a collection of his essays on health care in capitalist states (1986). A collection currently in press will provide a useful set of essays on the British health care scene: M. Bury, M. Calnan and J. Gabe (eds), *The sociology of the health service* (London: Routledge).

On the American health care system, see J. Hiatt, (1987) and J. Califano, (1986) *America's health care revolution*, for two recent if general treatments, as well as T.R. Marmor and J. Morone (1983), *Political analysis and American medical care*. However, the best sources of material on the American system are in journals such as *Health Affairs*, the *Milbank Memorial Fund Quarterly*, the *International Journal of Health Services*, the *New England Journal of Medicine*, and the *Journal of Health Policy, Politics, and Law*.

Comparative analyses of the health systems of Britain and the United States are few and far between: D. Fox (1986) analyses health planning initiatives to the mid-1960s; and V. Rodwin's (1984) *The health planning predicament* (Berkeley: University of California Press), a comparative study of four nations including Britain and the United States, is another exception. Other comparative studies of health care and welfare systems across various states include: R. Mishra (1987), *The welfare state in capitalist society* (Brighton: Wheatsheaf); S. Ringen (1987); and A. De Swaan (1988). J. Scarpaci (ed.) (1989) *Privatisation of health services in industrial societies* (New Brunswick: Rutgers University Press) is a cross-national study of privatisation in various states.

6 Privatisation in transport: from the company state to the contract state

David Banister

Introduction

After 1945 there was an extensive programme of nationalisation which formed part of Herbert Morrison's plans for the reconstruction of British industry. The British Transport Commission was set up to provide an 'efficient, adequate, economical and properly integrated system of public inland transport and port facilities within Great Britain'. Nationalisation covered the railways, docks and harbours, and road freight. The Conservatives reversed the decision on road freight in 1953. The 1968 Transport Act established six nationalised transport industries – British Railways, British Waterways, British Transport Docks Board, National Freight Corporation, National Bus Company and Scottish Bus Group.

What were the reasons behind government ownership and control of national transport assets? Gordon (1981) in a review of the Canadian position has listed five possible motives behind a policy of nationalisation: intervention might control natural monopolies which could operate against the national interest if they were private monopolies; nationalisation might further the economic growth objectives of governments and ensure political cohesion (the railways were an example of this process in Canada); equally, nationalisation could assist in regional development in isolated locations where the private sector might not invest; government intervention could be argued for bailouts of failed private firms (for example, Rolls Royce and British Leyland in Britain) or for pioneer ventures that might be too risky for the private sector (for example, nuclear power generation); finally, national interests might argue that the government acts as a rent collector in terms of the profits from the exploitation of natural resources.

However, probably more important than any of these individual explanations was the time at which these decisions were made. The 1970s marked a watershed in political and economic thinking. Prior to that time Keynesian arguments seemed most important. There were clear welfare objectives in economic policy and the enormous process of post-war reconstruction in Europe and Japan required the state to play a key role. Decision-making within this society was *pluralist* where power was regarded as being widely distributed between groups without any one group having an overall control and the state's role was essentially neutral as it acted as mediator between the different interest groups. For example, Taebel and Cornehls (1986) attempted to identify who these interest groups might be within transport – they suggested seven ideological dimensions, with three pro-car groups, one anti-car group, one pro-public transport group, one balanced transport group and a heterogeneous group which had ecological interests. However, as stated in Roger King's introduction, the pluralist approach has become untenable as the number of interests have increased along with people's expectations.

Within the transport sector, this pluralist phase in the 1960s and early 1970s was best illustrated by the controversy over the motorway programme (for example, Starkie, 1982 and Grant, 1977). It was here that the state had to intervene to prevent wide-ranging consumer concern over the perceived disbenefits of motorway construction swamping the interests of industry, as manifest in the road lobby and the national goal of an efficient road transport system. The review of the highway inquiry procedures helped to diffuse consumer actions (Department of Transport, 1978). Elite theorists have argued that industrial interests have often encouraged state involvement to ensure market stability and reduced competition, thereby increasing their own vested interests (Whitt, 1982). The Chicago School of public choice theory takes a similar line and argues that all regulatory agencies are liable to capture by the industry that they are supposed to be controlling (Dunleavy and Duncan, 1989).

Corporatism developed in the 1970s as a more positive approach to policy-making as well as a response to world recession, high inflation and unemployment triggered off by the rises in oil prices in 1973 and 1979. This period was one of retrenchment where the state formed a series of reciprocal relationships with major organised interests. It seemed at the time to be in the interests of both national and business concerns as the latter were seeking state protection against competition, a defensive mechanism in volatile world markets. Industry operating as monopolies or quasi-monopolies within the domestic sector used the state to plan for growth with minimal competition both within the domestic and international markets.

State involvement as partners with industry or as the controlling influence in nationalised enterprises now stood at the centre of decision-making. However, this position was inevitably short-lived, as a result of both external and internal events. The 1970s were uncertain times in economic terms as world trade stagnated, demand fell and unemployment as well as commodity prices rose. The response from industry was to cut back on output, reduce manpower levels and to reduce levels of investment. This in turn led to labour disputes and demands for higher wage settlements to match increased prices. At the governmental level taxation was increased, the balance of payments deficit was increased, and standards of living were at best maintained.

It was against this background that a radical alternative was introduced, namely the move to the company state and eventually to the contract state where the role of the state is to facilitate the operations of private companies. Initially the aim was to move towards a market economy based on well-tried neo-classical economic principles. The role of government was to be reduced to that of a facilitator so that the nationalised industries could have more freedom to determine their own policies. The government stood to gain by reducing its financial commitment to supporting state industries and so keep electoral pledges to reduce levels of taxation. From these fairly modest beginings a full-growth ideology has developed which involves both privatisation and liberalisation. The ideology is simple, namely that organisations are more efficient in the private sector with the normal commercial pressures that competition brings. Action has been swift (see Table 6.1).

Since its initiation there have already been two distinct phases in the move to the company and contract states. The first stage outlined above is the selling of nationalised industries to the private sector together with a process of liberalisation of constraints so that the market can operate without state interference. The role of the state is to ensure that competition is maintained and that public concerns are met, principally in the areas of safety and conditions of work. This is the *company state*.

The second stage takes the process further and involves the dismantling of government itself. The role of the state is reduced as the market not the state becomes the arbiter. As this process occurs, the role of government changes from its pluralist and corporatist mode to that of a neo-liberalist (which is essentially a transitory and a popular role that encourages ideals of self-interested competitive individualism and is fundamentally antistatist) to a *dirigiste* role. Most of the responsibilities of government in directing large nationalised companies will be carried out by those companies now in the private sector, and many of the functions traditionally performed by government will now be handled by agencies either set up as autonomous units or appointed as consultants to advise. This is the *contract state*.

Privatisation and the company state

The arguments

Privatisation can be defined as the packaging of productive assets into a limited liability company and the sale of at least a majority of shares in that company to individuals (Rees, 1986). This is privatisation in its purest form, but as will be shown later there are many variations on the basic form including franchising and contracting-out as well as partial or hybrid privatisations.

It seem that privatisation is one reaction to the perceived failure of the public sector and the welfare state set up some forty years ago. The arguments put forward by the New Right suggest that public bureaucracies are inefficient suppliers of services because there are no measures of productive efficiency. Public sector operations are often monopolies with limited opportunity for bargaining, restricted competitive pressures and a lack of external constraints. Within the bureaucracy itself individual departments tend to try to maximise their own power through bidding for the largest possible budget (Tulloc,

Table 6.1: *Privatisation in transport in the United Kingdom to December 1988*

National Freight Corporation: road haulage operator.
February 1982   Sold for £53m to a consortium of managers, employees and company pensioners. The government paid back £47m to the Company's pension fund to cover previous underfunding.

Associated British Ports: ports and property development.
February 1983   Part of equity sold.
April 1984   Remainder sold by tender offer.
    £34m raised.

British Rail
    Some non-essential assets sold.
    British Rail Hotels sold in 1983 for £30m.
July 1984   Sealink Ferries sold to Sea Containers Ltd for £66m. Proceeds retained by BR with subsequent adjustments to the borrowing limits.

Jaguar: luxury car manufacturer which had become a subsidiary of British Leyland.
July 1984   Sold for £294m.

British Airways: one of the leading international airlines.
January 1987   Sold for £892m.

Rolls Royce: aeroengine business bought by the government in 1971.
May 1987   Sold for £1360m.

British Airports Authority: operates seven of the principal airports in Britain including Heathrow and Gatwick.
July 1987   Sold for £1280m.

National Bus Company: consists of 72 subsidiaries which run most bus services outside the main metropolitan and other urban centres.
December 1988   Sale completed with gross proceeds of £323m. Net surplus to government after all debts paid of £89m.

1965). The inefficiency of bureaucracy contrasts with the cost-consciousness of the private sector. However, this simplistic view of the public sector based on budget-maximising considerations does not do justice to the complexity and varied nature of organisations (Ascher, 1987).

A more complex explanation is the move to redress the balance between the public and private sectors which seems at least in the government's view to have moved too much in favour of the public sector. Since 1979 the Conservative government has tried to reduce the power of the unions and their own commitment in terms of public expenditure. The traditional Left explanation for these radical changes in policy has been the move away from the public service ethos with its notions of loyalty to the organisation and the general public to a primary concern over cost efficiency. The organisation becomes fragmented into several cost centres and there is a loss of local autonomy and workers' rights. This spiral leads to increased social costs through redundancies, less job security, heavier workloads and a deterioration in pay and conditions. Additionally, the distribution of these impacts is uneven as there is a greater negative effect on women and part-time workers. The social and welfare issues are seen as secondary when placed against overall efficiency.

A second basic argument put forward to support privatisation is that the private provision of services is inherently more efficient as there is a simple measure of performance, namely profitability (Rickard, 1988). These supply side benefits can be increased through reductions in regulatory controls, giving more freedom to management and making firms accountable to their shareholders. Liberalisation is an essential part of the process of privatisation so that enterprises can operate as close to the market as possible. However, it is unclear whether ownership is a key determinant of this success. Some companies bought out by management and workforce have increased both productivity and profitability through profit-sharing schemes, but such shemes can also work in the public sector. Privatisation without liberalisation will lead to private monopolies and liberalisation without privatisation will lead to state capitalism and the maintenance of public monopolies.

Giving more freedom to management is crucial as it allows capital to be raised in a variety of ways on the financial markets, and releases the enterprise from the external financing limits imposed by the government in the 1980s on all publicly-funded transport enterprises. Similarly, deficits sustained by public transport operations have had an unwelcome effect on the government's public-sector borrowing requirement. Privatisation also contributes directly to exchequer revenue and reduces the public-sector borrowing requirement as the ratio of government expenditure to national income is reduced. Supply side economics would take this argument further and suggest that inflationary pressures are reduced, tax cuts can be introduced and this in turn would allow more private investment to take place so that productivity, output and profitability can all increase. This powerful logic is countered by the argument that these gains are short term. The longer-term impacts of selling national assets may result in higher taxation as the government is forgoing revenue from these nationalised industries. In effect the government is borrowing against future income streams (Rees, 1986).

Privatisation raises this crucial issue of control. One argument is that privatisation will reduce trade union power and that this in turn will lead to increased efficiency and less wage inflation. However, an extensive programme of trade union legislation has already been introduced, restricting many of their powers (for example closed-shop agreements). The main impact may be less central government intervention in local labour disputes. Many privatisations have occurred in growth industries where one would expect labour relations to be good.

Another reason for privatisation may be to widen share ownership and to create a society which has a direct interest in the success of individual companies. Each individual should have the opportunity to select their own holdings in privatised assets rather than being 'forced shareholders' in nationalised companies (Rees, 1986). However, the evidence here seems to suggest that many members of the share-holding democracy are not concerned about the principle of share ownership but in 'stagging' underpriced shares on a rising market to make a quick profit. Only about half the original shareholders retain their shares. The power of the small shareholders is very limited as it is the large national and international interests that have the controlling vote in all companies not run and owned by their management and/or their workforce.

These complex and theoretically attractive arguments have been raised in support of privatisation. Kay and Thompson (1986) have suggested that the case is less than clear. The policy of privatisation does not have a sophisticated rationale, rather it lacks any clear analysis of purposes or effects, and hence any objective which seems achievable is seized as justification. The outcome is that no objectives are effectively attained, and in particular that economic efficiency has systematically been subordinated to other goals, in particular political goals.

The balance

It seems from this short review that the arguments for privatisation are far from clear. Apart from the ideological view that the public sector involvement in service provision is too great, and the unclear economic arguments that the rigours of the private sector will reduce inefficiencies, the success of the move towards the company state is only seen through individual examples. Again, this conclusion may reflect equally on the absence of suitable theories of management of public enterprises, the lack of consistent objectives for public enterprises and their vulnerability to exploitation by government.

If greater involvement of the private sector is seen as a means to adjust the balance between the private and public sectors, then the question becomes one of defining the conditions under which services should be provided by the market. Williamson (1975) identifies the following five situations where internal provision offers significant advantages over contracting or franchising in the market:

- Where flexible sequential decision-making is needed to cope with uncertainties in the environment.
- Where only a small number of competitors are present, and there is a likelihood of opportunistic and predatory pricing behaviour.
- Where a divergence of expectations is likely to occur between the internal purchaser and the external seller.
- Where operational or technological information gained from experience is likely to give one supplier a strategic advantage over all others, thereby reducing competition.
- Where a transition-specific 'calculative relation' between parties is inappropriate and 'quasi-moral involvement' between those supplying and organising the service is necessary to enforce provision.

The presence of one or more of these conditions may result in preference for public provision of a particular service even if it costs *more*. In the transport sector it is difficult to envisage a situation where at least one of the above conditions is not met, but the important supplementary factor to note is that cost efficiency should not be the overriding concern when determining the appropriate level of transport service provision. As Vickers and Yarrow argue (1988), competition may be the main mechanism by which internal efficiency can be improved. However, where there is no competition the balance of advantage is less clear cut with a key determinant being the effectiveness of regulation.

There seems to be a fifty-year cycle with the switch from private to public ownership in transport. In Britain in the 1930s bus regulation was seen as a solution to market failure as competition was seen as undesirable in an industry with major externalities. In the United States regulation was effective from 1887 to 1935 with control over entry to avoid destructive action by new operators, but this effectively gave existing operators monopoly pricing power (Bailey, 1986). This institutional inertia seems to exist in both public and private transport operations with the threat of competition being the trigger to impel the incumbent to act efficiently. The theory and practice of competitive markets is clearly stated through the economics of contestability, sunk costs and barriers to entry (Baumol, 1982 and Gwilliam, 1989). The incentive mechanism works towards improved internal efficiency and the elimination of X inefficiency or the failure of firms to make maximum use of inputs in producing given levels of output (Liebenstein, 1966). If internal cost and allocative efficiency can both be improved there is a double gain in terms of social welfare. As stated earlier, it seems that liberalisation is a necessary condition for private sector involvement in transport, but that private sector involvement does not seem to be essential for efficiency. The pendulum has swung away from public transport services being provided in the public sector to services being provided in the private sector. This redressing of the balance with the private and public sectors working together may lead to a period of instability prior to a more stable market equilibrium position being reached. It is this transition stage through which transport in Britain is now progressing prior to emerging fully in the company state.

Experience

Transport has been the forefront of the government's privatisation pro-gramme. There have been two distinct phases in this process, with the first extending from 1979 to 1984; the transport enterprises included in this group were the National Freight Corporation, Associated British Ports, some of British Rail's non-essential assets and Jaguar (see Table 6.1). These sales were either to management (e.g. NFC), or a single buyer (e.g. Sealink), or as a limited stock exchange flotation (e.g. ABP). At this stage it seems that the government was not clear on the possibilities of privatisation or the most appropriate means by which assets could be transferred from the public to the private sector.

The second stage has extended from 1987 to 1988 and represents a much stronger ideological argument. It is here that the government has through extensive publicity encouraged a wider share ownership and has made provision for small investors to 'buy' a part of a newly privatised company, often at an advantageous price. This group of sales has all been of significantly larger scale than those in the first phase. The four transport privatisations in the 1982-4 stage realised about £500 million and the four sales in the 1987-8 group have realised nearly £4000 million (see Table 6.1).

In this review of experience three short examples will be presented, one from the first stage (the National Freight Consortium), one from the second stage (British Airways), and one nationalised industry which has not yet been privatised but is high on the list of possibilities if the Conservatives continue in power (British Rail). A comparison will be made between the options available to British Rail and those adopted by Japanese National Railways which was restructured and privatised in 1987.

The National Freight Consortium has been presented as a major success story in the privatisation programme (see Table 6.2). The National Freight Corporation was the largest road freight haulage organisation in the United Kingdom but it had experienced management and financial difficulties in the 1970s. Sir Peter Thompson, its chairman originally proposed a management and employee buyout, and the government approved its sale in February 1982. Some 77 per cent of the workforce took up the options of share ownership and this amounted to 83 per cent of the new National Freight Consortium's equity. With a large part of the workforce committed to the company, the NFC's brand of industrial democracy allowed immediate changes in the management structure. Since that time the road freight industry has benefited from the growth in the economy as a whole. The NFC has also benefited from the trend within freight distribution to contract out as much of the road freight as possible. Consequently, their position as the United Kingdom's largest freight carrier has been more than maintained. It is now the largest freight transport operator in the Western world outside the United States. Over the last seven years the NFC has diversified its operations including entry into the property market and the lucrative premium end of the removals market, particularly in Australia and the United States. This expansion has resulted in a growth in profits of 28 per cent over the last year to £47.4 million, and individual employees have seen the value of their investment increase by 47 times since privatisation. As a result of its own commercial success, the NFC has now been floated on the Stock Exchange to allow further growth, but control of the company still remains with its own management and employees (see Table 6.2).

It seems that the NFC has indeed been a considerable success in the private sector, and it has taken full advantage of buoyant economic conditions and positive changes in freight distribution practices. However, the key to

Table 6.2: *National Freight Consortium*

Activities:	International network of removals, parcel deliveries, freighting and contract distribution. Operates in the UK, USA and Australia.
Divisions:	British Road Services Group Pickfords Removals Pickfords Travel Lynx Express Delivery Special Services Group Tempco Union
Workforce:	29,100 employees of whom 20,000 are shareholders. 83 percent of equity held by staff before share flotation.
Pre-Tax Profits:	£47.4m on turnover of £911.4m (1987). £37m profits in 1986 – rise in profits of 28 per cent.
History:	The National Freight Corporation was sold to a consortium of managers, employees and company pensioners for £53m (February 1982). £1 invested in 1982 worth £48 in 1988. Interests of management and employees safeguarded by restricting the transferability of National Freight Consortium shares. Floated in February 1989 to give a stock market valuation of £950m.

the success has been the flexibility within the organisation and employee accountability both in terms of management practices and ownership. For example, a bonus structure has been introduced which is related to the performance of the company and of each individual within the company. An individual could have obtained a 44 per cent increase in salary (1987) through an inflation increment (2 per cent), a merit rise (12 per cent) and a bonus profit-related payment (30 per cent). Local ownership and privatisation of medium-sized companies does seem to work, particularly if the economic conditions are favourable.

The British Airways privatisation was of a different order and much more complex than that of the NFC. BA has been an attractive candidate for privatisation because it was profitable, and a change in ownership had already been facilitated in 1984 when it was set up as a Public Limited Company (Department of Transport, 1984). BA operates an international network of routes to 145 destinations in 68 countries with some 170 aircraft (1986). Most of the debate over the privatisation of BA really reflected its dominant market position and the difficulty that any UK or European-based airline would have in competing with it. This dominance has now been compounded with the acquisition of British Caledonian (December 1987) which was its chief national competitor. The combined strength of the BA/BCal company increases its local dominance and competition must now be viewed on a global scale.

BA's privatisation was delayed by the Laker litigation over predatory practices and by the renegotiation of the Bermuda 2 agreements over the North Atlantic routes with the USA. As noted in Vickers and Yarrow (1988), BA was easy to privatise as it had been managed according to commercial criteria in the public sector. They also note that the share flotation was aimed at existing shareholders and not at widening share acess. Even then the issue was heavily oversubscribed with an immediate premium of 44 pence (68 per cent) on the partly-paid price of 65 pence (full price 125 pence) for those who 'stagged' their shares. The sale in January 1987 realised £892 million.

However, it was over the intervening three years (1984–7) that the most fundamental changes had been taking place within BA. Internal efficiency had been significantly improved through a new management structure. Productivity had been increased and the labour force cut from 54,000 to 36,000. Financial gains had been made through savings in fuel costs, greater efficiency within the aircraft fleet and currency gains through the strong pound. All these positive factors were compounded by the strong growth in the demand for air travel with an increase of 7.4 per cent per annum in the 1980s in the revenue passenger miles to a 1988 figure of 1,048 billion revenue passenger miles of world air travel. This growth is expected to continue at a rate of 5.8 per cent per annum to the year 2000 when the total amount of air travel will almost have doubled to 2,068 billion revenue passenger miles (Department of Transport, 1989).

Most of these improvements in financial and productivity performance occurred before privatisation (Vickers and Yarrow, 1988). The delay in privatisation due to the Laker litigation and the North Atlantic route negotiations allowed these changes to take place, but the basic question seems to be that the threat of privatisation may be a sufficient incentive to efficiency gains. There is, however, no reason why such gains cannot be obtained in the public sector, as illustrated above, particularly if they are combined with strong management and leadership such as that demonstrated by Lord King.

Our third case is one in which privatisation has not yet taken place, but it is strongly anticipated that it will take place in 1991 if the Conservative party wins the next general election. British Rail has high fixed costs tied up in track and other infrastructure (e.g. stations) and high sunk costs (e.g. rolling stock and staff), and it is difficult to privatise in a form which will not merely create a private rather than a public monopoly. It is obviously unrealistic to duplicate the track so that active competition can take place. Some mechanism is required to ensure that private operators have equal access to the track.

Three options are at present being considered. The first is to have a separate *track authority*. Starkie (1984) has proposed two companies: one of which, 'British Rail', would own the infrastructure, control the trains and the overhead administration; another company or more than one company, 'British Trains', would own its rolling stock and compete to run services. The latter would also pay an agreed price to the Rail company for the use of their infrastructure. A variant of this option, favoured by the Adam Smith Institute

(Irvine, 1987), is where British Rail would keep the track and let others lease access to run services. There are already examples of private freight operations running services on British Rail with BR drivers but their own locomotives and rolling stock (for example, Foster Yeoman). This arrangement would be extended over the whole network on a service by service basis, or private operators could take over all services on particular routes (for example London to Southend or London to Gatwick and Brighton). A fee would be payable to the track authority (British Railways) for the use of the infrastructure, a form of toll rail pricing.

The second option is the *breakup* of the complete operation either on a regional or a sectoral basis – prior to nationalisation in 1948 the railways operated on a regional basis, and privately-run companies with public subsidies provided services in geographical regions. This option is favoured by the Centre for Policy Studies and seems to be the one that the government will support. The Secretary of State for Transport unveiled the alternative proposals at the Conservative Party Conference in the Autumn (1989). Alternatively, the sectoral breakup option would be based on the five existing operational sectors – InterCity Services, Provincial Services, Network South East, Parcels and Freight.

The final option would be to privatise BR as a whole so that it would become a *private monopoly* with heavy regulation. Effectively, this option would require least change and it is not unnaturally the one favoured by the BR Board. Apart from the options, certain other questions remain unresolved. Privatisation makes subsidy difficult. BR has had a Public Service Obligation to provide services on social criteria, particularly in rural areas and for commuters. This subsidy amounts to about £600 million (1989) but will be reduced over the next three years to about half that level. The question here is how that subsidy should be allocated, which in turn depends on the package eventually decided upon by government. It may be allocated to the new Regional Companies or it may be allocated to tendered services, as has happened with bus services since 1986 (Tyson, 1988).

Rather than discuss the three options in detail, a comparison will be made with Japanese National Railways which were privatised in April 1987 (see Table 6.3). JNR has suffered from very similar problems to those faced by BR. There was too much government involvement in the railways, which in turn led to unclear management objectives and responsibilities. The public railways were limited in their opportunities to pursue other business activities. This contrasts with the private railways in Japan which are often small parts of much larger diversified organisations. For example, the Tokyu Railway Corporation which operates in the Tokyo metropolitan area is part of the Tokyu Group with an annual revenue of over 25,688 billion yen (£11.6 billion) of which the Railway Corporation only accounts for 8.6 per cent of the total (Sakita, 1989). Other difficulties facing JNR include an ageing (and expensive) workforce and inflexible unions. External factors such as competition from other modes of transport (e.g. car and air) together with rapid urbanisation and population decreases in rural areas have all resulted in falling levels of demand and an enormous accumulated deficit (ECMT, 1988).

Table 6.3: *Privatisation of Japanese National Railways*

Restructured on 1 April 1987 in 12 Private Corporations

Company Name	Total Track (km)	Number of Employees	Type of Business
East Japan Railway	7,657	82,469	Passenger
Central Japan Railway	2,003	21,410	Passenger
West Japan Railway	5,323	51,538	Passenger
Hokkaido Railway	3,177	12,719	Passenger
Shikoku Railway	881	4,455	Passenger
Kyushu Railway	2,406	15,000	Passenger
Japan Freight Company	(10,011)	12,005	Freight
Railway Telecommunication		570	Telecommunication
Railway Information Systems		279	Computer Services
Institute		550	Railway Research
Shinkansen Property	(2,012)	64	Shinkansen Leasing
JNR Accounts Settlement		(2,520)	Account Settlement
TOTAL	21,447	201,059	

Notes:
Figures in brackets under total track relate to freight operation route and Shinkansen route lengths.
Employee figures in brackets are not permanent employees.
Those former JNR employees being retrained are not included.

Accumulated Deficit of 37.1 trillion yen (£170 billion) to be paid off by
    16% shared by the three JR Group Corporations intended to operate
    as profit-making (East Japan, West Japan, Central Japan).

    23% levied from the same three JR Group Corporations as a
    Shinkansen user fee.

    21% realised from land sales.

    2% raised from selling stocks in JR Corporations.

    38% raised from the general public through long-term bonds.

Source: Based on Sakita (1989).

The restructuring followed the recommendations of the Commission on Administrative Reform of JNR (East Japan Railways, 1987):

- To consolidate overall railway operations.
- To reduce total number of employees.
- To limit long term liabilities.
- To enlarge the new corporations' scope for business.

In preparation for privatisation (1985–7) the numbers of employees were reduced by 34 per cent (see Table 6.3), forty loss-making services were replaced by bus or other rail services, new timetables were introduced to speed up and increase the frequency of InterCity trains, investment was reduced and JNR land sold off, but fare increases were kept to a minimum (ECMT, 1988).

JNR adopted the Regional Company option to privatisation and twelve new companies have been set up. Passenger services are now run by six companies with one freight company running all freight services. Additionally, there are companies for telecommunications, computer services, research, Shinkansen leasing and account settlement (see Table 6.3). The three companies operating on the main island of Honshu are all expected to run profitably as is the freight company. The three companies operating on the other islands (Hokkaido, Kyushu and Shikoku) will still make losses and special funds have been made available to cover those losses. All companies are encouraged to diversify into non-rail activities as the complementary private rail companies in Japan have already done. Developments are encouraged that are likely to bring business to the railways such as the location of the Hiyoshi campus of Keio University along the Tokyu railway network (Sakita, 1989). Other developments have included shopping centres and housing estates. The notion of 'value capture', where property value increases along the new railways can be included as part of the development rather than as separate from the development, is an integral part of rail planning in Japan, but a potential which has not really been capitalised on in the United Kingdom (Morichi, 1987). In addition, value capture creates new demand for services and identifies where the market can be expanded. The huge accumulated deficit of JNR has been shared among the three companies intended to be profit-making and benefiting from the profitable operation of the Shinkansen lines. It should also be noted that over a third of the deficit will be paid through the issue of long-term bonds to private investors (Ohta, 1989 and Table 6.3).

It seems that the process of privatisation in transport is still in a learning stage with different approaches being adopted in particular situations. Each of the cases cited here offers some lessons for the company or privatised state. Apart from the privatisation of BR, other transport enterprises in the United Kingdom may follow. Top of the list is the privatisation of London Regional Transport and the separation of London Buses from London Underground. The buses would probably be spilt up on a geographical basis and the necessary reorganisation has already taken place, whilst the underground would probably be privatised on a line-by-line basis. Municipal and metropolitan bus operations in other cities in the United Kingdom would also follow. This would mean that there would be no public transport operations left in the public sector and the next stage along the route to complete privatisation of transport would be to sell off the road infrastructure so that the private sector would be responsible for its construction, its planning and its maintainence, and users would be charged directly or indirectly by them for use of road space.

Privatisation and the contract state

The arguments

With the extensive privatisation of transport services, the role of government must also change. Dunleavy and Duncan (1989) have identified three forms of ownership when it comes to running existing transport systems. Direct government provision occurs when facilities are fully tax-funded and provided free at point of use as with roads in the United Kingdom. Alternatively, services can be provided by quasi-governmental agencies (QGAs) such as public corporations, state equity holdings, hived-off municipal companies or those operated by quasi-elected local government organisations (QUELGOs). Finally, services can be provided by the private sector. Most of the debate has centred around the balance between the last two categories and the dynamics of changes which have been outlined in the previous section with the move to the company state.

The role of government as the producer and operator of much of the transport infrastructure and services has been reduced through privatisation, and the question now arises as to what role the government should now assume. Veljanovski (1987) suggests that if its role as producer is removed, the state now becomes the protector to ensure that the rules are followed. The irony here is that liberalisation is required to ensure that market conditions are favourable for competition, and to ensure that newly privatised companies can compete in the market. However, more regulation is often required to ensure that competition is fair, that monopoly positions against the public interest are not re-established and that public concerns over safety, environment and social issues are met. Liberalisation is needed for privatisation yet regulation is also needed to control the privatised companies. The response of the government has been to reinforce the controls on private companies through the Monopolies and Mergers Commission, to make more use of monitoring organisations to ensure that competition is fair (e.g. the Office of Fair Trading), and to establish agencies in the private sector that will carry out functions previously seen as part of the state's responsibilities (e.g. Vehicle Inspectorate). Additionally, the government has made much more use of consultants as advisers, thereby cutting down on the need for in-house expertise, and has also involved the private sector in discussion over future investment proposals. In particular, these discussions have been concerned over the increased role that the private sector could have in the funding and running of major new projects (e.g. the Channel Tunnel and the proposed Channel Tunnel rail link).

The next stage in the privatisation programme is to supplement the company state by the contract state which will act as the main controller of the newly privatised transport companies as well as those that still remain in the public sector. Wherever possible all these regulatory and control functions will be carried out in the private sector. France has followed this more *dirigiste* tradition which allows the state to be penetrated by companies (Newton and

Karran, 1985), with the use of private bodies for public purposes and to set clear commercial objectives for those private bodies which must still be accountable to government. So the role of both the central and local state is switching from the provider of all services to the role of stimulator, adviser and enabler (Hepworth, 1988).

In his rationale for privatisation, Dunleavy (1986a) includes a series of agency roles in his radical explanations. Of the five agency roles identified, it seems that central or local government would still act as delivery agencies to produce or supply goods where the market failed to operate satisfactorily. Central and local government would act as control agencies to route public resources where needed to people or to subsidise services, and to act as transfer agencies to pay out grants. Local authorities would have an additional role as contract agencies to put out tenders for contracted or franchised services, whilst the autonomous executive agencies would act in a supervisory role to regulate the industry. The function of both central and local government could be further reduced if private sector agencies were set up to administer delivery or contract agencies. Under contracting-out arrangements, public authorities continue to bear direct responsibility both for the provision arrangements and for the quality of service provided, although the work is actually carried out by employees of private firms (Ascher, 1987; Heald, 1984; Heald and Thomas, 1986). To this list of agency types could be added an agency that examines the efficiency of all transport functions remaining in the public sector. Its role would be similar to that of the Audit Office, but with a specific transport remit and it could be set up as an executive agency.

Experience

As the contract state is a relatively new phase in the privatisation programme, the experience is limited. Three different situations will be presented, one as it relates to controlling agencies, one as a new executive agency, and finally the closer involvement of the private sector as agents.

The Office of Fair Trading has recently been concerned over the possibility of predatory practices in the bus industry after the deregulation of bus services and the privatisation of the National Bus Company in 1986–8 (Transport Act 1985 and Table 6.1). There seems to be a reluctance for small new operators to compete directly in the market with established operators and new services have only been maintained when new routes have been identified. In the limited situations where on-road competition has taken place this competition has often been short lived with the established operator gaining eventual control over the route. The general prevalence of non-price competition in the commercial market and incumbent advantages suggest that the market may be oligopolistic or even monopolistic (Tyson, 1988).

The 1985 Transport Act imposed the normal requirement on the bus industry to register with the Office of Fair Trading any practices that might be considered restrictive. However, as Gwilliam (1989) argues, the control of predatory practices in the bus industry is difficult, as the product is

Table 6.4: *Vehicle Inspectorate as an Executive Agency*

Established 1 August 1988 as the first government executive agency.

Responsible for testing the roadworthiness of the 21 million vehicles in use on British roads.

Duties include: –   Heavy Goods Vehicle testing – 954,000 tests and retests in 1987/8.
Public Service Vehicle testing – 82,000 tests and retests in 1987/8.
Supervision of 17,000 garages which carry out 15 million MOT tests on cars, light goods vehicles and motorcycles.
Investigating 2,700 serious accidents and liases with industry on recall of vehicles.

Employs 1,600 people and has a network of ninety-one vehicle testing stations.

Annual turnover of £32.7 million with a surplus of £616,000.

The Inspectorate is required to break even.

Other transport organisations being considered for executive agency status:

Transport and Road Research Laboratory
TRRL undertakes a programme of applied research to provide scientific and technical advice and information primarily for the Department of Transport. The aim of the programme is to help set standards of design, construction and maintenance of highways, to assist in developing regulations for vehicle construction and use, to improve efficiency and safety of traffic movement and to aid policy development relating to road transport generally and to road safety and public transport in particular.

TRRL has 600 staff gross costs of £26 million and receipts of £2 million.

Vehicle and Component Approvals Division
VCA operates the National Type Approval schemes for passenger cars and goods vehicles and provides a service to vehicle and component manufacturers who wish to obtain internationally recognised type approvals for their products.

VCA has 70 staff and an annual budget of £2 million.

Driver Testing and Training Division
DTT provides driving tests for motorcycles, cars, heavy goods and public service vehicles and administers the register of approved driving instructors. DTT's costs are recovered by fees charged for its services.

DTT has a staff of 2,000 and a turnover of £40 million.

Driver and Vehicle Licensing Directorate
DVLD is responsible for registering and licensing drivers and vehicles in Great Britain and for collecting and enforcing vehicle excise duty. It also provides a wide range of services for the Department of Transport, other government departments, the police and various external organisations. The Directorate's headquarters are in Swansea with fifty-three Vehicle Registration Offices spread throughout the country. The computers at Swansea keep records of 30 million driver licence holders and nearly 22 million licensed vehicles.

DVLD employs 5,400 staff and gross costs of £130 million offset by £10 million receipts.

Source: Based on Department of Transport (1988)

heterogeneous and complex with the marginal costs and revenues of particular services varying enormously over both time and space. Without an in-depth investigation, it is difficult to establish whether a particular action is predatory or not. Even if it was established, it would probably be too late as the new entrant would have withdrawn from the market and the incumbent operator would have strengthened its position.

Gwilliam concluded that the OFT needs to establish clear guidance on acceptable behaviour, and suggested that any operator introducing a service or a pricing structure appearing to be predatory 'should maintain it for a prolonged minimum period as a condition for the retention of his operator's licence'. It may also be necessary to create an OFBUS (Office of Fair Bus Trading) which would 'combine protective powers similar to those in parallel organisations in the newly privatised monopolies with specialised fair trading responsibilities'.

These control agencies must be independent of government if they are to be effective. The Monopolies and Mergers Commission can only carry out investigations when instructed by the government, and even then it does not have unrestricted access to information or the ability to advise directly Parliamentary Select Committees (Curwen, 1986). The Audit Office which carries out efficiency studies on nationalised industries should also be completely independent and accountable to Parliament.

A second dimension of the contract state has been to divest the government of some functions through the creation of executive agencies. The Vehicle Inspectorate has become the first such agency (see Table 6.4) and is a direct output from the the recommendations of the efficiency unit report on improving management in government (Jenkins, Oates and Stott, 1985). The government has set the new agency the target of improving its cost efficiency by 3.7 per cent over the next two years (1989–91), and to develop new initiatives and performance incentives. The agency will be accountable to the Secretary of State for Transport and the Public Accounts Committee. The Secretary of State's announcement stated that 'the Vehicle Inspectorate is a large organisation by private sector standards and will benefit considerably from the greater autonomy, clearer objectives and a heightened sense of corporate identity which Executive Agency status will bring'. It seems likely that other transport Executive Agencies will be set up including the Transport and Road Research Laboratory, the Vehicle and Component Approvals Division, the Driver Testing and Training Division and the Driver and Vehicle Licensing Directorate (as summarised in Table 6.4). In each case it is argued that these services can be provided more efficiently in the private sector and that they should be operated on a commercial basis. With each of the proposals cited, this seems possible with the exception of the TRRL which is mainly a research organisation. Some of the TRRL's services can be sold both in the United Kingdom and overseas, but much of their research is on a contract basis to central government who would presumably be charged a commercial rate for that work.

Underlying the move beyond the company state to the contract state is the Government's aim to reduce its role as the provider of services, as the monitor of those services and as the regulator of those services. In the third situation the state has moved into a much closer partnership with the private sector, using its services where necessary and relying on its expertise and finance in putting forward new transport infrastructure proposals.

The government has made extensive use of consultants to supplement their own internal expertise. For example on the proposed BR privatisation the government has used Samuel Montague to prepare the case for breakup and Deloitte Haskins and Sells to advise on appropriate structures for privatisation. Similarly, BR have employed Lazard Brothers to argue the case against seven regional operating companies. Lazards foresees rising costs, operating inefficiencies and falling rail traffic if the network is not kept intact. Rail traffic could be cut in half with sharp rises in fares, cuts in rural lines and the creation of a top-heavy management structure. Similar use of consultants as agents is apparent in the four London Assessment Studies that are currently nearing completion. This partnership between government and transport consultants is not new, but with the move to the contract state, much more research and advice is being put out to tender on a competitive basis.

However, a more fundamental move is to involve the private sector not just in an advisory role, but as the main agent for the development of new infrastructure. Michael Portillo was appointed in August 1988 as the new minister with special responsibility for the generation of private sector cash for railway and road schemes. Privately – funded transport infrastructure already completed is limited to schemes such as London City Airport built by John Mowlem at a cost of £30 million. However, several schemes are now under construction, including the Channel Tunnel (£4.7 billion), the Dartford Thurrock Bridge (see Table 6.5) and the Docklands Light Railway extension to Bank (£150m). Schemes under consideration are numerous and include rail links to the Channel Tunnel and from Paddington to Heathrow Airport. Also included are light rail systems in Docklands (the extension to Beckton), in Manchester, in Wolverhampton, in Bristol and in several other cities. Road schemes under discussion or tender include a new east coast motorway from London to Scotland via the Humber Bridge, a second Severn Bridge, and the duplication of the M25 along the most heavily congested south–west sector. It is the government's intention to transfer the risk for large capital infrastructure investments from the public to the private sector (Rickard, 1988). These risks would include cost overruns, technical deficiencies in construction and subsequent high maintenance costs, and estimations of future levels of traffic demand. It is also argued that the private sector can more readily innovate, for example through the provision of car-only toll roads, the greater use of tunnelling in urban areas and the joint development of facilities.

The questions of risk and funding are crucial to whether development takes place. The possibility of implementation of the recent Central London Rail Study's proposals for two new full-sized rail tunnels extending from west to east (Paddington to Liverpool Street) and from north to south (Euston/Kings Cross to Victoria) is dependent upon private funding (Department of Transport et al., 1989). It is argued that the schemes proposed will enhance land values and generate significant benefits to businesses and landowners, and

Table 6.5: *Dartford-Thurrock Road Bridge*

This road bridge will be completed in 1991 and it will be the first time this century that a major road has been privately funded in the United Kingdom.

Construction: By Dartford River Crossing Ltd
                  Trafalgar House plc 49%
                  Kleinwort Benson plc 17%
                  Bank of America 17%
                  Prudential Assurance 17%
                  Cost £170 million

Operation: The Company will take over the outstanding debt on the existing Dartford Tunnels from Kent and Essex County Councils and will operate both the tunnel and the new bridge as toll facilities.

The bridge will provide 4 lanes for southbound traffic and the existing tunnels will provide for 4 northbound lanes.

The Company will have a maximum of 20 years to recoup their costs and make a profit.

Tolls will not increase in real terms above the levels prevailing at 1 January 1986.

---

it is suggested that such beneficiaries would negotiate with railway operators over the choice of routes, alignments and the location of stations 'in return for a significant financial contribution to reflect the benefits they would derive'. Only in situations where expected revenues from fares and the financial contributions from developers are not sufficient to pay for the scheme would the government consider making a grant, but even then only if there are sufficient non-user benefits (e.g. in the relief of road congestion).

It seems that the concepts of value capture exploited by the private railway companies in Japan could be successfully explored in the United Kingdom. The proposed financing of the two preferred options in the Central London Rail Study through the private sector does not seem to be possible as there are no clear direct advantages to developers involved, and the scale of the proposed development is large, being of the same order as the Channel Tunnel. A more likely scheme in London would be between Waterloo and Canary Wharf. Olympia and York, the developer, has proposed a new direct underground link to improve the accessibility to their major new office project and they are prepared to fund half the estimated £320 million costs. In total, it seems that Olympia and York is prepared to fund transport infrastructure to a level of about 10 per cent of the total development costs provided that the main beneficiaries are those companies renting space in Canary Wharf. It would seem that the cost-sharing option is the most likely way to involve the private sector, with the developer sharing operating expenses and contributing to costs integrated with or connected to their developments.

Although still in its infancy the government, having nearly completed its programme of privatisation to create the company sector in transport, will now be examining the extension to the contract state where many of its own functions are divested. The arguments are similar to those behind the company state and are based on cost efficiency, management accountability and clearly stated commercial objectives. The question remains as to whether the state has any role in the provision and regulation of transport infrastructure and services in the market economy.

The role of government in the privatised state

Historical evidence suggests that goods and services deemed essential should be provided by the public sector at a fair price. Merit goods such as public transport can be provided directly by the state or through carefully controlled private operators. Public goods such as air traffic control with important externalities also have to be provided by the public sector (Hensher, 1986). This historical view has now been reversed with the extensive programme of privatisation and the move towards the company state.

Traditionally, public service provision involves the state in both planning and delivery of a range of services which are indirectly financed (in whole or in part) from taxes. However, that simple traditional position has now been changed with the state playing a greater variety of roles (see Table 6.6). The regulatory role would include environmental, social and safety factors in transport, the grant mode covers situations where the state provides financial support for an activity but does not produce or plan it (e.g. concessionary fares are provided by the local state) and under the contract mode one would include road construction and maintenance. The state has withdrawn from the production of all modes of service provision and its role as the planning agent and financial backer has also been reduced. With the move towards the contract state all of these functions may be lost (see Table 6.6) as the private sector takes over the financing of transport infrastructure and agencies become increasingly important in the planning and control of transport services.

Vickers and Yarrow (1988) have suggested that the following four developments in public policy could help improve performance:

- The introduction of greater competitive pressures on those public corporations that have enjoyed protected market positions.
- The creation of specialised regulatory agencies entrusted by government with duties covering price controls and the promotion of competition. These should be stronger than the regulatory bodies established as part of the privatisation programme.
- The creation of a specialised agency (Audit Office) for the sole purpose of conducting efficiency audits.
- The widespread use of performance-related incentive schemes for the management of public corporations.

Each of these developments has at least in part been achieved. The first through privatisation or the threat of privatisation, even though public

Table 6.6: *A Typology of Service Delivery*

Modes of service provision		Involvement of the state	
	Planning	Financing	Producing
Regulated	Yes	No	No
Grant	No	Yes	No
Contracted	Yes	Yes	No

Source: Based on Sonnenblum, Kirlin and Rees (1977)

monopolies have in some cases been replaced by private monopolies (e.g. British Airports Authority and British Airways). Some have argued (e.g. Thompson, 1988) that, although privatisation was originally aimed to maximise competition, the focus has increasingly switched to the concern to transfer assets from the public to the private sector as monopolies and that competition is notional and not real. Hence, although one moves from the regulated state through liberalisation to privatisation, there is eventually a need for further regulation. The second development has been achieved through the setting up of agencies within the contract state to control the new privatised companies and to carry out functions traditionally done by the public sector (for example, OFT, Executive Agencies). The Audit Office has already monitored efficiency within the transport sector (for example, National Audit Office, 1988). Finally, even within transport enterprises within the public sector, much more clearly stated performance-related targets are being pursued, for example British Rail has a clear directive to reduce its level of public subsidy and to make the user pay the full costs of their travel. Indeed, BR has been very successful in maintaining a large network at minimum cost to the taxpayer.

From the arguments presented here it may seem that there is no role for the state in transport provision. Service production has been switched to the private sector, and many of the new regulatory and control functions have been set up as private executive agencies or as agencies within the public sector. The state has been removed from its role as producer and to some extent from its role as a protective state to ensure that the rules are followed.

However, there is still a crucial role for the state. The state should still intervene where the market fails to ensure that all people have access to transport and facilities. The disadvantaged would include those people on low incomes, those with physical or age-related disabilities, and those who suffer from isolation in both rural and urban locations: a social responsibility. The state should still intervene where there are significant externalities, such as the use of resources, land acquisition and assembly, safety and environmental concerns with transport: an environmental responsibility. The state should still intervene where transport interacts with other sectors, such as the generation effects of new developments so that wider land use implications can be considered: a development responsibility. The state should still intervene where transport has national and international implications so that the national and local interests either in the short or the long term can be included prior to decisions being made: a national responsibility.

So although the state has divested some of its responsibilities as the producer and regulator of transport services, it still has a vital role to play in at least the four areas of responsibility noted above. These responsibilities cannot be left to the company or the contract state, and must still remain with an organisation which is accountable to the electorate through the ballot box and not to the shareholders through the company accounts.

Guide to further reading

The topic of privatisation and transport is a new one and there is not a vast literature available. Key references mainly come from the economics literature. Included here would be John Vickers and George Yarrow (1988) which presents the economic theory behind privatisation, the arguments for public enterprise in the United Kingdom and a series of case studies including a chapter on transport industries. Other books covering similar ground are John Kay and David Thompson's edited volume (1986) *Privatisation and regulation – the UK experience* (Oxford: OUP) and V.V. Ramanadham (ed.) (1988) *Privatisation in the UK* (London: Routledge and Kegan Paul). Both of these books examine the differences in ownership structures, the rationale for privatisation and attempt to answer the crucial question of whether public enterprise has in fact failed or not. Kate Ascher (1987) focuses on the different types and forms of privatisation and the contracting-out of public services. Again, the scope is much wider than transport as the case study material comes from local authority services and the NHS.

Within transport the published evidence is even less comprehensive. Z.J. Haritos (1987) in *Transportation* 14, 3, pp. 193–207 contrasts the different objectives of public and private sector companies, questioning whether in transport accountability and economic efficiency are achievable goals. David Starkie (1984) puts forward the case for separating the ownership of railway track and the operation of rolling stock. The former should be owned by one company, whilst services could be run in competition and at a price by a range of companies on that track.

An international perspective on privatisation and the use of private capital to fund major transport infrastructure can be obtained from the recent ECMT Round Table 81 (Paris, May 1989) on the possibilities for, and cost of, private and public investment in transport. Three keynote papers give very different national perspectives on the principal directions and priorities from Britain, West Germany and France.

Part IV   The local state and consumption

7. Tensions in the management of consumption: property struggles in housing and planning

Malcolm Harrison

Introduction

This chapter looks at some tensions which can arise within government programmes when the demands of centralised power come up against the interests of people at 'grass roots' level. In particular, questions are raised about the potential for challenges from below focused around rights claims. Prospects for such claims in policy environments in which close 'peak-level' relationships have been built up between governmental agencies and major external organised interests are considered. The arguments are developed with reference to consumption-management and social policy (rather than industrial relations), and the main case studies are taken from housing and land-use planning. We shall see that there is considerable scope for challenge from the grass roots or mass level on a collective basis, especially where grass roots claims can be allied with notions of private rights and property. This situation should not be interpreted as an aspect of a pluralistic politics. Instead, relatively closed national decision-making systems are tied in with constituency-building or incorporation processes at mass level which not only provide legitimation for privileged access by intermediating bodies, but also reinforce the expectations and rights claims of households. On this interpretation, the potential for conflict may be effectively a '*structural*' feature of consumption-management in some Western economies, arising from pressures to combine security or continuity in corporate capital accumulation with electoral success, public credibility and individualistic systems of 'citizen rights'. Resistance to peak-level power may originate in rights claims which have been nurtured within structures of state-organised consumption. In particular, claims focused on property may become the stakes around which opposition develops. Encouragement of mass-level incorporation strengthens the ability of some grass roots groups to mount such challenges, because people's expectations are raised and their claims enhanced. Contrary to the formulations of economic liberalism, however, grass roots property rights claims may require *collective* assertion. Indeed, given their potential as a means of political mobilisation, such property claims could fit well into the political programmes of the Left in Britain and other Western states. In this sense private property might prove in the long term the 'Achilles heel' of corporate power within capitalistic societies. In the more immediate future, for governments making social or environmental policies there will continue to be problems in resolving the resulting tensions within specific policy areas and legislative programmes.

Decision processes, organised consumption and social policy

Western welfare states exhibit a variety of combinations of modes of intervention, representation and implementation in fields of social policy, welfare and environment. States are involved in a wide range of activities (outside the provision of direct wages), shaping consumption by groups and categories of households. The ensemble of modes in a particular country can include legal provisions, controls and sanctions, services supplied directly through state agencies, support through the tax system for types of savings or consumption of goods, privately-run services encouraged or sponsored by the state, occupationally-linked benefits, and so forth. The overall pattern may be conceived of in terms of a *structure of organised consumption* (Harrison (ed.), 1984 and 1986), in which state agencies intermesh with major outside actors. The patterns of relationships and forms of intervention alter with shifts in power, and each country follows a distinctive historical path (despite some common tendencies).

One important variable is the extent to which policy-making and implementation are dependent upon close links with outside financial and industrial organisations. Parts of consumption-management systems can involve deep interpenetration of governmental agencies and selected major business interests that are accorded privileged status and access (see, for instance, Craig and Harrison, 1984). Scholars explain the special place occupied by business within decision processes in a variety of ways. Stress may be placed on a balance of class forces in which such interests remain strong, or perhaps on functional necessities requiring the state to respond to business needs. Certainly the role of industrial and financial corporations is not merely an interest group one (see, for instance, Lindblom, 1977, pp. 170, 172, etc.): their privileges may range from an attribution of status in informal consultation processes to a grant of particular legal powers (such as provision for compulsory acquisition of land). Of course, these corporate interests rarely have the field entirely to themselves. Policies related to welfare and consumption may also be influenced by religious movements, professional groups and trade union representatives.

The present chapter, however, is concerned only with countervailing pressures that may come from the *consumers* of services, assistance and benefits, and be based on their material concerns. The focus of much academic work has been on negotiation of policy at the peak level of national decision-making, and on intermediate, 'meso' or local levels where representatives of interests similarly come together to reach accommodations over the shaping of policy (see for instance Cawson (ed.), 1985). For analysis of welfare institutions and organised consumption, however, this emphasis should be supplemented by consideration of events at mass level. In the case of industrial relations, tensions between peak and mass-level concerns are well understood, and grass roots representation is in any case institutionalised via trade unions and their organisations. Outside this, the picture is less clear. Management of consumption involves not only complex relationships between major organisations and government, but also processes of constituency-building, incorporation and legitimation at mass level. These processes may not coexist easily with the drive for mutual accommodation with the private suppliers or financiers of services and goods.

In considering mass-level representation and incorporation, it is important to appreciate that the politics of consumption cannot be read off in a simple way from industrial relations and a concept of unified class struggle. In many fields conflicts based in industrial relations now often take second place to social cleavages and political issues related to groups of consumers, ethnic or gender categories, or residential communities (see for instance Rex, 1986; Rex and Mason (eds), 1986; Gilroy, 1982). More generally, the relationships consumers have with government and powerful private intermediaries differ from relations between employees and their managers. The struggles of consumption require separate review (even if the ultimate primacy of connections with production is acknowledged). Areas of social and environmental politics embody distinctive aspects of what Marxists might see as the reproduction of the social relations of capitalism. To varying degrees households are drawn into particular life styles through the systems of support, regulation and sponsorship that social policies and consumption-management involve. Ideas associated with encouraged forms of household consumption and welfare can foster or maintain various attitudes about commodities, stigma, patriarchy, entitlements and so forth. Put simply, organised consumption has both material and ideological aspects which are sometimes one step removed from industrial class conflicts. Social policy is the site of numerous struggles, but not all connect in a *simple* way with the conflict of capital and labour.

One obvious implication is that consumption cleavages may occur on an intraclass basis, reinforcing tendencies for fragmentation of working-class interests. The management of consumption thus provides a base for 'divide-and-rule' tactics by elites, weakening the reformist demands that come from below (Harrison, 1984). In British housing policy, for example, financial and administrative aid for owner-occupation has been treated by some anti-collectivists as a means of undermining working-class solidarity and support for the Labour party (for a relevant empirical study see Williams, Sewel and Twine, 1987). Whether or not such attempts at direct manipulation are effective (and there must be doubts about the independent political influence of any isolated item of consumption), it seems reasonable to suggest that, in the long term, processes of selective ideological, political and material incorporation of households occur. Benefits contribute systematically to the material well-being and status of certain types of households, encourage the maintenance of particular attitudes and help constitute individuals as 'citizens' with varying ability to share in the life of the wider society. These citizens are 'represented' as consumers by a number of intermediating agencies claiming to speak on their behalf (we note specific examples later). Certainly the British post-war welfare state settlement incorporated some groups more than others: the term 'differential incorporation' seems appropriate (see Rex, 1986, pp. 65–72; Rex and Mason, 1986, p. xii) to indicate the impact of the organisation of consumption (and welfare systems in particular).

Incorporation, however, raises difficulties for governments, since it implies security of material rewards for households that are drawn in, and it requires underpinning with convincing concepts about representation and rights. Attempts to incorporate (or claims to represent) mass-level interests (even selectively) carry with them possibilities for threats emerging from below which can become obstacles to privileged peak-level decision-making. Notions of entitlements and rights take on special significance in such contexts. Before turning to our case studies, therefore, we must look at rights claims as possible bases for political mobilisation.

Rights struggles: Anglo-American divergence?

The North American scholars Bowles and Gintis have argued that 'democratic sentiments' may encroach upon the capitalistic economy, and that progressive social change in liberal democratic capitalist societies 'has followed the logic of collective opposition to oppression suggested by Marxian theory, while adopting the liberal language of rights' (Bowles and Gintis, 1986, pp. 5, 25). Rights thus have had an important function in the promotion of representative government and democracy.

It is natural that writers from the United States should stress rights, since notions about citizenship and legal redress are so important there. Individual rights claims can play a crucial political role as a focus or resource around which battles develop (cf. Scheingold, 1974), and through which peak level power can be resisted or challenged. In his classic work of the 1940s, 'An American dilemma', Myrdal referred to what he called the 'American creed', within which beliefs in equality and the right to liberty held firm places. In considering the creed's applicability to race relations he felt it was, 'expressive and definite in practically all respects of importance . . . . Most of the value premises with which we shall be concerned have actually been incorporated for a long time in the national Constitution and in the constitutions and laws of the several states' (Myrdal, 1944, p. 24). The implication was that movements for equal rights in the United States could call upon a set of widely-held beliefs about the importance of such matters, and on various legal and customary institutional supports. In post-war America legal challenges have formed part of the pressure brought by civil rights reformers (alongside other tactics), and among government's responses have been legal measures to combat discrimination (see for instance Issel, 1985, pp. 163, 171–90, etc.). The concept of formal citizen rights thus has provided a weapon to be deployed by ethnic minorities, feminists and other groups against certain kinds of vested interest.

We must consider, however, whether mobilisation on the basis of rights claims is feasible where circumstances are less favourable. Does Britain in particular offer an instructive contrast? At first sight it seems so, for citizens' legal rights to challenge executive or corporate power (and even control of information held by government: see Marsh (ed.), 1987) have been only weakly developed. British people have few constitutional safeguards, and personal inequality is actually embodied in the parliamentary system (through hereditary peerages giving special opportunities to participate in governing processes). Outside Northern Ireland, 'civil rights' have rarely been a key issue for grass roots mobilisation in recent decades. Instead, energies have been engaged more often in workplace-based struggles, with trade unions and the Labour party as the means for channelling demands. Individual, community or household rights claims rarely occupy the centre of the political stage. Lacking firm constitutional basis, citizen participation and challenges to executive action have been allowed rather at the *discretion* of governments. Equal opportunities legislation has been influenced by reformers, but equally by desires to maintain social order, provide tokens of ministerial concern, or bring Britain into line with other countries. Thus despite the supposedly shared Anglo-American heritage, rights claims have been less prominent in recent British politics than in the United States. There has been no well-developed tradition for grass roots mobilisation here along lines which would complement trade union activity.

Even in Britain, however, significant exceptions exist. Struggles against private landlordism, for instance, have led to various laws protecting occupiers. Within environmental politics there has been pressure for rights of access to the countryside (pursued in one period through 'mass trespass' on the estates of landowners). In more recent years there have been demands for so-called welfare rights, for rights of equal opportunity in employment, and so forth. Furthermore, as noted in our introduction, there are 'structural' relationships to be considered. The very way in which consumption is managed may *itself* generate potential for struggles built around rights claims. This point will now be considered more fully.

Demands by peak-level organisations for privileged access in policy-making in Britain often rest on claims to represent broader interests at household level. At the same time the structures of organised consumption can generate sets of entitlements and forms of savings or accumulation at grass roots. Consequently, in some policy-making contexts expectations arise within political constituencies about meeting the 'needs' of households in various ways, about protecting their entitlements and accumulated resources, and about mechanisms for accountability to them. With occupational pensions, for instance (where the state is involved through the tax system, as an employer, and through providing a legal framework), governments are under pressure not only to respond to fund managers, but also to provide safeguards for members. Although participatory procedures for rank-and-file beneficiaries have not yet developed far in this sphere (for a thorough analysis see Schuller, 1986), the question of accountability has begun to appear on the political agenda (Britain's National Union of Mineworkers, for instance, has attempted to influence pension-fund investment policies, although unsuccessfully). For present purposes we may interpret such pressures in terms of individual rights claims being collectively asserted. State encouragement of organised consumption has contributed to a growing set of grass roots claims or entitlements, some with the potential to form a basis for collective mobilisation. While the struggles will always concern power, notions of rights may have a part to play as political resources. The situation is not entirely new, but the increased relative importance of consumption in politics gives consumer rights a heightened significance.

This analysis leads to an unexpected conclusion. Although people in the United States appear better placed to utilise rights claims in popular struggles, such claims from British consumers nevertheless represent a serious *potential* threat to centralised power. The concentrations of influence so marked in Britain's system of organised consumption, the success of the incorporation process at mass level, and the centralised nature of British politics, mean that major institutions could be vulnerable if challenged on rights grounds. Depending so much on relationships with the central state, working within nationally-determined legal frameworks, and claiming to speak on behalf of the welfare of consumers, some major private sector institutions are in a potentially exposed position. Whether serious challenges actually emerge will depend on the degree of involvement and commitment of households, as well as the orientations and effectiveness of the political Left. In some cases (as with occupational pensions) there is of course a clear link to the politics of industrial relations.

Property and participation

Private property is sometimes seen as a factor inhibiting liberty, democratic accountability and human development. Yet it can be a force for the weak as well as the strong. As Proudhon might have put it, property can be both theft *and* liberty. There are links between democratic accountability, private property rights and participation.

To present our case, it is first essential to distinguish it from economic individualism and some normative variants of pluralism. A stress on private rights could imply arguments linked to economic liberalism and a crude methodological individualism, ignoring the complex realities of human behaviour and interaction. Indeed, such a danger *is* implicit in many rights-based approaches, including those pursued by economists of the American 'property rights school' (for relevant comments see Harrison, 1987; Bowles and Gintis, 1986; Schaffer and Lamb, 1981). What is presently argued, however, is very different, for it involves a notion of struggle in which mobilisation might be on the basis of individually-held rights or rights claims, but via *collective* organisations (such as local authorities, residents' and tenants' associations, consumers' organisations, and so forth). By contrast, economic liberalism tends to downgrade the role of local participatory processes in favour of market relations and individual choices unfettered (or unorganised) by custom, kinship or 'community'. As Bowles and Gintis have noted, economic liberalism may undermine accountable collective forms of expression and organisation below the level of the central state itself: liberalism has 'conspired with the imperatives of the capitalist economy' to erode all collective bodies standing between state and individual, except for the capitalist corporation (Bowles and Gintis, 1986, p. 177).

Given this tendency, uncertainty surrounds the scope of local participation in Western economies. Governments may seek to by-pass policy-making processes which involve local participation of a pluralistic and open kind. Such participation reflects, in many cases, a set of partly-acknowledged grass roots rights claims (see Harrison, 1987) that may challenge the market freedoms preferred by economic liberals and the 'corporatist' accommodations reached at peak level. Organisations capable of focusing such claims collectively may come under attack at times when governments are emphasising markets and profitability. In Britain, for example, recent reductions in local government powers could be interpreted in this way. Various measures since 1979 have reduced local government's role in education, land-use planning, housing, and transport, as well as abolishing some local authorities altogether. A second central government strategy is to restrict the agenda for local debate, or to require altered processes of consultation which enhance the role of business (see, for example, King, 1985, pp. 207–8, 212). One point deduced from such developments is that collective expression of grass roots views does not fit easily with trends in the wider capitalistic economy. At the same time there are great differences between our conception of rights and those forms encouraged within market-oriented systems.

Opposition between the requirements of business activity and the pressure for participatory rights at grass roots is not a new phenomenon, nor is it confined to Britain. Australian case studies show how business interests there sought to replace certain existing local arrangements for land-use planning by a 'corporatist' mode of mediation within which they could be assured of direct involvement in the planning process while potential opponents were excluded. In Melbourne this was achieved 'by dismissing the elected council and removing planning functions to the regional level' (Saunders, 1985, pp. 154–64).

Of course even where collective representation is allowed to influence decisions below state level, the relevant organisations may not *themselves* be immune from 'take-overs'. Local authorities, for instance, might be 'colonised' by private sector interests, sometimes with central government approval. The relationships need not be corrupt, but may imply less open decision-making and a more privileged type of politics (see comments below on 'planning gain'; and Reade, 1984; Simpson, 1987).

Although rights of citizen participation and grass roots property rights are not the same, they overlap. Grass roots property rights can be implicit in participatory processes built into parts of public policy-making, and are capable of expansion in several areas where consumption is managed through private agency/public sector cooperation. Where participatory claims can be linked to private property rights held individually at grass roots level they may be difficult to suppress. 'Property' reinforces or adds legitimacy to the challenges from below. This point will be made clearer by some examples from recent Conservative government activity in Britain.

Tensions in land-use planning

Planning concerns production interests as well as consumption of environment by households. Conflicts often occur when proposals by property developers are opposed by residents of an affected locality. Local people may defend their consumption of the residential environment (in its broadest sense) by attempting to participate in decision-making processes: through elected representatives, civic and amenity societies, and so forth. Very often pressures for large schemes come from corporate organisations or nationally-based firms which central government wishes to encourage. It is not easy, however, to override local claims. Indeed, the emphasis placed in consumption politics on home ownership tends to reinforce local resistance to change, and enhances the idea that residents have legitimate claims over a host of activities conducted on property 'owned' by others nearby. People have come to expect to participate over issues that may affect property prices, views from house or garden, local road traffic, shopping arrangements, and the perceived 'character' of their towns and villages. Furthermore, they expect to participate not merely as isolated individuals, but collectively through the system of electoral representation.

It is important to understand how this situation has come about, for in origin it was not a matter of generally accepted civic rights but was closely tied to property claims. Land planning stands out as one of the few areas of British public policy where traditions of public participation and judicial supervision of executive action have developed. One reason is that private property is involved. As Harden and Lewis explain, planning is the only field in which the overwhelmingly *ad hoc* and discretionary nature of processes of advice and inquiry gives way to a legally structured framework. The origins and development of that framework depended crucially on 'the categorization of compulsory purchase and planning restrictions as derogations from the common law rights of owners of land'. Thus it was the 'property connection' which provided 'institutional opportunities for judicial challenges to decision-making leading to demands for the extension of formalized procedures and rights enforceable ultimately through the courts' (Harden and Lewis, 1986, pp. 174–5). From a narrow legal starting point for directly affected property-holders, rights and expectations have broadened over time so that planning has become more open to pluralistic pressures at local level than most other policy activities. By formal rights and administrative customs people now expect to be informed of proposals and to have a say (see Mordey, 1987), a trend which can inhibit or delay bargains among powerful public, private and semi-private organisations. This trend has been reinforced by central government's support for life styles and choices associated with personal mobility, owner-occupation and individualised consumption-maximisation for the better off. Expectations, furthermore, go well beyond the power of veto over the actions of immediate neighbours (see Harrison, 1987). These rights, of course, are exercised to an extent collectively, through elected representatives, local authorities and other local organisations, and participants may be prepared to accept the need for a range of decision-making principles of a universalistic kind (rather than only expecting their own protection).

One paradox of owner-occupation is that while housebuilders are often presented in the national political arena as the favoured deliverers of the 'property-owning democracy' (see for instance Ambrose, 1986, pp. 190, 194), they conflict with local resident owner-occupiers over planning proposals. Approval of land release for housing schemes is essential for major builders upon whom government relies for the further extension of owner-occupation. Indeed, the industry is often presented as operating very much in the 'national interest' (as if it represented the needs and views of potential occupiers), and land allocations by planning authorities in effect are nowadays expected to take this into account. The industry's relationship with central government is close, and appears to have some 'corporatist' characteristics (see Rydin, 1984, 1986). Consequently Conservative governments in recent years have sought to reduce obstacles to development, and to by-pass local resistance. Simmie has charted events in south-east England, noting the power of producer interests and the possibilities and limitations of countervailing local electoral pressures in relation to Structure Plans (in recent years the main formal policy tools for land planning) (Simmie, 1986). Producers of housing, especially large volume housebuilders, are concerned with maximising the designation of land for housing purposes in Structure Plans, and have promoted their interests especially through their 'production association, the House Builders' Federation (HBF)' (pp. 76–7). Simmie writes, 'As the new Conservative administration assumed office . . . . it came under pressure from house producers to speed up the workings of the formal planning system . . . and for the system to allocate more land for house production even in the greenbelt around London' (p. 77).

Joint studies of housing land availability involving the private sector were encouraged by central government, and local authorities were pressed to be more responsive to developers (see Department of the Environment, 1980 and 1984; see also Rydin, 1986; Ambrose, 1986, chapter 7, etc.). More generally, government proposed various alterations to planning procedures (see Minister without Portfolio, 1985), some of which passed into law, and several of which were aimed at reducing the scope of local authority controls. Even so, government's overview of planning could not openly become too one-sided, given the strength of local conservationist and protectionist sentiments. Ministers have been able to influence directly the outcomes of planning appeal cases, where central government considers – via the planning inspectorate – developers' requests for the overturning of negative local authority decisions on applications for permission to develop. Even here, however, the impression has not been of a very *dramatic* shift away from traditional planning criteria (for a recent study see Heycock, 1986). In fact throughout the post-1979 period political tensions have continued to constrain ministers especially in lowland England:

> Ranged on one side have been house producers using internal pressure, 'old boy' networks, sanction threats, inducements, national media and secret politics to persuade a sympathetic national government to modify the formal planning system in their favour. . . . Ranged against the house producers . . . have been 'green' pluralist political pressures . . . . This . . . has even affected central government policies via pressure from Conservative, shire county MPs. (Simmie, 1986, p.81)

Central government has modified some locally-prepared plans in the interests of developers, but parts of its programme have met with delays and even defeats (notably in respect of green belt policies: see Short, Fleming and Witt, 1986, p. 274, etc.; Ambrose, 1986, p. 202; Simmie, 1986, p. 80; Rydin, 1986, p. 3). On the local side one response has been for authorities to try to obtain some form of 'planning gain' for the community in return for schemes going ahead (Short, Fleming and Witt, 1986, p. 274). The increase in bargaining for such compensatory local planning gains from developers may owe something to a 'downgrading' of formal plans. It may imply, furthermore, close relationships between developers and local authorities at the expense of open decisions and wider participation (for some issues here see Simpson, 1987). This is a reminder that antidemocratic tendencies exist locally as well as nationally.

Away from the prosperous shires and suburbs, central government has in some places introduced new administrative machinery which can more readily accommodate the requirements of developers and private finance. The leading example is the setting up of Urban Development Corporations, circumventing normal planning procedures (which have relatively pluralistic consultative features). The activities of one body, the London Docklands Development Corporation, have been the subject of a devastating critique by Ambrose (1986, chapter 8). This 'QUANGO' apparently pursued a market-oriented 'demand-led' strategy that ran counter to the views and aspirations of many local interests. Ambrose sees the organisation as a prime example of the blurring of distinctions between public and private sector agencies (pp. 226–7). Local people here were unable effectively to resist the developments encouraged by central government, despite the magnitude of the physical changes involved. One hypothesis might be that their rights claims were accorded weak legitimacy not merely because of the current configuration of electoral political forces (where Conservative governments need pay little regard to the representation of the interests of the poor), but also because of the property ownership patterns (see information in Ambrose, 1986, p. 225, etc.). Putting this argument the other way round, where owner-occupation is more firmly entrenched, local claims to be consulted and participate in neighbourhood planning are treated more seriously.

Tensions in housing policy

Recent events related to building societies and council housing show clearly how grass roots rights claims may conflict with the development of public policies fully responsive to the desires of business interests. The 1986 Building Societies Act (ch. 53) created a framework for diversified activity, allowing scope for various commercial and entrepreneurial operations previously treated as falling outside the long-established remit of societies as 'mutual' organisations (see Chancellor of the Exchequer, 1984; House of Commons Debates, Building Societies Bill, 19 December 1985). This change reflected a wider trend for state-encouraged commercialisation, and for greater integration of mutual bodies into the mainstream London-based financial sector. The legislation catered for extension of financial services by the societies, new types of lending, enlargement of housing-related services and more direct involvement in housing provision and management. It also made arrangements covering mergers, and conversions to company status.

The Act was a result of close cooperation following a period of years in which building society representatives and central government had increasingly engaged in policy discussion and negotiation with a measure of mutual accommodation (see Craig and Harrison, 1984). One feature of the increasing involvement of building societies in housing policy has been the claim that these organisations in a sense 'represent' the aspirations of ordinary households, small investors and borrowers. Acknowledgements of building society claims to an expanding role in housing policy have thus rested in part on notions of the public interest, and the societies' perceived ability to meet 'needs'. As formally mutual organisations rather than conventional companies, the societies have been in a good position to build up this image. There are even attempts to justify new activities like investing overseas as 'services to members'. Thus a building society representative in the Parliamentary second reading debate stated:

The Bill gives power . . . for the major societies to operate in the EEC. That is important today because many working people retire to Spain or Portugal and buy a villa. It is important that while buying that villa they have the help of their own building society, the one that they are used to . . . . Such people are not tax exiles; they are rain exiles. (House of Commons Debates, Building Societies Bill, 19 December 1985, col. 607).

This illustrates how remote some people at peak level are from life at grass roots, but also how peak-level power draws upon the notion of service and representation as a source of legitimacy. In the creation of the Bill itself this claim to represent – and its legal basis in mutual status – provided a barrier to full and immediate commercialisation. Government had to place constraints on management freedoms, at least initially. Indeed, the Act requires voting support at grass roots level before any leaderships' schemes to convert into commercial companies can go through. Some societies have drawn back for the moment from conversion, but the Abbey National's leaders have pressed ahead. They have run into a storm of protest, with organised opposition developing among rank-and-file members. Unfortunately for the objectors, management can control the flow of information, timing of meetings and so forth, as well as being able to offer substantial financial inducements to secure a favourable vote. Consequently the 'protest vote' is likely to be muted, (although the final outcome remains unclear at time of writing).

One significant aspect of these events has been political party alignment, for the Labour party has appeared as defender of the mutual tradition and – by implication – of the collective private property rights of borrowers as 'shareholders' (see House of Commons Debates, 27 July 1988, etc.). Given current rising levels of mortgage defaults and high interest rates, there is scope for Labour to stand legitimately as the champion of owner-occupiers. On the government side there are delicate policy issues. They must be cautious about rapid commercialisation that threatens the rights and property of householders, and have been unable to disregard completely the issue of representation. Owner-occupiers need not be compliant tools of corporate interests. It is worth remembering that in the 1930s there was a famous legal challenge to the building societies from house buyers, underlined by mortgage strikes on some speculative estates in the south-east (see Craig, 1986, pp. 97–107). If there were today effective means of activating and giving collective expression to claims and aspirations from the grass roots, then the path of building society development might be reshaped in directions very different from those being taken at present.

Turning to council housing, again we may obtain insights from legislation. In 1980 the new Conservative government emphasised the rights of public sector housing tenants. The 1980 Housing Act (ch. 51) included provisions for a 'tenants' charter' drawing upon previous Labour proposals (see Secretaries of State for the Environment and Wales, 1977, p. 130, para. 51), but with the addition of a right for most local authority and some housing association tenants to purchase their dwellings at a discount. Subsequent legislation has strengthened the 'right to buy', but the broader notion of a package of occupier rights was not without side-effects for the government. A number of property rights had been conceded in 1980, including a measure of security of tenure and some rights of consultation over estate management. Although the 'right to buy' remained significant, as time passed Conservative policy began to focus on those council houses less likely to be sold to sitting tenants. One approach involved local authority 'deals' for the acquisition and refurbishment of entire council estates by the private sector, often with subsequent selling on of houses into owner-occupation (see Usher, 1987). Central government became heavily implicated in encouraging this process, and many local authorities responded positively. Some, however, ran into difficulties because their bargains with the private sector necessitated removal of existing sitting tenants, who could prove reluctant to go (see for instance Cowan, 1985). Consequently, having conferred security of tenure in 1980, the government in 1986 provided councils with additional grounds for possession against their own tenants in such cases, to facilitate what had become known as 'municipal winkling' (see Housing and Planning Act, 1986, ch. 63). Although won by legislative power, this political battle reflected badly on the government and those councils (including one Labour-controlled one in particular) that attracted media attention over it. In seeking to carve out new opportunities for private sector/public sector interpenetration here, government found the notion of tenant property rights – which it had earlier adopted – something of a nuisance! Certainly it was not easy to remove such rights without at least providing token compensation (such as home loss payments: see Housing and Planning Act, 1986, ch. 63, s. 9(7)).

More important than these estate refurbishment schemes is the general intention to dispose of council housing, with its tenants, to private institutions, housing associations and trusts, and to encourage councils to delegate management reponsibilities to outside agents (see Housing and Planning Act, 1986, ch. 63, ss. 6–11; Housing Act, 1988, ch. 50). A number of interlocking motives may be discerned, including reducing the influence of Labour party-run local authorities (and their ability to employ 'direct labour' workforces), increasing variety of rented housing tenure and creating scope for private investment.

Although this third goal is important, there have been limits on how far government has been able to manoeuvre cooperatively with private institutions, or create new chances for them. The 1986 legislation conceded council tenants a voice (or vote) before their estates could pass to new landlords (see Housing and Planning Act, 1986, ch. 63, s.6, s.10). Tenants also generally would in theory retain the 'right to buy' subsequently (although see Usher, 1987, p. 55). In effect, while the feeling that tenants were entitled to occupier property rights helped establish the 'right to buy' in 1980, by 1986 it had begun to present obstacles or costs for other forms of privatisation. There was active opposition among tenants to specific estate privatisations, and it looked likely that the right to vote would impede future disposals. The 1987 Bill led to more opposition, and government was pressed hard on voting rights. For ordinary transfers of estates to new landlords, ministers stood firm on voting arrangements containing a pro-transfer bias (see Housing Act, 1988, ch. 50, s.103, (2); House of Commons Debates, Housing Bill, 30 November 1987, etc.). They retreated, however, on Housing Action Trusts (HATs). These were to be agencies set up by central government to take over council estates in selected places. After some improvement work, dwellings were to be passed on to various other landlords. Initially, provisions did not allow for any tenant ballots over HATs, and homes were never to return into council hands when a HAT ended. During passage of the Bill, government gave way on both these points (Housing Act, 1988, ch. 50, s.61; s.84). It may be that ballots, which tenants' groups had fought for, will now lead to HATs being rejected in several cities. The future of the programme is in doubt at time of writing.

The 1987–8 period confirmed that tenants will take organised political action when they feel threatened over security of tenure, rent levels and the imposition of unfamiliar landlords. This contrasts markedly with the politics of the 'right to buy', where collective opposition was slight (even though poorer tenants faced diminished rehousing prospects because of sales of the better dwellings). It was hard to mobilise opposition to giving households more rights over the homes they already lived in, and central government capitalised on this. To take individual rights *away* from tenants, however, is very different. Although the 1988 Act has been 'sold' to the public in terms of increased tenants' choice, it really creates new substantial rights only for landlords and investors (for instance see s.93). Many tenants are well aware of this.

Conclusions

Although it would be wrong to overstate the role of rights claims in political struggle in the United Kingdom, some rights in law or established custom do offer a feasible basis for resistance to peak-level power. The construction and maintenance of political constituencies at mass level through the organisation of consumption has involved conceding a range of entitlements or rights, and the development of large expectations. This is certainly so with owner-occupation, and with the closely-related 'consumption of environment' where owner-occupiers are politically important. It is also true for council house tenants, even if recognised entitlements here are much weaker. Consequently, although cosy bargains can be struck by governments and major private institutions, their manoeuvrability may be restricted by demands from below. Where there is potential for effective collective mobilisation on the basis of recognised consumer rights, a strong grass roots counter-force to peak-level power may develop. Although not the only force at work, property claims could form a significant component of such challenges.

It is important to stress that the conflicts arise from what have become 'structural' features of some capitalistic economies. Government is not simply 'overloaded' because of rising expectations in a pluralistic political context. Instead, the management of consumption develops in response to a shifting balance of class and other forces. This management process becomes crucial for the reproduction of the social relations of capitalism, and differential incorporation (and constituency-building) occur as part of it. Incorporation, however, provides bases not only for social control but also for forms of resistance. Sometimes the potential for mobilisation around rights claims will remain merely latent. One path for left-wing political parties might then be to seek to activate and channel the claims.

Guide to further reading

Two general books which contain useful comments on the politics of consumption are P. Dunleavy (1980a), and P. Saunders (1986). Relevant shorter pieces include P. Dunleavy (1986), 'The growth of sectoral cleavages and the stabilisation of state expenditures', *Environment and Planning D*, 4, pp. 129–44; P. Saunders (1984) 'Beyond housing classes: the sociological significance of private property rights in means of consumption', *International Journal of Urban and Regional Research*, 8,2, pp. 202–7; V. Duke and S. Edgell (1984) 'Public expenditure cuts in Britain and consumption sectoral cleavages', *International Journal of Urban and Regional Research*, 8,2, pp. 177–201; M.L. Harrison (1986). For some readings on property rights see P.G. Hollowell (ed.) (1982), *Property and social relations* (London: Heinemann) and C.B. Macpherson (ed.) (1978), *Property: mainstream and critical positions* (Oxford: Blackwell). See also A.M. Honoré (1961), 'Ownership', in A.G. Guest (ed.), *Oxford essays in jurisprudence* (Oxford: Oxford University Press). For a radical review of current property rights ideas, and further references to the literature, see M.L. Harrison (1987).

8. Housing and the state: privatisation, policy reform and plurality?

Robert Smith

Introduction

Although only a minority of Britain's housing stock has been directly provided by the state, nevertheless government interventions in the housing system through policies of both regulation and subsidy have had a considerable impact upon the housing market as a whole. The growth of home ownership during the twentieth century, and particularly since the Second World War, has been significantly influenced by government policies whilst the development of the owner-occupied sector has had a clear impact upon other parts of the housing system.

The state in Britain is significantly involved in the housing sector of the economy, with signs of intervention to be found throughout the housing system, and not just in the mode of provision. The state takes action to influence the production, consumption and distribution of housing services, including both direct provision in the form of council housing to rent and indirect measures which affect behaviour in the private market. Traditionally, attempts have been made to modify the quantity, quality, price and ownership of dwellings, although the emphasis of overall policy has varied over time, reflecting changing circumstances and differing political priorities.

As an alternative to an integrated universalist housing service, which would have required the nationalisation of private housing, the state has sought a managerialist role in housing, not allowing the market to operate in an unfettered way, instead using measures to control and regulate in such a way as to ensure an adequate supply of reasonable quality housing at prices which people can afford. Thus there is a tendency for housing 'problems' to be seen in terms of numbers and/or standards rather than in distributional and equitable terms. However, since the 1970s, and particularly post-1979, the thrust of central government policy towards housing has shifted. It has always been part of Conservative philosophy to place a heavy reliance on the market to solve the problems of 'what' and 'how much' to produce, as well as 'for whom', but under Mrs Thatcher the advocacy of free market solutions has been relentlessly pursued.

In the province of housing successive governments have accepted the continuation of a dominant private sector and assumed that direct public subsidies and the expansion of council housing provision were merely temporary expedients (Malpass and Murie, 1987). Since 1979, under the Conservatives, considerable strides have been made to encourage further the growth of owner-occupation, limit the role of public provision in rented housing, stimulate the housing association and private rented sectors and promote the transfer of council housing to alternative landlords. The purpose of this chapter is to examine these trends in housing policy and the shifts in equilibrium between central and local government and the state and voluntary/private sectors.

The growth of home ownership

There has been a dramatic metamorphosis in the pattern of housing tenure in this country over the last seventy-five years, with owner-occupation first developing as a significant tenure form between the two World Wars, becoming the largest single tenure in the mid-1950s displacing the private rented sector. Since 1971, owner-occupation has accounted for a majority of the housing stock in England and Wales, and by 1987 it represented 66 per cent of the housing stock (Association of Metropolitan Authorities, 1988, p.11).

For almost forty years all British governments, of whatever political persuasion, though with varying degrees of emphasis, have sought to promote home ownership, with the role of the state in direct provision being essentially residualist, whilst regulating and shaping market forces in the private sector. The last Labour government (1974–9) clearly believed that the continued expansion of owner-occupation represented either a shift in tenure preference or a reflection of long-held housing aspirations which could be satisfied by growing real incomes. Anthony Crosland had argued in 1971 that Labour was in favour of home ownership, which was good for savings and self-reliance and, above all, was what many people wanted (Crosland, 1971, pp. 18–19). The Labour government's review of housing policy, which began in 1975 and which was finally published in 1977, endorsed this view (Department of the Environment, 1977). Labour's last term of office saw the introduction of a number of specific measures designed to bolster home ownership and the 1977 housing policy review suggested a number of schemes which might increase the effective demand for owner-occupation, primarily by reducing the financial burden in the early years of home purchase. In many instances the policies suggested in the 1977 Green Paper have been implemented or strengthened since 1979 by successive Conservative governments. In terms of owner-occupation, differences between the polices of Mrs Thatcher's government and those pursued by the last Labour administration are essentially ones of emphasis and not direction. However, the retreat from direct public provision of housing opportunities has been advanced several steps, and a still greater reliance placed upon the private market in meeting housing needs and demands.

Since 1979 public expenditure cuts, low levels of new council sector housebuilding, rising real rents, and a shift of subsidies away from renting and in favour of owner-occupation, have all combined to convey housing still further into the private domain. As Whitehead has commented, the Conservatives had three main objectives when they were returned to office in 1979 (Whitehead, 1983). These were:

1. To reduce the level of public expenditure on housing.
2. To substitute private for public finance.
3. To transfer the dwelling stock from public to private ownership, primarily by expanding owner-occupation.

The reasoning behind this approach was both practical and ideological. At the more pragmatic level the most pressing need on entering office was seen to have been to reduce the Public Sector Borrowing Requirement (PSBR), and capital expenditure on housing was a relatively easy target. The more doctrinal arguments were based on a view that the economy in general, and the housing system in particular should be made to function more effectively through the more widespread use of market mechanisms.

Alongside these arguments there was another reason for the change of emphasis: that policies designed to increase the level of owner-occupation were politically very popular. Whilst all the major political parties have had a long-standing commitment to the expansion of home ownership, it is one controversial policy – the Right to Buy for council tenants – which has been crucial in stimulating this continued growth in the 1980s. Shortly after the May 1979 General Election the Prime Minister argued:

Thousands of people in council houses and new towns came out to support us for the first time because they wanted a chance to buy their own homes. We will give to every council tenant the right to purchase his [sic] own home at a substantial discount on the market price and with 100% mortgages for those who need them. This will be a giant stride towards making a reality of Anthony Eden's dream of a property owning democracy. It will do something else – it will give to more of our people that freedom and mobility and that prospect of handing something on to their children and grandchildren which owner-occupation provides. (Hansard, 1979)

The political controversy over the right-to-buy, introduced by the 1980 Housing Act, is not related to the encouragement of owner-occupation but in the extension of central government control and the loss of local autonomy. There is a long history of council house sales, dating from much earlier than 1980, and substantial sales have taken place under Labour administrations (Forrest and Murie, 1988). However, since 1980 over a million council homes have been sold into owner-occupation. Coupled with a very low level of new public-sector completions, the scale of state housing in Britain has been in absolute as well as relative decline since 1979. The success with which the Conservatives have been able to facilitate the transfer of public rented housing into owner-occupation has also been aided by the low public esteem of local government in general and council housing in particular (Raine, 1981).

Government housing policy in the first half of the 1980s was concerned principally with the promotion of home ownership. In addition to the mandatory Right to Buy the Conservatives have encouraged the development of a range of initiatives designed either to increase the supply of relatively low-cost homes or stimulate effective demand for home ownership by increasing access to mortgage finance and lowering the cost of entry to this tenure. Whilst many of these initiatives were in existence before 1979, they have been given a higher profile and considerable promotion by the Conservatives (Booth and Crook, 1986), with local authorities and housing associations induced to implement these discretionary policies. However, apart from the Right to Buy the other specific low-cost home ownership initiatives have had only a limited impact. Much of the increase in the level of owner-occupation which has taken place during the 1980s can be accounted for by traditional processes of speculative private construction and a continued transfer of former privately rented housing into home ownership.

If the focus of government housing policy during the early 1980s was the extension of owner-occupation, in the latter part of the decade priorities have changed. The 1986 Housing and Planning Act, although it contained clauses extending and consolidating the earlier Right to Buy provisions, was described (perhaps, with hindsight, prematurely) by the then Housing Minister John Patten as 'the last great push of the right-to-buy campaign'. Although the 1986 legislation did introduce more generous discounts, particularly for those living in flats, the thrust of the Act's housing provisions was to enable local councils to transfer their housing management functions to housing associations, housing trusts, building societies or other private sector bodies. Alternatively, councils were empowered to devolve management to tenant cooperatives. This approach to the council rented sector has been taken much further under the 1988 Housing Act.

The privatisation of local authority rented housing

Council housing has existed in Britain since the middle of the nineteenth century, although prior to the First World War the focus of local authority housing policy was on public health initiatives designed to improve conditions in the private sector slums (Burnett, 1978). It was not until just after the First World War that council housing developed on a national scale in response to a dislocation of the private market and severe shortages. It was accepted by government that local authorities should, as a short-term expedient, mount a large-scale subsidised house building programme to provide the 'Homes Fit for Heroes' (Orbach, 1977; Swenarton, 1981). As Clapham has noted, council housing first emerged for a mixture of pragmatic and ideological reasons (Clapham, 1989); it was as much a response to a political problem, with a shift of the balance of class forces towards the working class, as a housing problem (Malpass and Murie, 1987).

During the 1930s council housing took on a more residual role, with circumstances favouring the development of owner-occupation and the power of labour weakened by economic recession. The state undertook a more specific housebuilding programme, providing for those displaced by slum clearance (Merrett, 1979; Daunton (ed.) 1984). However, the Second

World War once more saw the disruption of the housing market and the subsequent need for a strategic response to housing problems, with local authorities once again the chosen agents. From 1945 until the mid-1950s local authorities led the way in the production of new housing, until the private sector once more asserted its dominance, and councils were again relegated to a secondary role. However, continuing housing shortages and the need for further redevelopment in the 1950s and 1960s meant that local authorities continued to develop at a significant rate, such that by 1971 29 per cent of households in England and Wales rented their homes from a local authority or New Town Development Corporation. Unfortunately, it was during this period that much of today's problematical council housing was built. Resources and prestige have been concentrated in the development of housing to meet output targets set by government. Much of the building was at high density, and often of high-rise and non-traditional construction (Dunleavy, 1981). This period of mass public housing provision threw up a range of physical and managerial problems, and dissatisfaction grew with the style of local authority management and development. Indeed, much of the explanation as to why council housing has been under attack from central government during the last ten years rests upon perceptions about the way it has been managed.

Whilst managing the housing stock constitutes a major service of district councils, with some local authorities being among the largest landlords in Western Europe, housing departments form only a part of the complex local authority structure. As a profession, housing management has been slow to evolve and, as noted above, has often played second fiddle to a range of other functions. Local authority housing management has often had a bad press, frequently being described as inefficient, bureaucratic and paternalistic (City University Housing Research Group, 1981). It is possible, at least in part, to rebut many of the criticisms (Association of Metropolitan Authorities, 1986) and studies have shown that council housing is managed at least as efficiently as other parts of the rented sector (Department of the Environment, 1989). However, in recent years, and partly as a matter of political ideology, the Conservative government has sought to introduce more diversity into the rented sector and onto council estates.

It was noted in the previous section that when first elected in 1979 Mrs Thatcher's government was committed to 'rolling back the frontiers of the state', and that a major element of this programme was the sale of council houses to their tenants. In more recent years the Conservative government have considered how the ownership of rented housing might be diversified. In March 1987 John Patten, then Minister of Housing, argued: 'at the start of the century a fundamentally wrong turn was taken which led to inefficient public and private rented sectors – we must give rented customers the same satisfaction as home buyers' (Patten, 1987). This theme was taken a stage further after the 1987 General Election by the new Housing Minister, William Waldegrave, who asked a number of fundamental questions about the role of council housing. He concluded:

It is an oddity confined largely to Britain amongst European countries that the state goes landlording on this scale. The next great push after the right to buy should be to

get rid of the state as a big landlord and bring housing back to the community. . . .
Meanwhile, the council can concentrate on their front line housing welfare role, buying
the housing services they need or subsidising those who need help, and undertaking the
wide range of regulatory, enforcement, planning and other tasks which are the essence
of the public sector. (Waldegrave, 1987)

Although the 1986 Housing and Planning Act enabled local authorities to
transfer their housing stock to other landlords, this has been taken much
further under the provisions of the 1988 Housing Act. The 1988 legislation
gives council tenants the right to transfer to other approved landlords if they
wish to do so, making it easier for local authorities to voluntarily transfer their
housing stock to other landlords and making provision for the establishment
of Housing Action Trusts (HATs) to take over the management of specific
housing estates. It is the government's clear objective to reduce the direct
role of local councils in the provision and management of rented housing
and increase the scale of activities of other agencies, including housing
associations, cooperatives and private landlords. Diversification of ownership
and management is seen as the solution to the perceived problems of council
housing.

In part, these further initiatives to privatise rented housing and further
residualise the council sector represent a continuation of central government's
attack on local authorities and the increasing centralisation of housing policy.
At the same time a shift in emphasis from simply encouraging wider home
ownership to extending choice in the rented sector recognises that the scope
to promote owner-occupation still further may be quite limited and that a
lack of opportunities in the rented sector may be contributing to problems of
increasing homelessness, a lack of labour mobility, and a degree of inflexibility
in the housing system.

It can also be argued that the 1988 Housing Act involves a recognition of the
failures of council housing, and not just by the Conservatives. The influential
Inquiry into British housing (1985) sponsored by the National Federation of
Housing Associations and chaired by the Duke of Edinburgh argued for a
more flexible tenure pattern, the creation of a strong social housing sector
made up of approved landlords, and the development of a new strategic
role for local authorities. The Audit Commission has highlighted the
management difficulties faced by local authorities and the wide variation
in housing management performance by individual district councils (Audit
Commission, 1986). The Institute of Housing, the leading professional body
in the housing management field in the United Kingdom in its 1987 report,
Preparing for Change, urged local authorities to cast 'a vastly more critical eye
over the performance of the housing services' which they provided (Institute of
Housing, 1987). Whilst not advocating immediate action, the Institute's report
also suggested local authorities might need to take the initiative in disposing of
some of their housing stock to alternative agencies. This was seen as preferable
to disposal imposed by government. Other commentators have also called for
the introduction of a range of tenures upon council estates, which would help
sharpen the performance of local authorities (Power, 1987).

There are clear arguments in favour of widening choice for households in
the council sector, but what is required is a rational system that ensures that

tenants have a real say in the ownership and management of their homes. The problem with the Conservative response encapsulated in the Housing Act 1988 is that it ignores many of the positive initiatives taken by local authorities in the housing field in recent years. Many local councils have decentralised housing management and repair services to the local level whilst others have played a pioneering role in promoting tenants' management cooperatives (Clapman, 1987). The work of the Priority Estates Projects (PEPs) has also secured significant improvements on some of the most unpopular council estates, as well as developing mechanisms which will enable tenants to have a much greater say in decision-making (Power, 1984). There is a case to be made that local authorities have already taken significant initiatives to improve the responsiveness of housing services and available opinion poll evidence shows council tenants to be reasonably satisfied with the service provided (Market and Opinion Research International, 1988; Department of the Environment, 1989).

Much of the debate around the issue of local authority stock transfer has focused upon the potential effects of introducing competition. Concerns have been expressed that local councils will be unable to meet their statutory responsibilities to the homeless and that the council sector will be further residualised with the most disadvantaged remaining as local authority tenants on the least popular estates. In addition the financial regime in which local authority housing operates (which is subject to substantial change under the provisions of the Local Government and Housing Act, 1989) may become more restrictive, further reducing investment in the maintenance of the stock and forcing up rents. This may increase the propensity of local authority tenants to transfer to alternative landlords. Further arguments have been put forward pointing out that transferring council housing out of public ownership undermines local democratic accountability.

What is clear is that local authority housing is under attack from central government. Yet at the time of writing there is little available evidence of the extent to which council tenants may wish to choose alternative landlords (Gallup, 1988). Nor is it clear who might succeed local authorities as the new landlords of council housing. Some local authorities have begun to assess their future role in housing provision, exploring local solutions to the perceived problems, such as transferring all or part of their stock to new or existing housing associations. Other local housing authorities are seeking to improve the efficiency and effectiveness of their housing service so as to compete under Tenants Choice. There remains a considerable degree of uncertainty as to the extent to which a new breed of private landlord might enter the rented market and take over the ownership and management of council estates.

At the time of writing the role of the local state in housing in Britain is very uncertain. It is the intention of central government to remove local authorities from their monopolistic position within the rented sector and to break up the ownership and management of council housing. There are a number of scenarios for change, and by the twenty-first century the involvement of the local state in housing may be very different from what it is today. What happens will depend not only upon central government policies but also the views of consumers, the response of local authorities (and their ability to show themselves as effective managers of rented housing) and the extent to which alternative landlords emerge to supplement or replace the role of local councils in the sphere of rented housing.

Housing associations and government housing policy

The success of the Conservative government's strategy to diversify the ownership and management of rented housing in Britain is, to a considerable extent, dependent upon the response of housing associations. Since the early 1960s successive governments, both Labour and Conservative, have sought to widen housing choice for the consumer through the promotion of the housing association movement. In part this has been a response to the continued decline of the private rented sector and partly to avoid a complete monopoly of rented accommodation by local authorities. Although still a minority tenure, housing associations have come to play an increasingly important role in helping to solve the problems of poor and inadequate housing, both through the provision of new housing and the rehabilitation of older dwellings. In parallel with the view that the direct state provision of housing is not necessarily the most appropriate response to housing problems has come a growing interest in the potential of the housing association movement, from whose nineteenth century pioneering activities council housing is seen to have originated. Clearly, support for the non-statutory sector is essential to facilitate the disengagement of the local state.

Since the mid-1970s, whilst the council housing sector has been in decline, the scale of housing association activity in the housing system has increased significantly. Yet this has only been possible due to the generous arrangements for subsidy to associations originally incorporated in the 1974 Housing Act and the fact that a greater share of public capital investment in housing has been channelled through housing associations than in the past, and this at the expense of investment through local authorities (Hills, 1987).

It would be naive not to recognise that part of the rationale for encouraging the growth of housing association provision lies in a dissatisfaction with the actions of some local authorities. At the same time one cannot ignore the fact that one of the attractions for central government of channelling investment through housing associations is that they present no democratically elected party political opposition to central government. This makes them a more malleable and directly controllable vehicle for implementing state policies (Murie, 1985).

Since 1974 central government has created a financial climate conducive to the development of housing association provision, but only by offering a particularly generous level of grant support. The increasing reliance of housing associations on central government funding has made the voluntary housing movement politically very vulnerable, and has allowed central government to implement more effectively their own housing policies without having to rely exclusively on local authorities (Karn, 1985). It is therefore somewhat paradoxical that at a time when the government is seeking to remove local authorities from the provision of additional general family housing it has also introduced a new and yet less generous financial regime in which housing associations must operate. The shift towards mixed public–private funded housing association schemes (with lower levels of average capital grant) may deter some associations from developing additional housing to rent, because of either the need to charge higher rents (perhaps beyond the reach of their traditional consumers) or the increased financial risks to be carried by the association. Central government may become reliant upon fewer associations than in the past to continue to provide new opportunities in the rented sector.

Despite the significant growth in housing association activity since 1974, the sector still accounts for only about 3 per cent of the total housing stock. However, if the government's policy of Tenants' Choice is to be implemented effectively then housing associations (either new or existing) seem the most likely new landlords. This is particularly so given that the Housing Corporation (Scottish Homes in Scotland and Tai Cymru in Wales), which is responsible for supervising and funding housing associations, is also responsible for the approval of new landlords under Tenants' Choice provisions of the 1988 Housing Act. However, the majority of existing housing associations are small-scale and often community-based, and the extent to which they would be willing and able to accept the management of transferred stock is a matter for question. There appears little chance of a large-scale takeover of local authority housing by existing housing associations. As the Director of their representative body, the National Federation of Housing Associations, has remarked, 'that would be like a flea swallowing a cat'. At the same time, most associations are likely to proceed cautiously, if at all, in this direction in order to retain their local management style and traditional customers, as well as the goodwill of local councils.

The potential is perhaps greater under the 1988 legislation for council housing to be transferred to new local authority housing associations: unitary housing organisations to be established by district authorities independent of the local council. A number of local authorities have considered strategies along these lines as an essentially defensive measure against the perceived threat of Tenants' Choice. At the same time, this notion offers potential financial and housing management benefits. It is, as yet, impossible to quantify the likely extent of voluntary transfer of council stock to local authority housing associations, but a number of district authorities have shown interest in this option, particularly where they fear the loss of a valuable asset to predatory private landlords.

The state and private landlordism

In seeking to revitalise the rented sector the government is also looking to an increased provision of rented housing by private landlords. The private rented sector in Britain has been in decline since 1915 (Whitehead and

Kleinman, 1986). The reasons for this decline are complex but include rent control and regulation under the Rent Acts as well as the relative financial advantages associated with the other major tenures, resulting from specific government policies. Private renting now accounts for only about 8 per cent of the United Kingdom housing stock, and only about a fifth of all rented housing.

However, as part of the Conservatives' restructuring of the rented sector under the 1988 Housing Act new lettings have been deregulated (taken out of rent control), so that private landlords can let at market rents, and tenants' security of tenure diminished. In themselves, it seems unlikely that such reforms will reverse the long-term continued decline in private landlordism, but these legislative changes have also been accompanied by government subsidies to encourage investment in the private rented sector. In particular, in the 1988 budget the Business Expansion Scheme (BES) was extended to allow companies providing housing to rent to benefit from tax relief on their investments. The BES scheme has stimulated interest in new investment in the sector, but it is questionable whether the initiative will prove successful in the long term in stimulating and retaining investment in the private rented sector of the housing market.

Finally, the provisions of the 1988 Housing Act do allow 'approved' private landlords to take over the ownership and management of council housing, if the tenants so wish. However, as with housing associations, it is too early to predict their likely involvement. Although some new companies have been established, most notably Quality Street, their future role in providing and managing housing is unclear.

Conclusions

This chapter has shown that during the last decade central government housing policy has been concerned with the restructuring of housing tenure, the extension of privatisation (and thus the residualisation of council housing), and increasing central control (with concomitant diminished local accountability). During the late 1970s and early 1980s the focus of central government housing policy was the promotion of home ownership, widening access to this tenure for those on the margins of owner-occupation. Between 1976 and 1986 the level of home ownership in Britain rose by 10 per cent. The Housing Act 1980 has been instrumental in the extension of home ownership, most controversially through the introduction of the Right to Buy which, whilst providing opportunities for purchase for some, placed severe constraints on local authorities, diminishing their own autonomy.

The corollary of this growth in owner-occupation has been a contraction in the scale of the rented stock, and in particular the number of dwellings rented from local authorities. The response of central government has been to seek to extend privatisation to the rented sector by encouraging a renaissance of private landlordism, the continued expansion of housing association activity, and demunicipalisation. The shift in strategy was first made explicit with the introduction of the Housing and Planning Act 1986, but it is with the 1988 Housing Act that the government's objectives towards the rented sector have become manifest.

The intention of the 1988 legislation is to recreate an essentially private rented sector, with a key role for housing associations but a diminished one for local authorities. The arguments put forward by the proponents of demunicipalisation are the need to introduce competition into the rented sector (and break the often monopolistic position of local councils), the increased opportunities for consumer choice, the ability of diverse, often small-scale landlords to represent their tenants more effectively and the opportunity to exclude party politics from the management of housing. Defenders of public housing would argue that it is only local party political control over housing which will be diminished, and that the provisions contained in the 1988 Housing Act represent not only a further attack on local government but also an extension of centralised control over housing policy at the local level.

Housing policy during the 1980s has undergone considerable reform. The future role of local authorities is uncertain, and in the longer term there may be significant changes in the way in which council-provided housing is owned, financed and managed. Government policy towards housing has been set in the context of widening choice for the consumer, in providing more effective and responsive local services, in emphasising the role of local authorities as strategic enablers rather than providers and managers and in replacing council housing authorities with a multiplicity of alternative model landlords, including housing associations, trusts, tenant cooperatives, private landlords and building societies. Current trends in housing policy reflect the Conservative philosophy of reducing state dependency and encouraging a more competitive, market-oriented individualistic approach to housing provision and management. However, they also represent a loss of local control over policy, and it remains to be seen to what extent the radical proposals enacted in the late 1980s will solve underlying structural problems within the housing system.

Guide to further reading

The literature on British housing has grown considerably in recent years and is likely to continue to expand in relation to both contemporary issues and the changing nature of policy and the housing system. Given the pace of change in both policy and practice, readers are advised to refer to key journals such as *Housing Studies, Housing Review, Roof, Inside Housing, Voluntary Housing, Policy and Politics, Urban Studies, Housing Associations Weekly* and *Journal of Social Policy*. And the following selected references: Paul Balchin

(1989), *Housing policy: an introduction*, (London: Routledge, 2nd edn); Martin Daunton (1987), *A property owning democracy?* (London: Faber and Faber); Peter Malpass (ed.) (1986), *The housing crisis* (London: Croom Helm); Anne Power (1987), *Property before people* (London: Allen and Unwin); David Clapham (1989); David Clapham and John English (eds) (1987); Ray Forest and Alan Murie (1988); and Peter Malpass and Alan Murie (1987).

9 The state and education

Roger Duclaud-Williams

Introduction

Britain and France are often pictured as polar opposites in terms of widely diffused attitudes towards the state. Dyson and Birnbaum in particular have provided us with analyses in which the French state dominates society whilst the British state, if there is one, is dominated by society (Dyson, 1980; Birnbaum, 1982; Birnbaum and Badie, 1983; Birnbaum, 1980; Birnbaum, 1988). These contrasts can be made in terms of elite and popular culture and by reference to institutional arrangements. It will be possible to examine whether the existence of a state tradition in the French case and its absence in the British case is reflected in the state's role in education.

This intellectual problem is a real one because even the briefest survey of the history of education in these two nations shows a very striking contrast between the early emergence of state responsibilities in France and their much later and more hesitant appearance in Britain. Although in both cases compulsory free education was an achievement of the last decades of the nineteenth century, the French state had been active in certain educational questions much earlier. Gallican pressure forced the Jesuits out of France in the 1760s, thus preventing them from carrying on the educational work to which they were traditionally devoted. Napoleon's establishment of a network of *lycées* in the first decade of the nineteenth century was intended to provide the emperor with a politically loyal and technically competent cadre for his bureaucracy and army (Prost, 1968). In the Guizot law of 1833, the administrative arrangements were established which were to make possible a nationwide network of elementary schools for boys. At almost the same time the British Parliament was reluctantly voting its first small contribution to assist the religious bodies in the provision of elementary education, and state responsibility for the secondary sector was only fully assumed with the Education Act of 1902, almost a century after Napoleon's initiative in precisely the same area (Bishop, 1971).

The question, therefore, naturally arises, how far do these undeniably clear historical contrasts have any relevance for the state intervention in the provision of education in the 1980s? How far can such divergent legacies retain their distinctive national character when both nations, faced by important economic problems, are scrutinising educational provision with a view to maximising its contribution towards the resolution of economic difficulties? We shall argue here that these distinctive national traditions do retain considerable importance but that they do not have quite the impact on the process of policy-making which one would naturally anticipate. In particular, it will be argued later that it is the British, not the French, state which retains the greatest degree of autonomy in the elaboration of its objectives and the greatest capacity to overcome political resistance – but more of this paradox later.

This chapter is organised into three sections. In the first section we postpone the consideration of nationally distinctive policies and institutions in order to consider the more general question of how changing economic, social and political circumstances in advanced industrial society are affecting the role of the state in the provision of education. In this section the argument is pitched at the general level of educational provision in the contemporary West. The aim is to provide a background against which more specific nationally distinctive arrangements can be considered in the subsequent sections. In this section we ask whether the contemporary state is extending the range of its educational responsibilities. We conclude, in the face of much academic argument to the contrary, that there is no evidence to support the proposition that the role of the state is expanding and likely to continue to expand.

The second section is concerned with the key question of the extent of state responsibility and examines the position of the boundary between the state and private educational provision and the character of the relations between public and private provision in Britain and France. Clearly any examination of the state in action must try to describe in some detail what the state does and what it does not do. We shall argue here that the significance and meaning of the private – public distinction varies crucially between levels of educational provision and between nations. No single model of typical relationships between private and public provision can be identified therefore, even within these educational systems. We also conclude that, despite the reputation of the French state, private forms of educational provision in higher education compete with public universities and offer an alternative which is more attractive to many politicians and students. This alternative privately sponsored model of selective and vocationally-oriented higher education is all the more significant because its existence and appeal constitute a strong implied criticism of the publicly financed universities.

In the third section of the chapter we shall consider the question of interest groups and their impact on policy. The aim in this section will be to discover whether the corporatist trends which have been detected in the state's relationship to the economy, and by some students in state welfare provision, manifest themselves in education and, if they do not, then to decide exactly what kind of pluralism emerges in British and French educational policy-making (Cawson, 1982; Harrison (ed.) 1984). We are concerned in this section with one of the key dimensions of any study of the state, namely autonomy. We shall argue here that it is the British state which possesses a greater capacity to act autonomously and a greater ability to overcome political resistance.

The state and educational provision

The second and third sections of this chapter are focused on state boundaries and state autonomy respectively. They examine a series of arguments about national distinctiveness. It is necessary to set the discussion of the differences between two national systems within a wider context. It is therefore the purpose of this section to ask whether it is possible to identify any general trends, in advanced industrial societies, which are enlarging or diminishing the role of the state as educational policy-maker.

There are a number of reasons for taking very seriously the view that the role of the state as educational provider has been expanding in the 1970s and 1980s and will continue to do so. Since the first oil shock European governments have been wrestling with what we have come to call 'the economic crisis'. This has meant, in education, a preoccupation with minimising public expenditure and increasing returns to the economy in the form of a more skilled and more adaptable workforce and attitudes judged as more sympathetic to the employer's point of view and more conscious of the need to create wealth.

There is a paradox in this argument which needs to be resolved. It is widely agreed that the 1970s and 1980s have seen the ideas of the New Right and of a variety of anti-Keynesian economists growing in influence. How, it may be asked, can the economic crisis of the 1970s and 1980s be held responsible, at one and the same time, for encouraging the growth of conservative ideas and helping to enlarge the state's role as educational policy-maker?

The paradox can be resolved in either of two ways. Policy-makers have sometimes reasoned that, if the market can be relied upon in the long term to promote the attitudes and produce the skills which it requires, this cannot be the case in the short term. Initially, given the power of vested academic interests and the regrettable apathy of business in educational matters, the state is the only actor with enough power to re-orient the educational system in a more productivist direction. The state must therefore intervene in order to correct the undesirable consequences of its own earlier interventions.

A second view is more sceptical about the impact of market forces on a public system of education even in the long term. On this argument education has too many public goods characteristics for an efficient level of provision to arise without substantial state intervention of a permanent character. Those who adopt this line of argument emphasise the tendency of employers to poach rather than train, and the difficulty for employers in reconciling the short-term need to cut costs and the longer-term need to invest in training.

We may conclude therefore that the economic difficulties of the 1970s and 1980s have increased the appeal of neo-liberal and conservative ideas but have provoked European states into a more activist and interventionist attitude towards education. High levels of unemployment among young people have also frequently led to an extension of public provision, although in this case the motives for government intervention are normally more social and political than economic. If this line of argument can be sustained, then it provides the essential context within which we should consider our British and French cases. The next step in the argument therefore involves explaining why this attractive general proposition does not provide the key to understanding the changing role of the state in relation to education. The argument to be developed here is not that economic change has not provoked more state intervention but rather that this tendency coexists with many others, some of which are working to produce opposite results. A variety of forces are at work here, some expanding and some reducing the role of the state, and there is no evidence requiring us to prefer expansion to reduction, or vice versa, as the most likely outcome. If liberal economic ideas are propelling the state towards more interventionism, what are the influences tending in the opposite direction, which may, in some political systems, be more influential?

The arguments to be considered are of two sorts – pedagogic and bureaucratic. Both are well illustrated by the French case. Recent French governments of both Left and Right have tried gradually to move away from traditional relationships between teacher and pupil, school and parent, and school and administration.

In 1977 the decision to operate the first four years of French secondary education on essentially comprehensive lines began to be implemented. The pedagogic problems thrown up by this entirely new situation were considerable. The official reaction to these difficulties was contained in the Legrand report of 1982 (Le grand, 1982). Most of the recommendations contained in this report were adopted by the then Minister, Alain Savary.

The authors of the report argued that secondary education had to adapt itself to a new situation in which its clientele was socially and intellectually much more heterogeneous. This necessarily meant allowing the schools more freedom to adapt to their social milieu. The report also argued that teachers should progressively develop new forms of relationship with one another and their pupils. Teachers were to be encouraged to abandon a view of themselves as conduits for a particular body of knowledge defined in disciplinary terms. Their relationship with pupils was to have a pastoral as well as a strictly instructional dimension, and collaboration between teachers was to become more important. We should note that, although a change of minister in 1984 produced a shift in pronouncements and policy away from the progressive towards more traditional and conventional definitions of the role of the school and teacher, the new Minister continued to endorse the Legrand report, although less enthusiastically than his predecessor, and the same is true of his successors since 1986.

The shift from schools as identical units in a larger bureaucratic whole towards schools as communities enjoying substantial autonomy, and the associated shift from a narrow to a broader teaching role, are supported by certain long-term social trends and do not seem to be too dependent on the swing of the French political pendulum. In a recent definitive account of French educational change in the twentieth century Prost has emphasized the influence on educational practice of changing relationships between parents and children within the family. He refers particularly to the shift from children as objects of ambition and control to children seen as objects of parental love (Prost, 1968).

There is a second category of argument which is bureaucratic. Many French observers have been only too conscious of the problems associated with hierarchy and bureaucracy in education. 1984 saw massive demonstrations in France fuelled by parental fear about over-dependence on and powerlessness in relation to the educational bureaucracy. The increasing importance of research in higher education and the increased attention now being paid in many countries to more flexible, less conventional forms of education, directed primarily at adults, are both developments which are strongly anti-bureaucratic in their implications. Both suggest the limited usefulness of centrally-conceived and state-dominated plans for educational provision. One of the important themes developed in much writing on the 'crisis of the welfare state' is the disfunctional character of bureaucracies for many educational and welfare purposes.

All observers of recent British educational developments are rightly convinced that centralisation in education has been on the increase since at least 1976. It is equally evident that a trend in quite the opposite direction can be observed in France. Although in both countries differences of emphasis and approach exist between parties of the Left and Right, it nevertheless seems fair to argue that these tendencies, in both countries, have operated and are likely to continue to operate irrespective of short-term political fluctuations. In Britain the process of expanding central government's role began with Callaghan's Labour government of the 1970s but has been much accelerated since the Conservatives came to power in 1979. In France, the Right under Giscard D'Estaing was committed to gradual decentralisation in the years between 1974 and 1981, but it was the socialist Left between 1981 and 1986 which was able to implement these reforms. At present, in France, it is spokesmen for the liberal Right who are urging a more cautious socialist Minister of Education to proceed more rapidly towards decentralisation and thereby necessarily to a degree of state disengagement.

The argument of this section has been that, although all European states have had to face a similar external economic challenge, this has not produced similar responses. It might seem, a priori, that an economic challenge of this sort would lead to an extension of the state's role in education. In practice, nationally distinctive values and institutions, in the French case a reaction against bureaucracy and statism, are sufficiently important to override and cancel out the centralising and statist implications of economic difficulties.

Private and public provision

In considering the relations between private and public provision of education in Britain and France, it is necessary to treat separately three distinct areas of educational provision. We shall consider first mainstream primary and secondary provision, secondly higher education and finally the rapidly growing area of industrial training and youth training.

Mainstream provision

The bulk of private provision in this sector takes a quite different form in France from England. Approximately 15 per cent of French pupils between the ages of 6 and 18 are educated in institutions which are commonly described as private. More than 95 per cent of these institutions are Catholic. However, to describe them as Catholic and private conceals more than it tells. Whereas in the early decades of this century most teachers in these schools would have been convinced Catholics and many would have belonged to teaching orders, today the rapid decline in the practice of catholicism in France makes it quite impossible for Catholic schools to recruit staff of this sort. Surveys of the attitudes of parents sending their children to these schools show that most of them do not attach great importance to the provision of a specifically Catholic education and have chosen a Catholic school because of the stricter discipline, the absence of children from ethnic minorities, or simply because their children have, through exam failures, been excluded from state provision (Ballion, 1982).

Although these schools retain the right to charge parents, and a minority of institutions do have substantial fees, they receive public funding on a pro rata basis with the public sector. They are also required to teach the nationally determined curriculum and enter their pupils for nationally set examinations in exactly the same way as schools within the state sector. Whilst therefore these schools have a private status in law, it would be more accurate to speak generally of the contractual sector. The use of this term is intended to indicate that, in exchange for public funding, these institutions have agreed to provide a form of education which in most important respects does not differ from that provided within the public sector. The contrast between the position of the contractual sector in France and that of the preparatory school and public school sector in England is too evident to require any further emphasis.

If we were, ignorant of history, to seek to explain the emergence and continuation of a private or contractual sphere of educational provision, we would surely expect to find that the private sector was offering either a very different or a very superior product to parents. The French case confirms these expectations but in rather an unexpected fashion. Given the importance of state subsidy to the contractual sector, many schools are willing to make only nominal charges and therefore the real cost of choosing a Catholic rather than a state school is slight. Under these circumstances it is clearly not necessary for these schools to be markedly different to be nevertheless in a position to attract sufficient pupils. Their position in the educational market does not seem to be either contracting or expanding markedly.

The same logic applies in the English case. The cost to parents is much greater and so too is the distinctiveness of the educational product purchased. An interesting parallel nevertheless exists between the two cases. In both it would appear that the degree of educational distinctiveness has been in decline in recent decades. Demands from public school parents for academic success above all have forced the market-conscious public schools into a position where they are more and more seeking to offer a superior version of the same rather than something distinctive (Salter and Tapper, 1985; Walford, 1984). The loss of distinctiveness in the French case is due in part, as already noted, to long-term dechristianisation but is also attributable to a decision on the part of the Catholic hierarchy to prefer survival to distinctiveness. In pursuit of this policy, state subsidies have been accepted and genuine independence sacrificed. In both cases therefore the extent to which private provision is in a position to stimulate innovation through competition with the public sector is in decline.

It remains, before leaving mainstream provision, to note one rather nice paradox. Whereas in England private provision is somewhat more distinctive and certainly distinctive as to the social composition of the families served, the political salience of the issue raised by such provision is rather low. This at least is a conclusion suggested by the policies of the Wilson and Callaghan Labour governments. By contrast, in France, where the provision in the contractual sector is educationally much less distinct, the political salience of the issues raised by such provision can hardly be underestimated. We can establish this point by referring briefly to the events of 1983-4. In this period, in pursuance of an electoral undertaking given by François Mitterrand in his campaign for the presidential election of 1981, the socialist government was seeking to negotiate a closer relationship between the state and contractual sectors of education. Since, as already noted, the integration of the Catholic into the state system was already far advanced, it is difficult to see why quite so much importance was attached to minor administrative changes designed to move a little further in the same direction. Nevertheless, a great deal of emotion was poured into a campaign, led by the Church and supported by Catholic parents, in defence of the contractual sector whose very existence was said to be threatened. Culminating in massive demonstrations in which more than a million parents were involved, this campaign succeeded in forcing the President to disavow his own Minister of Education, who subsequently resigned, and to withdraw the Bill. It would seem that, in England, where private provision does retain at least some degree of genuine independence and is therefore in a position to offer a genuine choice to the limited number of parents able to take advantage of it, the existence of private provision has not so far created any very serious problems for the governments of either the Right or the Left. In France, however, where the educational significance of the contractual sector is much less, the political importance of the relationship between public and private provision is much greater.

Resolving this paradox is relatively straightforward. The conflict in France is more symbolic than educational. The teachers' unions, who overwhelmingly dominate the left-wing pro-integration coalition, present themselves as defenders of liberal values which are not truly menaced by contemporary French catholicism. The Catholic Church, and its parent allies, defend passionately a faith which is not in danger, and educational autonomy, most of which they have already given up. It must also be conceded that the teachers' unions in the public sector have a material interest in integration because of the recruitment possibilities which it might offer. The core of the explanation of this much ado about nothing therefore lies in the 1981 socialist electoral success, the power of teachers and their unions within the socialist party, and the mixture of corporate interest and ideological hostility to 'private' provision within the teachers' unions (Duclaud-Williams, 1985). In the English case the educational and political issues are real enough but a Labour government would need to feel itself in a very strong position before it would risk challenging the right of parents to spend their earnings as they see fit. The weakness of the Left's position here, and therefore the explanation of low saliency and inaction, lies in a popular mental map of society which is extremely individualistic – individualistic, that is, in the sense that it lays all the emphasis on the benefits of education to the individual and ignores the significance for the community of different forms of educational provision. Individual benefits are more direct, more tangible, and therefore more perceptible, than social costs.

Higher education

Let us begin by examining the arrangements for the provision for higher education in France, which are notably more complicated than those in Britain. Most observers are struck first by the very clear distinction between the prestigious Grandes Ecoles, with their highly selective recruitment policies, and the much less prestigious universities open to anyone with a *baccalauréat* pass (Suleiman, 1977). If one's aim is to provide a summary description of the social and educational function of institutions, then the above distinction is crucial. But, if one is interested in examining the role of the state, one has to deal immediately with the problem raised by the fact that the above distinction comes nowhere near matching a distinction between public and private forms of provision. Some of the Grandes Ecoles are privately financed and charge fees, whereas others, generally the most prestigious of all, are public institutions and do not. In the former category come a great number of institutions of higher education in the business education and engineering spheres and in the latter, at the pinnacle of the system, we find institutions such as the National School of Administration, the Ecole Polytechnique, and the Ecoles Normales Supérieures. The sector of the Grandes Ecoles is therefore given a certain homogeneity by the tendency of these institutions to serve a socially privileged clientele by their highly selective recruitment policies, by the considerable degree of autonomy which they enjoy, and by their tendency to avoid the use of permanent staff and to rely as far as possible for teaching on outsiders from the public and private sector employed on a part-time basis. It would seem that these characteristics, which bind the sector of the Grandes Ecoles together and give it a certain distinctive character, are more important than any characteristics associated with the distinction between the public and private sector. It is true that the three public institutions mentioned above lead the majority of their students into careers which begin in some form of public service, whereas the private, engineering and business schools do not. This difference, however, appears relatively minor when compared with the similarities mentioned above. The essential homogeneity of the sector and the consequent irrelevance of the public private distinction is further underlined when one remembers that many of those who begin their careers in the public service complete them in either the private or the semi-public sectors (Suleiman, 1974; Rémond et al., 1982).

If we shift our attention to a lower point on the higher educational pyramid, it still seems difficult, in the French case, to attach any great significance to the private–public distinction. One might begin at this level by distinguishing between the universities as public institutions on the one hand, with their relatively unselective recruitment and nominal fees, and a range of private establishments charging substantial fees and enjoying a real degree of educational autonomy. If such a distinction could be maintained as an accurate description of provision at this level, it would correspond to a rather neat distinction between the responsiveness of the state to democratic pressures for maximum provision at public expense and the responsiveness of the market to those in a position to pay. Such a neat distinction collapses, however, once we take into consideration the University Institutes of Technology which, although administratively part of the public university system, select their students carefully and acknowledge openly the emphasis on the vocational which is otherwise much more typical of private institutions. Whether we distinguish between elite and non-elite institutions, or between the vocational and the liberal, or between the possession of some institutional autonomy or the absence of such autonomy, we fail to find a distinction which fits the private–public divide and we are obliged to conclude that the private–public distinction is irrelevant for anyone seeking to provide an accurate description of what is really going on in French higher education.

Precisely the same conclusion is suggested by an examination of British provision. In the past it has been possible to distinguish between the less-favoured and more tightly controlled public sector, consisting of polytechnics, colleges of education and colleges of higher education, and the publicly funded, but legally private, university sector. Today such a public–private distinction seems much less relevant than it once was. The government and UGC now discriminate more openly between institutions and subjects (Carswell, 1986). This diminishes considerably the distinctiveness of the university sector. When British provision is contrasted with French, one is immediately struck by the much greater homogeneity of institutional arrangements in the British provision despite the public–private distinction referred to above. British students and their parents do not pay fees. Institutions within both sectors are rather undogmatic in their attitude towards the vocational liberal distinction, possessing departments awarding qualifications of both sorts. Recruitment is selective and competitive on both sides of the private–public boundary. One could distinguish on a number of grounds between Oxford and Cambridge and other institutions of higher education. They are clearly much more closely associated with the political elite, enjoy considerably more autonomy than other institutions, and possess wealth and a capacity to raise funds in the private sector which other institutions of higher education cannot rival. Again, the distinction between the private and the public does not seem particularly important because of the similarities of operation on both sides of the boundary line, and where a significant boundary can be drawn dividing Oxford and Cambridge from other institutions of higher education, it is a boundary within the private sector rather than one at its edge.

Industrial and youth training

In this area of educational provision some quite remarkable parallels emerge between British and French forms of state involvement (Brown and Ashton (eds), 1987; Cohen and McRobbie (eds) 1987; Dubar, 1980; Vaudiaux, 1974). In both cases we find an area of rapid expansion with a steadily increasing level of public financial support but accompanied by a pronounced tendency to devolve to employers' decisions about organisation and content of training courses. We see in this sector a variety of emerging forms of collaboration between private and public actors. We can undoubtedly identify here a system of public policy-making which leaves much freedom for both formulation and implementation in private hands.

How can we explain the emergence of a pattern of public–private interaction and policy-making which is so unlike that observed in other sectors of educational provision, where the role accorded private actors is much more limited? A number of complementary explanations suggest themselves and seem to apply with equal force to both the French and British cases. First, and this applies more to the youth than to the industrial side of the training sector, the waning of optimism about educational progress had led by the 1970s to a conviction that policy could not simply continue raising the school-leaving age and in this way making more of the same available to new age-groups and social groups. A belief in the benefits to the community from education and a particular urgency behind its extension in a period of youth unemployment continued to encourage increased public spending but many were convinced that the school, as conventionally conceived, was not the institution through which this education could most appropriately be provided. Hence the increased interest in education outside the school and the need to involve employers.

Policy-makers in the 1970s were also convinced that the new education ought to be primarily vocational. Once the task to be performed had been defined in this way, an obvious justification for a much increased role for employers was created. Finally, it should not be forgotten that of all the sectors of educational provision so far discussed, this is far and away the most recent in origin. The fundamental French law in this area dates from 16 July 1971 and the major British administrative actor in the field, the Manpower Services Commission, came into existence just three years later. Expanding rapidly during the 1970s under conditions of severe economic difficulty, practice in this sector was bound to be influenced by what we may briefly describe as the new realism, or, alternatively, the new liberalism. A belief in the unavoidable malfunctions of bureaucracy and the advantages of new private or semi-public forms of public service provision was more explicitly developed in France. The development of policy in this area in France has been particularly influenced by centrist political ideas associated with figures such as Jacques Delors and, more recently, J.P. Soisson (Soisson et al., 1986). Although the Thatcher government's important initiatives in this area have sometimes been advertised as *laissez-faire*, in fact we are dealing here not with privately provided profit-driven activities but with an area in which public and private money and public and private responsibilities come together.

In this section frequent use has been made of the terms private and public. The ambiguity of these terms hardly needs stressing. In using them we may wish to refer either to the legal status of an institution, or to the sources of its finance, or to whether administratively it forms part of a hierarchy which in theory is capped by government. Whatever formulation of the private–public distinction we choose, no clear national or sectoral pattern emerges. The most important contribution of institutions genuinely autonomous of the state to educational provision seems to lie, in France, at the level of higher education and, in Britain, through the public and preparatory schools, in primary and secondary provision. Whilst the French state has used powerful financial and legal instruments to make a great deal of progress towards the integration of the formerly private, but now contractual, Catholic school sector, it has acted in a much more restrained fashion with respect to private institutions of higher education. It would be quite wrong to conclude, for example, as one recent student of this topic has done, that the role of the state in France is much greater or more fully developed than is the case in Britain (Smith, 1983). Public finance and control are obviously the dominant forms of provision in both cases. If we asked how such a disorderly and difficult-to-comprehend pattern of provision has arisen, the answer seems to lie in the rather unpredictable operation of two quite contradictory and opposite trends. On the one hand we find institutions which once enjoyed considerable distinctiveness and autonomy and were private in many senses of that word, but which have progressively become more integrated into a system of educational provision which is state directed and predominantly public. This is the case of the Catholic schools in France and the British universities. Working in quite the opposite direction, we have institutions which were created by state legislative action and which, whilst retaining their public, financial and legal status have, for a variety of political reasons, slipped through the state's fingers. We have here the quite different cases of the French universities, whose student recruitment policy is so obviously only grudgingly accepted by governments of the Left and Right, and the public Grandes Ecoles, which often with the assistance of a sponsoring department other than the Ministry of Education, defy the imposition of any coherent state policy in the realm of higher education (Schinn, 1980; Vincent, 1987). With this two-way movement both towards and away from effective state control constantly in operation in both countries, it is not surprising that a rather complex relationship between public and private spheres emerges.

State autonomy and organised interests

When considering the relationship between the state and interests organised and unorganised, one is immediately struck by a certain similarity in the trend of recent developments in Britain and France. In both cases the shift has been, in the post-war period, towards the involvement of a larger number of interests, towards greater involvement of non-educational actors in educational policy-making, and consequently towards a rather greater politicisation of the decision-making process. With respect to the last of these trends, the change has been less marked in France because, even in the relatively closed world of educational politics of the 1940s and 1950s, educational issues were frequently matters of public and political controversy.

Evidence of these emerging trends in Britain and France is not difficult to find. French student politics first began to impinge on the national scene in the early 1960s when students were involved in anti-torture campaigns and in support of the nationalist cause in Algeria (De Maupeou-Abboud, 1974). In the wake of the events of 1968, French trade unions reached an important collective agreement in 1970 which provided the framework for legislation on vocational training and adult education in the following year. The general trade unions had never previously entered the educational policy arena. In Britain these trends were first evident in the emergence of a movement for the reorganisation of secondary education along comprehensive lines and in the opposition which this movement excited (Kogan, 1971; Ranson and Tomlinson (eds), 1986). The political parties, groups of locally organised parents and threatened grammar schools were the major actors in this field, but, as controversy over the comprehensive question tended to die down in the 1970s, tension grew between those who wished to defend the traditional liberal conception of education and those who, in the cause of modernisation, were intent on shifting educational provision substantially in a vocational direction. Associated with this last trend was the emergence of substantial conflict between teachers and their organisations on the one hand – as advocates of a broader and more varied curriculum – and politicians, civil servants and some within the inspectorate, who were sceptical about the value of many of these teacher-promoted curriculum innovations and were interested in promoting the idea of a national core curriculum (Lawton, 1980). Some of these developments in the character of the educational policy-making arena had their origins outside education. The promotion of the vocational was clearly related to economic difficulties and the intensification of international competition, but other forces, tending to produce similar results, were located within the educational system.

At this point in the argument one might be tempted to conclude that the entry of new groups into the field, the opening up of a previously relatively closed sub-government of education to external influences, and a general increase in politicisation, would sharply reduce the degree of genuine autonomy of the state as educational policy-maker. We shall argue that quite the opposite is the case. The best way of making this general point may be through making use of a particular example. The twentieth-century state is an economic as well as an educational actor. Most educational institutions derive the bulk of their incomes from public sources. We have here, therefore, a structurally determined conflict, which can be more or less intense, between the state which is conscious of the need to facilitate the creation of wealth, and the world of education which, insulated from the market to a great degree, is less conscious of this need. When British and French governments in the first half of the twentieth century tried to promote technical education because they believed it could make some contribution to more rapid economic growth, they were generally confronted by a hostile or indifferent range of educational interests. The 1944 Education Act was intended to create a tripartite system of secondary education but the third technical leg simply failed to materialise (Albu, 1980).

The opening up of the educational debate, and particularly the entry of employers, parents and trade unions into the arena, has considerably strengthened the state's hand. It is doubtful whether the substantial shift in a more vocational direction in recent years in Britain and France could have been achieved without this political support. A particular example has been used by way of illustration, but the argument is, in fact, general. Increased pluralism gives the state a greater choice when choosing its allies. It also implies an increase in the range of respectably advocated views and, in this way, also provides the state with greater freedom for manoeuvre.

So far we have concentrated on similarities in the direction of developments in our two cases. A closer examination reveals some important and interesting differences. The formal organisational arrangements of French educational provision have always been more centralised than those of England and Wales. These formal arrangements have not always produced the results intended by their creators, but they did reduce the range of interests with which the state had to deal. Therefore, whereas British governments in the 1940s and 1950s consulted and negotiated with teachers' organisations and organisations of local authorities, the latter were entirely absent from the French educational debate. If we are to pursue the logic of the argument developed so far, namely that increased pluralism also increases the effective autonomy of the state, we must conclude that the French state was weakened by this absence of pluralism. This was indeed the case. The French teaching unions grouped together in the FEN, with close links within the Ministry of Education and in the parliamentary parties of the Left and Centre, exercised much more influence than English teachers have ever been able to. There are a number of factors, the impact of which we would need to examine in order to understand fully why the French state was more vulnerable to teacher influence than the English state, but part of the explanation undoubtedly lies in the two-sided rather than three-sided character of many educational debates in France in the immediate post-war period. In the 1950s teacher opposition was sufficient to bring to nothing a number of government reform initiatives designed to reorganise the early years of secondary education in order to increase equality of opportunity (Aubert et al., 1985; Hamon and Rotman, 1984).

Undoubtedly the capacity of the French state to overcome resistance was increased by the constitutional changes of 1958 and the emergence in 1962, for the first time in France, of a stable majority in Parliament. But it is my contention that, despite these much discussed constitutional and political developments, and despite the increasing pluralism of the world of French education, both of which have tended to improve the position of a once parlous state, today French governments still enjoy substantially less real autonomy than their counterparts on the other side of the Channel.

Before trying to explain how it is that a political system which possesses a genuine state tradition possesses also a less powerful and less autonomous state than we do in England, with our absence of a state tradition, it would be well to devote some space to substantiating the contrast to which attention has been drawn. The argument can first be made by citing examples of contested policy initiatives which have been implemented in Britain but effectively obstructed in France. Most recently, we have seen the French government's capitulation to student protest and its abandonment of proposals which made only a very slight movement in the direction of allowing universities to operate a more selective student recruitment policy (Boumard, Hess and Lapassade, 1987). We may contrast this with the Conservative government's Education Reform Act of 1988. Here was a piece of legislation universally condemned by the educational world and the world of local government and, more significantly, by many within the Tory party, which nevertheless passed into law virtually unamended. As evidence of the ability of British governments to overcome opposition, we may also point to the way in which educational provision for 16 to 18-year-olds, organised by the MSC, has expanded rapidly despite opposition from teachers, local authorities, and probably from within the Department of Education and Science. On the French side we may also cite the failure of the socialist government to carry its proposals for integrating the Catholic schools more fully into the public system. Church and parental opposition in this case forced the President to withdraw a bill to which he and his party were strongly committed. But these examples of successes and failures are only suggestive. British and French governments do not encounter the same problems or the same intensity of political opposition and in these circumstances it is difficult to come to firm conclusions about the genuine extent of state autonomy and power. One may go some way towards the elimination of these methodological difficulties by concentrating in rather greater detail on a particular policy initiative where the problem to be faced and the means to be employed in dealing with it are as similar as possible. These conditions come close to being satisfied with respect to the problem of adjusting the supply of trained teachers to the need for them. A brief comparison of the way in which British and French governments tackled this problem in the 1970s will be used here to support the argument that British policy-makers have more real power and freedom of manoeuvre than their French counterparts.

If supply was to match demand, governments in both countries had to increase the numbers of teachers in training extremely rapidly during the 1950s and 1960s. This increased demand came in part from the progressive impact of a higher birth-rate, but was much more related to an increased demand for schooling beyond that which was compulsory. The British government, collaborating with the local authorities who are the direct providers of training places, succeeded in organising an extremely rapid expansion of provision in the 1960s. By the early 1970s the problem was quite different, the birth-rate was now falling and demand for non-compulsory schooling was expanding much less rapidly. It was now necessary to close training colleges or reduce their intake and redeploy the staff of these establishments on a large scale. It is on the downward swing of the pendulum that governments are most likely to encounter stiff resistance but again this problem seems to have been handled in a manner which suggests that the state and local authorities were relatively unconstrained in England and Wales. Table 9.1 gives some indication of the rapidity of the increase and the subsequent decline.

The position in France was, from the policy-maker's point of view, much less satisfactory. As demand, especially for secondary teachers, increased, the French government tended to abandon the traditional recruitment routes and qualification levels which had previously been regarded as necessary. In the secondary sector graduates without any teacher training and sometimes those who had not yet passed their final university examinations, were given temporary contracts without security of tenure. At the primary level young people were employed who had not been through the training colleges, the conventional route for qualification as a primary school teacher, and the government had resorted instead to those who were only qualified with a baccalauréat or, in some cases, did not even possess this qualification. The demand for secondary school teachers was also met in part by promotions from the ranks of primary school teachers. This promotion was in principle only possible when candidates had passed an examination testifying to their ability to teach in the secondary sector but, in practice, these examinations, and the courses leading to them, do not seem to have either upgraded or filtered applicants in the manner which was required. The consequences of these policy failures have been frequently denounced by well-informed observers of the French educational scene but most recently by Schwarz in 1981 looking back on the 1960s and 1970s (Schwarz, 1981; Périé, 1987). Table 9.2 gives some idea of the extent to which French governments had increasingly to resort to unsatisfactory expedience in order to recruit the required number of teachers.

To what British assets or French handicaps can we point in explaining this contrast? It is important to remember our aims in the examination of this balance sheet. We are to some degree interested in the problem for its own sake, that is to say in trying to understand why the same problem has been dealt with more effectively in Britain than in France, but this is not our principal concern. Our aim must be to use the case of education to help us to understand the underlying strengths and weaknesses of the state in Britain and France. This means that where we point to the importance of an explanatory factor which relates to the form of educational provision, whilst we may help to advance our understanding of the management of teacher supply, we will not have advanced our understanding of the state. Where, on the other hand, explanatory factors emerge whose relevance seems more general, then our conclusion may legitimately apply not simply to the management of

Table 9.1: Teaching staff (new entrants, total enrolments and successful students for initial teacher training by sex for England and Wales)

Thousands

	1965	1970	1975	1980	1982	1983	1984	1985	1986
England and Wales									
All new entrants	34.8	46.6	40.8	18.9	18.3	17.7	16.8	17.3	17.9
Men	11.2	14.7	13.3	7.1	6.3	6.0	5.2	5.1	5.2
Women	23.6	31.9	27.5	11.8	11.9	11.7	11.7	12.2	12.7
All enrolments	76.5	115.6	104.3	35.8	32.1	32.8	32.6	34.9	35.8
Men	23.2	33.8	29.9	10.9	9.5	9.5	8.6	8.5	8.6
Women	53.3	81.8	74.4	24.9	22.6	23.3	24.0	26.4	27.2
All successfully completing*	21.7	35.9	40.7	21.3	18.3	15.2	13.9	13.8	13.5
Men	7.8	11.0	13.4	5.9	5.1	4.3	3.9	3.9	4.1
Women	13.9	24.9	27.3	15.4	13.2	10.9	10.0	9.9	9.4

Note:
* Numbers for men and women are estimated from 1980.

Source: Education Statistics for the United Kingdom, 1986.

education but to the autonomy and the administrative and political capacity of the state.

The first factor to which we must attend concerns the organisation of the teaching profession in our two countries. The English profession is much more unified organisationally than the French. By this I mean to refer to the fact that the English teaching certificate qualifies a teacher to work in any primary or secondary school. The arrangements for pay, qualifications and terms of service of French teachers are infinitely more complicated and sub-divided. This means that the problem of ensuring an adequate supply in France is inherently more complicated because teachers of different sorts are required at different levels and are recruited through different channels. This problem of French heterogeneity is further complicated by the fact that recruitment to the most prestigious corps in secondary teaching, the *Agrégés* and *Certifiés*, is conditional on success in an exam, and the examiners are always members of the corps to which the candidate aspires. These examining juries, as they are rather appropriately called, have a notorious tendency to fix the level of achievement required for success at a level which fails to provide the ministry with enough teachers.

At this point administrators have recourse to the relatively unqualified, non-tenured staff already referred to. When these temporary staff were first recruited in large numbers in the 1960s, the intention was that only those who succeeded in qualifying themselves by the normal route would eventually win tenure. In the event, the influence of the teacher unions and the slowness of the administration in organising a sufficient flow of well-qualified secondary teachers, meant that most of these teachers eventually obtained tenure and

Table 9.2: Temporary teaching staff in secondary education

	1962–3	1972–3	1977–8	1981–2	1983–4
Total	13,130	31,155	39,794	32,616	30,678
Temporary staff as a percentage of whole	12.6	16.8	14.0	11.3	10.5

Source: Périé (1987), Table 3, p. 73.

were often able later, on the basis of seniority, to win access to the corps from which they had previously been excluded by examination failure. In seeking to understand the contrast in the position between Britain and France, we must also remember that the attitude of English institutions of higher education towards the examinations which they organise is such that government can be fairly confident of a high percentage rate of return, in terms of qualified teachers, for the places which it makes available in either colleges of education or university departments of education. The vast majority of students entering these courses will complete them and successfully qualify.

We must now ask ourselves to what extent the factors to which we have drawn attention are specific to the educational sector or relate more generally to relations between the state and society? In fact, both particular and general factors seem to be at work here. Let us consider first the problems created for administrators by the self-recruiting character of the more prestigious secondary teaching corps. We have here a limited degree of professional self-government. We might first explain the ability of these teachers to win such privileges by pointing to the extremely socially restricted access to French secondary education in the period before 1940, and the close links between the teachers in secondary and higher education (Ringer, 1979). If these aspects of the situation are emphasized, then the explanation seems more educational than general. However, on closer examination, explanatory elements general to French society and politics also have some importance.

The nearest English equivalent to the French secondary teacher who was an *Agrégé* before 1940 would have been a graduate teaching in a grammar school or public school. Unlike their French counterparts, these teachers did not develop a strong sense of shared corporate identity and interest, in large part presumably because they were employed by a wide variety and large number of employers – charities and local authorities. A common employer and a unified set of terms of employment in addition to a shared and highly valued qualification gave the French *Agrégé* a much stronger sense of identity. The point here is that the dispersed pattern of authority in the English case and its concentration in France served to stimulate, in the French case, a limited degree of professional self-government. We may properly consider this a general rather than a specifically educational factor for two reasons. First, the tendency to concentrate and centralise the exercise of authority, whether in the provision of public services or for other purposes, in France is a general tendency and not one particular to education. Second, we know from studies of the French civil service that this tendency towards self-government and self-recruitment by examination is well developed outside education and seems to find strong reinforcement in certain values prominent in French political culture (Suleiman, 1974; De Baecque and Quermonne, 1981; Crozier, 1964).

Further, it would appear that the concentration of formal authority in the French case is related to difficulties of management in another way. The contrast with the English position again helps to make the matter more clear. When R. A. Butler in 1944 decided to concede equality of status for teachers in primary and secondary education, he clearly did not imagine for a moment that this would mean that there was any danger of non-graduates teaching in the higher forms of grammar schools, let alone public schools. He clearly, and probably quite rightly, calculated that the attitude and traditional practices of local authorities, and even more importantly, headmasters, would continue to ensure that teachers were properly qualified to do what was expected of them. Where, however, a single central body is responsible for teacher appointments, as has always been the case in secondary schools in France, the Minister himself must take steps to ensure that only properly qualified teachers are appointed. In such circumstances it seems almost inevitable that the available teaching posts will be graded and classified and that a central authority will specify the level of qualification necessary for appointment to a particular post. An inability or unwillingness to delegate important discretion on this question to regional, departmental , or school levels, forces a central authority to tie its own hands in this way. Again we are describing here the necessary consequences of a high degree of centralisation in the management of personnel on a large scale rather than a particular feature of French education.

Let us now summarise the argument of this section. We began by noting an increase in the extent of competitive pluralism in the relations between the state and organised interests in post-war Britain and France. We then went on to conclude that this tendency had given the state more room for manoeuvre. It is worth noting here that the direction of development described is the very opposite of that which some students of corporatism purport to identify (Schmitter and Lehmbruch, 1979). When policy-makers at the national level felt that their capacity to act in what they conceived to be the general interest, and their ability to demonstrate publicly that they were acting in the general interest, were compromised by too close an association with particular established educational interests, they reacted, in Britain and France, not by attempting to incorporate and take in the existing established interests but by promoting rival groups and in this way acquiescing in and accelerating the growth of pluralism which was itself a result of social trends quite outside governmental control. So far the argument is concerned with the identification of common trends. From this point onwards our attention turned to an equally important contrast in the relationship of the state to the educational policy arena in Britain and France. We argued that the French state, although strongly supported culturally by a set of beliefs requiring and expecting the state to act vigorously in defence of the general interest, and whilst appearing to be much better placed than the state in England with respect to bureaucratic resources, was nevertheless much more tightly constrained and seemed to possess much less freedom of manoeuvre than the state in England. The conclusion to this chapter seeks an answer to the question: how can we explain this contrast in state autonomy when the distribution of cultural and institutional assets points to a conclusion opposite to that which we have reached?

It is only proper to recognize at this point that the conclusions of this section are directly in conflict with those of Dennis Smith in his recent comparative study of the state's role in education (Smith, 1983). He argues that, as a result of the experience of revolution, the modern French state has acquired great organising and coercive capacity. The state in France, in his view, has used and continues to use its power to limit any tendency for the educational sector to assert autonomy. By contrast, he paints a picture of English policy-makers who are preoccupied with crisis avoidance. These policy-makers defer to powerful educational interests and have tended in the past to respect conventions and practices which support educational autonomy.

It will be clear to the attentive reader that there is much evidence in the preceding pages which contradicts Smith's conclusion. Smith is too ready to see formal centralisation as evidence of real political power. He also seems unaware of the significance of genuinely private forms of French higher education and of the autonomy possessed by prestigious institutions within the public sector. He takes no account of the way in which powerful organised interests, such as the teachers' unions and the Catholic Church, have been able to thwart time and again the carefully-laid plans of successive French governments. He is led astray by a tendency to infer from history, when observation of contemporary French hesitations and British decisiveness provide a more accurate picture.

Conclusion

It is important to make clear at the outset that the contrast to which we have pointed, between a cautious and tightly constrained French state and a bold and assertive English state, although to some degree controversial, is by no means unsupported by evidence coming from other policy arenas. Before going any further, it would therefore seem sensible to ask how this contrast has been explained in the existing literature and at the same time to discover whether these explanations can be applied to the educational arena.

Ashford's comparative study of central local relations in Britain and France points to conclusions which are parallel to those contained in this chapter (Ashford, 1982). Relying principally on a study of the reorganisation of local government in England and Wales in the 1970s and the blocking of similar reforms in France, Ashford concluded that the French state was pragmatic and cautious whereas policy-makers in England were often assertive and dogmatic. We shall confine our consideration here to the descriptive and explanatory aspect of this debate and leave to one side the difficult normative question of whether greater constraints on French policy-makers are ultimately productive of more effective government, and whether the greater freedom of manoeuvre accorded policy-makers in Britain tends to lead them to over-hasty and over-political, and therefore ineffective, policy-making.

Ashford relies principally for his explanation on the greater interpenetration of national and local politics in France. It is this French interpenetration and British insulation of national politics from territorially-based pressure that gives rise to these contrasting styles of government policy-making (Bulpitt, 1983; Grémion, 1976). The author's own research on the relations between local politicians and the process of educational policy-making at central and local levels in France indicates that the explanation which is perfectly correct in the sphere in which Ashford applies it cannot be extended to education (Duclaud-Williams, 1983; Duclaud-Williams, 1985; Duclaud-Williams, 1988). French teachers and educational administrators successfully exclude local politicians from any significant degree of influence over most educational questions. Territorially-based conflict over the distribution of educational resources does exist but is managed within the educational bureaucracy in a process of competition between levels and areas.

The Anglo-french contrast to which we are seeking an explanation has also been observed in the sphere of housing, finance and construction (Duclaud-Williams, 1978). The principal explanatory factor relied upon by the author of this comparative study is the impact in the British case of intense programmatic two-party competition. Again we find ourselves identifying here a factor which cannot be exported from one policy arena to another. British party competition is certainly generally more programmatic than French, but the impact of policies generated by the political parties is extremely uneven across policy arenas and major recent British educational policy initiatives have not been at all closely related to explicit electoral undertakings (Rose, 1980). A further related factor which is relevant in the case of housing concerns the ideological saliency in British political debate on housing questions of where to draw the line between public and private provision, both of which are conceived of in rather stereotyped terms. State intervention in housing in France has taken a variety of administrative and financial forms, many of them mixing elements of the private with elements of the public, and the existence of these institutional arrangements has been inimical to an over-simplified private versus public provision debate. Again, although this factor may not be confined in its importance entirely to the housing sector, it certainly cannot be extended to education. We have seen already in the first section of this chapter that forms of educational provision do exist in France which are neither public nor private in the stereotypical senses of those terms, but the existence of these arrangements has so far at least failed to take the sting out of the debate concerning the role which ought to be accorded 'private schools'.

In the third section of this chapter it was argued that the frequent setbacks and hesitations which have been typical of French governments in recent years are not accidental or merely circumstantial. We related their occurrence to a tendency of government/teacher relations to dominate a wide range of educational policy issues, itself the product of formal centralisation designed to exclude local authorities and other non-educational actors from a role in policy-making. We have here, in its negative form, a specific national example of the general proposition that pluralism is positively associated with increased state autonomy. There has undeniably been a tendency to resort to this form of organisation in a range of French state interventions but it is not an invariable feature of French administrative organisation any more than reliance upon elected local authorities is invariably the preferred solution in the United Kingdom. What we can probably say, therefore, without too much fear of contradiction, is that French administrative practice is rather more likely to exhibit a high level of formal centralisation, that this is particularly so in education and that such centralisation is self-destructive. In a world of pervasively democratic assumptions centralisation simply becomes a mechanism through which the state deprives itself of potential allies and ties itself to a powerful partner.

But in our search for sophistication of explanation, we must not forget the obvious. The role of the Catholic Church as a provider of education is quite different from the role of the churches in England and Wales. The difficulty of maintaining a constitutional and political consensus within which democratic processes can operate, has for long also been more difficult in France than in the United Kingdom. Both of these factors, the first particular to education, the second of much wider significance, have been important recent causes of immobilism in French public policy-making.

An examination of contrasting roles played by the British and French states in a number of non-educational policy arenas has suggested that the explanations which apply in one arena cannot always be applied in education. This is so even where it is the same British/French contrast which requires explanation. In explaining the capacity of the British state to act autonomously and overcome opposition in the educational sphere, and the contrasted behaviour of the French state in educational matters, we nevertheless relied, for our explanation, principally on the unintended consequences of centralisation in the French case and the advantages of developed pluralism and dispersion of power in the British case. These are factors which are not exclusively educational and therefore have some cross-sectoral validity. The confused picture with which we are left is therefore one in which the same kind of contrast is thrown up by the examination of a number of different arenas but one in which the explanations offered mix factors particular to a given arena with factors of a more general cross-sectoral relevance. It seems to me that this limited degree of policy uniformity does entitle us to speak quite properly of characteristic features of the British and French state.

The position defended in this paper and that supported by Ashford and Mény is at odds, at least to some degree, with that defended by Zysman and Hall (Ashford, 1982; Mény, 1984; Zysman, 1983; Hall, 1986). In discussions of English and French economic policy these writers have stressed the power of the French state and the weakness of the English. There is no space here for an exhaustive examination of the problem posed by these writers for anyone wishing to defend the thesis of this paper but it would be wrong to ignore this conflict of academic views entirely.

Two key points need to be borne in mind in any attempt to reconcile these apparently opposed points of view. We should first remember that the phase of active and successful state intervention in the economy can be seen as a relatively short and rather exceptional interlude rather than as the most recent manifestation of a long tradition. Before 1936 the French state was protectionist but internally non-interventionist. The experience of economic policy-making in France since 1981 has tended to stress constraints, both domestic and international, and increasing modesty of ambition.

But a genuine contrast between the French state's role in the management of the economy and its role in other sectors may nevertheless exist. A possible explanation for such a contrast in the French case may lie in the difference between managing a public service on the one hand and regulating the behaviour of private actors by penalty and incentive on the other. When states chose to provide labour intensive public services in a highly bureaucratised and centralised manner, they locked themselves into constraining institutional forms and created powerful trade union or professional opposition. These difficulties are less apparent where state intervention in the economy is concerned. Policy-makers in the spheres of education and health do not possess any equivalent to the economic policy-makers' discretion in the granting of cheap credit. It would seem that the advantages of legitimacy and expertise which the French state enjoys when compared with the British state can be put to good use in the economic sphere, although they cannot in many other sectors. In Britain those responsible for making economic policy have not possessed these advantages and in any case have usually preferred not to intervene. If we may indulge ourselves in a little over-simplification, we may say that the contrast is between a French state, which invariably seeks autonomy and control but is frequently thwarted in welfare state arenas and more successful in economic matters, and a British state, where an opposite pattern of intervention and control exists.

Guide to further reading

Comparative and historical studies
M. S. Archer (1979), *The social origins of educational systems, Sage).*
F. K. Ringer (1979), *Education and society in modern Europe* (Bloomington: Indiana University Press).
J. Ben-David (1977), *Centres of learning* (New York: McGraw-Hill).
D. Müller, F. Ringer and B. Simon (1987), *The rise of the modern educational system,* (Cambridge: Cambridge University press).
R. Premfors, (1980), 'The politics of higher education in a comparative perspective: France, Sweden and the UK', *Stockholm Studies in Politics,* 15.
J. Ambler (1987), 'Constraints on policy innovation in education: Thatcher's Britain and Mitterrand's France', *Comparative Politics,* 20, 1.
R. D. Anderson (1986), 'Sociology and history: M. S. Archer's "social origins of educational systems"', *Archives Européennes de Sociologie, 27, 1.*

There is clearly an enormous amount of literature dealing with education in England but the following are particularly worth noting:

A. McPherson and C. D. Raab (1988), *Government education: a sociology of policy since 1945* (Edinburgh: Edinburgh University Press).

B. Salter and T. Tapper (1985), *Power and policy in education: the case of the independent schools*, (Falmer: Falmer Press).

D. Finn (ed.) (1987), *Training without jobs* (London: Macmillan).

On France see particularly:

Commission du Billon, (1981), *La France en mai 1981: volume 4, l'enseignement et le développement scientifique*, (Paris: La Documentation Française).

A. Prost (1968), *L'enseignement en France de 1800 à 1967 (Paris: Armand Colin).*

A. Prost (1981), *Histoire générale de l'enseignement et de l'éducation en France: Volume 4, l'école et la famille dans une société en mutation.*

A Prost, 1983, *Les lycées et leurs études au seuil du 21ème siècle* (Paris: La Documentation Française).

H. D. Lewis (1985), *The French Education System (New York: St. Martins Press).*

R. Périé, 1987, *L'education nationale à l'heure de la décentralisation (Paris: La Documentation Française).*

Pouvoirs (1984), Special Issue, 'De l'école', 30.

Part V Conclusions

10.Varieties of states and actions

James Simmie

Introduction

In this volume we have sought to examine, from an essentially empirical point of view, a selection of key state actions concerned with civil public policy. The focus has been on British state actions illuminated further by comparing them with actions, in the same policy fields, in other selected nation-state members of the Organization for Economic Cooperation and Development (OECD). Thus the type of state actions analysed in this book have been confined to those found in advanced 'Western' capitalist economic conditions.

Even this major limitation, as readers who have reached these conclusions will readily appreciate, still leaves an enormous variety of puzzling and seemingly inconsistent state actions being pursued by different states in the range of policies examined here. Nevertheless, we seek in this chapter to assemble some order from this variety by developing thematic conclusions drawn from the results of the analyses presented in the foregoing chapters.

This endeavour is organized around six main conclusions. The first two of these are concerned with the economic circumstances in which all the states studied were operating in recent times; and the different definitions and location of states and their constituent parts. These form the essential background to and machinery of state actions during the 1970s and 1980s.

The remaining four thematic conclusions are concerned with the description and 'middle-range' explanation of the varieties of state actions in different policy fields. The first of these draws attention to the structural contradictions, fragmentation and incoherence which affect much state action. The second looks at some of the effects of cultural differences and political ideologies on approaches to policies. The third theme examines the varieties of state forms and processes ranging from pluralist through corporatist to company and contract types which arise in nominally similar types of government. Finally, we seek to show how theoretical questions arising from these concerns may illuminate and increase our understanding of the significant varieties of state actions and policies.

These themes cross-cut deliberately the single policy focus on public versus private provision; forms of intervention/non-intervention; and intrastate relations used selectively to organize the individual policy studies so far. They also slice through the division of policy actions into central state concerns with production; local consumption; and the changing state levels at which different policy issues are resolved and provided. The reasons for doing this rather than, for example, summarizing the findings under each topic heading as if they were unrelated and unconnected, are that, when placed together and in the context of their complex surrounding circumstances, state actions follow a limited variety of logics. It is regarded as an essential task of a book such as this to attempt to specify what they are in different conditions and therefore to develop some explanations as well as descriptions.

The second reason for adopting cross-cutting themes is that a thematic perspective can point to similarities and differences in state actions despite the diachronic development of different policies. Again, the variety which appears in state actions at the same chronological point in time may underestimate more general characteristics if each policy is considered in equivalent contexts and stages of its own particular development to those of other policies.

Economic context

Thanks mainly to the benefits of hindsight, it is now possible to see that during the 1970s the capitalist world economy entered the depression phase of its fourth long Kondratieff cycle of growth and decline. This time around the crisis was exacerbated greatly by the oil price shocks of 1973 and 1979. This general economic depression was the most serious problem with which OECD states had to deal during the 1970s and 1980s. It was the single most important contextual parameter within which state actions could be devised.

John Mohan, David Banister and Roger Duclaud-Williams point out that the economic depression influenced thinking and action with respect to other policies such as health, transport and education. There is little doubt that its effects were felt in other policy areas as well.

The effects of depression were not confined to the basic shortages of money to pay for policies, ranging from regional economic incentives to the health service, which have featured so prominently in the news headlines throughout the 1980s. Roger Duclaud-Williams argues that resistance to governments tends to increase during the downward swing of the economic pendulum. He cites the difficulties experienced by both the British and French governments in adjusting the supply of trained teachers during the 1970s. David Banister argues that even the form of state decision-making was changed to corporatist and later company and contract in order to arrive at decisions that reflected the state's perceived requirements in time of economic depression.

All our authors have been analysing state actions in the explicit or implicit context of economic depression. This context has had a major impact on what those actions have been for two main reasons. In the first place, the four phases of Schumpeter's conceptual development of Kondratieff's long waves of economic development – namely, prosperity, recession, depression and recovery – all present nation-states with different limited ranges of policy options. In the depression phase these options are perhaps at their most limited. Second, as Ron Johnston maintains, economic power lies at the heart of 'complex civilized societies'. Thus, without wishing to argue for any mechanistic determination of state actions by economic structures or power holders, one general theme that does arise from the different contributions to this book, is the significance of the economic circumstances within which state actions are devised and implemented for what policies are arrived at and how they work out in practice.

Definitions and location of states and their constituent parts

In generating this book we assumed, rather too optimistically as it turned out, that defining the main object of study – the state – was not a major problem. We took as a working definition the simple concept of an 'organized political community under one government'. Contributors soon pointed out, however, that this definition does not get to grips with at least three main issues which affect greatly both the specific focus of empirical studies and their consequent findings. First, it does not indicate the variety and lack of singular uniformity which is an important characteristic of most OECD states. Second, it does not mention the significance of territory in defining a particular state for empirical purposes. Third, it may also be that, in practice, not all organized political communities under one government can really be defined as states.

Within the pages of this book the variety of political communities calling themselves states ranges from federal through nation to local. Wyn Grant raises the issue of federal states with respect to industrial policy in Canada. He questions whether the cultural divisions between English and French-speaking provinces are so great as to make it inaccurate to talk of the Canadian state as opposed to states. He also raises the problem of whether the same definition difficulty arises in the case of the United Kingdom because of the separate development administrations in all four countries. Thus, even within the United Kingdom, the nation-state, which at first glance appears to be the easiest to define empirically, definition issues are raised which have major impacts on what is to be analysed and therefore what information will be found.

The term 'local state' has also been used with respect to local government. It was assumed initially that such an entity was an empirical reality and that, following Cawson and Saunders' dual state theory, was often characterised by pluralist conflicts over policies mainly concerned with consumption. Ron Johnston raises important doubts about both these assumptions.

In the first place he questions whether the local state is really government or administration. He defines local government as 'day-to-day control by local politicians and bureaucrats'. Local administration is defined as 'local territories run by employees of the central state'. In his view local states only exist in cases of local government and not in circumstances of local administration.

In the second place he argues that states at all levels are necessary to and therefore concerned with production. This is particularly the case with the more overt concern with capitalist production shown in many metropolitan areas of the United States and, one might add, increasingly used as role models in the United Kingdom during the 1980s.

In conceptual terms we must conclude that defining the state as a unitary and uniform 'organized political community under one government' is very much an ideal type in the Weberian sense. In practice many politically defined states are not unitary, uniform nor even necessarily entirely under one government. Many of the contributions to this volume are concerned with a variety of divergences from this ideal type.

The first distinction that can be made between states is by activity. The second is by territory. Most contributors assume implicitly or explicitly that responsibilities for state activities are spatially delimited and that the coincidence of action and territory provide an operational definition of the state. Ron Johnston is the most explicit on this point. He argues that not only is the state necessary to production but also that it is spatially defined. This has important implications for his definition of local states within the context of nation-states. For him, a local state is therefore a 'territorial unit governed by representatives elected separately from those who run the central state'.

He goes on to argue that all but the territorially smallest modern states need an organizational structure of local authorities. Despite this the question of the balance between whether they should be primarily governments or administrations has been in question during the 1970s and 1980s. Taking as an example the changes taking place in the United States and United Kingdom during this period of economic depression, he argues that the numbers and functions of metropolitan administrations have increased in the former while the numbers and functions of local governments have been curtailed in the United Kingdom. A general conclusion that may be drawn from this observation is that where organisations lower in the state hierarchy are prepared or forced to act more as administrative agents of those higher in the hierarchy their numbers and functions may be increased during times of depression, primarily because they are seen as useful assistants in local production adjustments. On the other hand, where they seek to act as local governments (states) and maintain local consumption, this may be seen by both the central state and production interests as antithetical to the exigencies of economic depression, and they will be coerced into a more administrative role by reducing or curtailing both their numbers and their functions.

Ron Johnston also draws attention to another important aspect of space with respect to the context of state actions. This is that 'places'differ and are characterized by uneven spatial development'. This applies both to local and to central states. Different places also have different combinations of interests in their economies. There are also significant variations in state spending patterns in different places. One of the reasons why these territorial characteristics are important with respect to the definition of states and what actions they take is that they change much more slowly, if at all, compared with economic and political change. Therefore, in the short and medium terms at least, they form one kind of significant structural limitation within which states operate.

One final important territorial parameter which influences the possible actions of states is identified by Michael Moran. He illustrates its importance with respect to financial markets but it effects other production policies as well. It is that while most nation-state actions are confined within and aimed at internal policy issues, an increasing amount of economic activity is being organised on a global scale often by transnational corporations (TNCs). Individual states do not have powers over transnational space. The largest TNCs also have internal economies which control greater amounts of product than all but half-a-dozen of the world's nation-states. The scale and economic power of TNCs is therefore important in constraining the freedom of action of nation-states. Similar remarks could be made about the relationships between nation and local states and between local states and perhaps local business.

The main point to be grasped from this discussion is that the territorial extent of state powers is a major factor in determining the range of state actions that are likely to be found in any one place. Space is thus both an important element in both the definition of the state and in understanding the particular characteristics of state actions.

Finally, some candidates for definition as states are specifically excluded from this analysis. One such is the European Community (EC). While it is certainly an organised political community, possibly under one government, the European Parliament, it is still a collection of nation-states rather than a state in its own right. Primarily administrative divisions such as those between the different countries of the United Kingdom, following Ron Johnston's distinction, are also not defined as states for the purposes of this analysis.

Following the discussion above, the operational definition of the state used in this analysis is 'an organised political community under one government, exercising legitimate power and authority over a defined territory, and composed of politicians elected from that territory who are at least formally responsible for what state actions take place in that area'. It will be seen from the preceding chapters, however, that it is also necessary to specify the type, sector and spatial limits of the state in order to compare like with like when examining particular state actions.

Structural contradictions, fragmentation and incoherence

Given a reasonably coherent recognition of the significance and characteristics of contemporary economic circumstances and a definition of the states that are acting within those circumstances, we can now turn to the characteristics of particular states and understanding the actions they have taken. One recurring theme in the chapters above is the problem of structural contradictions, fragmentation and incoherence which seem to be characteristic of so much state activity when viewed with the benefit of cool hindsight.

One of the basic difficulties which lies behind these problems is that states are frequently attempting to do mutually inconsistent things at one and the same time. Ron Johnston draws attention to perhaps the best-known theoretical exposition of this difficulty. He quotes O'Connor's (1972) trilogy of necessary state goals of action. They are the necessities to: 'secure social consensus (an ideological and a policing function); secure conditions of production (by promoting accumulation strategies in capitalism, production strategies in socialism); and secure social integration (ensuring a basic standard of welfare for all)'. The pursuit of these three goals at the same time creates structural contradictions in state actions as several of our authors point out.

The interesting point to notice here, however, is that in capitalist societies it is to be expected that production will take precedence over consumption. This means that state actions to secure favourable conditions of production which are both within its own control and territory have an initially favourable momentum which often suppresses the expression of conflicts focused on production-oriented policies. This is illustrated in the chapters above by the absence or presence of their authors' concern with structural contradictions in the particular policies with which they are concerned. Thus, there is a noticeable absence of such concern in industrial and financial policy while, in contrast, it is raised as a specific problem in consumption management in general and education policy in particular. Malcolm Harrison argues that conflicts arise from what have become structural features of some capitalist economies. He cites as examples of these features: first, the need to combine capital accumulation with electoral success (perhaps not too characteristic of Thatcherite Britain); and second, the problem of maintaining public credibility and an individualistic system of citizens' rights. Roger Duclaud-Williams argues that there is a structurally determined conflict between the state's need to facilitate wealth creation on the one hand and its provision of education on the other.

It may be concluded from these authors' analyses that structural conflicts are inherent in state actions. They are focused on where the balances are struck between the unfettered pursuit of production goals versus the need to achieve periodic electoral success in order to continue to pursue those goals; the establishment of a property-owning democracy based on a system of individual citizens' property rights versus attempts to follow policies which effectively seek to remove some of those very same rights; the creation and private accumulation of wealth versus public payment for essential services such as education.

A second interesting point to emerge from the analyses above is the division between authors examining consumption and those analysing production policies. The discovery of and concern with structural contradictions is confined to the former, possibly because they are usually the responsibility of single ministries or departments so that attempts to follow mutually inconsistent objectives are present even within single state institutions. In contrast, the concept of fragmentation is almost exclusively referred to by those describing the making of production policies.

Despite a frequently asserted assumption that the state in capitalist societies is primarily concerned to facilitate private wealth creation and accumulation, and that this appears to be a rather clearer objective than those conflicting goals found in many consumption policies, both Wyn Grant and Michael Moran argue that states do not appear to be all that efficient at achieving this single goal. Wyn Grant goes so far as to argue that 'Industrial policy in most Western societies is a mess'. How can it be that the state in capitalist societies appears to be so bad at accommodating the collective interests of capital?

At least part of the answer appears to lie in the fragmentation of both the interests of capital and the institutions of the state. Fragmentation of the former are most clearly exposed by Michael Moran in his analysis of financial markets. He points to three major categories of cleavage in capitalist interests. The first is between national and international capital; the second is between different sectors of capital; and the third is between private and public capital. All these categories give rise to multiple differences of interest within and between separately controlled elements of capital.

Although nominally a single category of institutions, states do not appear to be generally more unified in their actions with respect to capital than the different elements of capital are themselves. Michael Moran, for example, says that 'Everywhere, state intervention is governed by a complex administrative division of labour and by jealousies and rivalries between the various state agencies at work'. Wyn Grant concludes that 'fragmentation exists in some form in most countries'. Both authors argue that this fragmentation is most evident in federal states such as the United States and Canada. It is also a characteristic of the United Kingdom, with institutional fragmentation between the Treasury, central banks, single industry ministries, separate national development agencies and even local authorities getting in on the act in recent years. Wyn Grant argues that the net result is that, in the crucial sphere of industrial policy, the 'fragmented state is uncertain of what its objectives are and how to attain them'.

Not too surprisingly, one result of this fragmentation is incoherence in policies. Wyn Grant notes this in the context of industrial policies. One of the reasons for it is the difference between the powers and objectives of strong central finance ministries as compared with the weaknesses and different goals of single industry ministries. Michael Moran adds to this the problem that states themselves are riddled with inter-institutional jealousies and rivalries. The net result is that many arms of states seem to expend as much time and effort on internecine politics as on devising and implementing economic policies.

Apart from the internal struggles which characterise state institutions, there are also those that arise because different fragments of states are also connected to different groups of external private interests. This leads to one of Michael Moran's conclusions that 'states are not independent actors'. Different parts of them are under pressure to produce policies that satisfy the interests of different economic sectors. Single-industry ministries connect their industrial sector's interests to government. Defence institutions, like the Pentagon, also foster particular industrial interests. Central finance ministries, which generally hold the purse strings, are also conduits of external interests to state economic policies. Many of these interests are mutually incompatible and their relative incorporation in state policies also leads to across-the-board incoherence in those policies.

The existence of incoherence is marked by frequent calls for policy coordination. Generally speaking, the more frequently these calls are heard the greater is the implication of policy incoherence. Wyn Grant also points out that such calls usually prove to be ineffective.

The third general conclusion that we draw from the comparative analysis of the state in action is, therefore, that its policies are frequently characterised by structural contradictions, fragmentation and incoherence.

Furthermore, these problems have proved to be persistent and difficult to overcome.

Political ideologies, cultural differences and their effects on policies.

Our fourth conclusion is that political ideologies and cultural differences play significant roles in the nature and content of state action. Virtually all our contributors mention the significance of the development (or re-emergence) of the ideologies of the 'New' Right during the 1970s and 1980s. They have contributed greatly to the widespread emphasis in most OECD countries on 'liberal', *laissez-faire* approaches in both economic and welfare policies.

In practice this ideological emphasis has meant that in industrial policies the basic principle followed has been increasingly one of a lack of state interference (Wyn Grant). This has been the approach adopted in most other civil policy areas particularly under Reagan in the United States and Thatcher in the United Kingdom. The guiding ideology has been that market allocations are usually the 'best and most desirable'.

One argument which has often been used to support this proposition is that market allocations are superior to bureaucratically controlled state actions because of characteristic failures in bureaucratic competence. This is noted in economic policy arguments by Wyn Grant, in transport by David Banister and in education by Roger Duclaud-Williams. Thus the ideological support for market allocations is often based not so much on their positive characteristics as on the perceived negative qualities of bureaucracies. The most serious of these is often argued to be the absence of a clear way of measuring their efficiency. In contrast, it is said that the efficiency of market allocations may be measured according to the rates of profit that they generate (David Banister).

This contemporary stance on the general desirability of market allocations as opposed to state actions produces a paradox which is at the heart of a book such as this. The paradox is that many contributors are discussing the numerous exceptions where the principles of market allocation do not appear to be capable of delivering the goods or, indeed, services!

The number and variety of these exceptions, in most policy areas, are sufficient to sustain the continuing ideological debate about the relative merits of markets versus bureaucracies. In industrial policy they include government contracts, protection against unfair competition, investment incentives, last resort banking and market failures in general (Wyn Grant). In financial policy the state will not usually allow the fate of losers to threaten the stability of the markets themselves (Michael Moran). David Banister quotes the control of monopolies which might operate against the national interest, the furtherance of economic growth objectives, the assistance of regional development, bailouts, new ventures and the collection of profits from the exploitation of natural resources as general reasons for state actions. In consumption management, Malcolm Harrison argues that 'contrary to economic liberalism, grass roots property rights may require collective assertion'. Finally, Roger Duclaud-Williams points out that services such as 'education may also have too many public goods characteristics for the market to provide'.

Thus, while it is the case that the ideology of *laissez-faire* espoused by the 'New' Right has had a significant impact on state actions during recent years, there is still a great deal of state intervention to combat market failures. The extent and variety of these interventions means that although the ideological debate has moved on it has by no means come to an end.

Among those who regard current circumstances as suiting their particular interests, however, the 'end of ideology' is a recurrent theme. It may be identified in claims that one aspect of public policy or another should not be the subject of 'political' debate. Our authors identify several examples of this claim. Wyn Grant argues that in many countries attempts are made to protect industrial competition policy from political influence. Ron Johnston concludes that a major difference between local 'government' in the United Kingdom and local 'administration' in the United States is that, in the former, local democracy is characterised by partisan politics whereas in the United States the main feature is 'non-political' pragmatic business. In some states this is taken to the lengths of banning political party activities, eliminating the ward bases of elections, placing limits on local government spending and allowing popular initiatives to determine some policies. Roger Duclaud-Williams also points out that in France teachers and administrators exclude local politicians from influence over most educational questions. This is also the case in housing, finance and construction.

Each of the above examples represents an attempt by one collection of interest groups or organisations to legitimise a particular status quo and not to have its continuation questioned in the political forums of the state. In many cases they are successful. This does not make the influence of ideology over state actions in these fields any the less.

In one respect the development and effects of ideology is simpler in consumption than in production policies. The reason for this lies in differences in the possession and control of information. Almost by definition, much of the information concerning consumption policies lies somewhere in the public domain. In contrast, much of the exploding volume of information about production is held privately.

Wyn Grant points out that one reason why bureaucracies are not very good at dealing with non-routine industrial policies is that much key information is concentrated with the companies. Private concentration is even greater in financial markets. There, not only is information concentrated in the private sector but information and intelligence are themselves major traded services (Michael Moran). The private possession of economic information, its circulation and transmission by new information technologies make it a particularly impenetrable resource. This makes it difficult for outside interests to conduct a sustained and informed ideological debate about its use and regulation. Very few external interests, for example, were able to participate in the debates over the 'big bang' City revolution of the 1980s.

This may be contrasted with often greater levels of participation and understanding where consumption policies are concerned. Malcolm Harrison and Robert Smith, for example, draw attention to the complex and paradoxical clash of *laissez-faire* and property-rights ideologies. In this instance, despite the complexities of the issues raised, individual householders can experience at first hand such *laissez-faire* proposals as the switching of the ownership of their accommodation from public to private landlords. They can react with both ideology and collective action to such proposals. Such conflicts may lead to the widespread rejection of Housing Action Trusts (HATs) in British cities. In passing, this also illustrates the importance of ideology in state actions.

Finally, the political cultures of different countries also affect the actions of their different states. Roger Duclaud-Williams points to the propensity to centralise authority in France. He attributes this tendency to prominent values in French political culture. Other countries differ in what their strong values are. But, religion, the Confucian work ethic and business esteem are all essentially cultural phenomena which have important effects on state actions in the respective countries where they form part of the predominant value system.

We may conclude, therefore, that part of explanations of state actions will often lie with ideology and culture. These are developed over long periods of time. They are often different not only in different nation-states but also in different parts of the same country. In both respects they are an important constituent of differences, both in state actions and in their variety and effects in different locations.

Varieties of state forms and processes

Our fifth concluding theme is that the ways in which states arrive at policy decisions and actions differ according to the structure, characteristics and numbers of external organisations or groups seeking to insert their interests into those particular policies and actions. Such differences lead to a variety of state forms. This variety appears in the foregoing chapters as pluralism, corporatism, the company and contract state. The question arises, however, as to why different forms are mentioned with respect to different policies. Is it serendipity among our authors or is there some logic behind the differences?

One similarity which appears to run through the differences is that where the supply of goods or services is conducted under more market conditions then corporatist or contract forms of state and external interest interrelationships predominate. Where supply tends towards more monopolistic conditions then company interrelationships tend to predominate. Second, where the consumption of goods or services takes place under more market conditions then contract forms of provision predominate. Conversely, where consumption is publicly provided then professional and bureaucratic state interrelationships with consumers are more normal. These relationships appear to be valid both at the level of the central and at the level of the local state. They can be illustrated from the different analyses presented above.

We shall examine first the supply of services under market conditions. Michael Moran shows with respect to financial services, and David Banister that deregulated and privatized transport services, are both subject to corporatist and contract forms of state interrelationships and regulation. Thus the existence and deep-rooted historical traditions of self-regulation helps to explain that when states intervene in the market supply of financial services they do so through corporatist forms. Intervention takes place through a wide range of representative associations and formally constituted self-regulatory organisations (Michael Moran). On the other hand, where the state switches the supply, regulation and control of services like transport from the public to the private sector then contract forms of state and supplier interrelationships are developed (David Banister).

Next we can point to examples of the supply of goods and services under monopolistic or oligopolistic conditions. One of the most remarkable changes in the organisation of production during the last two decades or so is the increasing concentration of, first sectoral and later intersectoral, economic power in the hands of limited numbers of monopolistic and oligopolistic TNCs. The United Kingdom economy has been in the forefront of such change. This has contributed to changes in the numbers of major economic institutions with which states must negotiate and consequently the form of those interrelationships.

Where industrial sectors were composed of more numerous economic organisations, then corporatist forms of interest intermediation tended to develop. As the size of companies continued to increase during the 1970s many became large enough to insist on dealing directly with states. Clearly, this change is most likely to effect industrial policy-making. With respect to this policy area Wyn Grant makes the point that corporatist theories have therefore proved less useful in understanding the making of industrial policies in the 1980s than appeared possible in the 1970s. Instead, what has emerged is the company or contract state.

The purpose of the company state is to facilitate the operation of companies. Interrelations between them are handled by newly established 'government relations divisions' which supersede the activities of the industry associations characteristically used in corporatism. Monopolies and oligopolies which are involved in the conditions of company states exercise relatively high levels of power with respect to the resulting state policies.

The contract state is also characterised by a set of conditions in which private bodies are used for public purposes. The main differences between the company and contract states are that in the latter the state has more autonomy in determining who does what and there is a greater degree of market competition between contractors.

Such conditions also apply where consumption is organised through market rather than bureaucratic forms. In the case of consumption, however, two phenomena seem to run in parallel. One is the empirical shift from public to contracted supply of services. The other is a consequent reduction in democratic, forms of citizen participation in the determination of the nature, quantity and quality of those services.

The shift to contracted provision is identified by John Mohan in health, David Banister in transportation, Malcolm Harrison in housing and Roger Duclaud-Williams in education. In the last of these a contracted sector has existed for some time in the form of the Catholic schools in France and the preparatory and public schools in the United Kingdom. Shifts such as these towards contract provision of services in market conditions have been the 'flavour of the month' during the 1980s.

In many cases they are associated with a withdrawal from liberal democratic forms of the development of state policies. As Ron Johnston argues, this has been most evident at the level of the local state. While such reductions in the powers and democratic control of local authorities has been proceeding throughout the century in the United Kingdom, the pace of this change has accelerated during the 1980s. Ron Johnston compares the more recent changes to the process of de-democratisation in the peripheral states of the world economy.

In this connection, Roger Duclaud-Williams raises the question of whether increasing the numbers of pluralist groups participating in state policy-making with respect to consumption services leads to more or less democratic control of those policies. In the case of French education, he argues that increased pluralism strengthens state autonomy because the state can then pick and choose between competing, respectable claims and then chart its own course. This illustrates the old principle of 'divide and rule'. Conversely, he argues that the centralised French state has paradoxically been comparatively weak with respect to education policy because only the professional providers of that service have been involved to any great extent in policy formulation.

Our conclusion from this discussion is that pluralist, liberal and democratic forms of state action are hard to find in practice. Despite the fact that this is conventionally advanced as the model of government in Western democracies, it forms more of an ideal type from which empirical reality differs in a variety of ways in different policy fields. We have identified the main forms of departure from this ideal type as corporatist, company and contract. The first are most common in production policy-making while contract forms are being used increasingly to provide consumption services.

Varieties of state actions

We are now in a position to draw some general conclusions regarding the major examples used in this book to illustrate the variety of state actions. These conclusions are in the nature of 'middle-range' explanations of those actions.

Turning first to industrial policies, Wyn Grant cites the major sectoral examples of how to deal with overproduction in the chemicals and dairy processing industries. We may note from the discussion so far that the chemicals sector is composed largely of oligopolistic TNCs. By definition their powers and activities transcend individual national boundaries. In such cases the nation-state is a constrained and relatively ineffective actor. Where it does act it is often in concert with the companies. In the example of overcapacity in the chemicals sector, however, dealing with this problem was left mostly to the companies themselves.

In contrast, the dairy processing industry is geographically confined within individual nation-states. It is also composed of numerous production and processing organisations. In these circumstances state policies were needed to reduce overcapacity. These were developed in concert with intermediary associations. This was therefore a fairly 'classic' case of corporatist forms of interrelationships between the state and producers.

In the case of financial markets, Michael Moran argues that state interventions are institutionally complex and differentiated. This reflects a similar complexity in those markets themselves. He lists the variety of state actions as ranging from ownership through direction, licensing and inspection. Although the general trend in recent years has been towards deregulation, states have been unable to abandon finance to the marketplace altogether. The reason for this is that financial markets would not work at all without the framework guaranteed by state power.

The state is required to intervene in financial markets first because those markets are now global. This requires nation-states to harmonise local regulations in order to prevent any other nation from cornering those markets. Thus, 'big bang' in London was forced on the City by the way New York markets were developing. The state had to change the local rules to accommodate required dealing conditions.

Second, the state is needed to ensure some degree of propriety in financial markets. Crises and scandals shake the critical factor of 'confidence'which is essential to the operation of financial markets.

Finally, the state is required to control the conditions of competitive struggles in these markets. This is because, at the moment, no individual organisations are sufficiently dominant to do this and, if they were, this would have significant implications for the competitive nature of those markets.

The variety and complexity of financial markets therefore gives rise to a range of state actions conducted in bureaucratic, corporatist and contract modes. The paradox of deregulation seems to be that state actions become different rather than less.

Deregulation is also the current fashion in transportation (David Banister). In this example state actions have been changing from those of public to contract provision. The state is able to make such decisions because of the geographical limitations of most companies and the existence of competitive markets in this policy area.

Again, deregulation tends to involve different rather than less state action. New roles have been developed, for example, for both the Monopolies and Mergers Commission and the Office of Fair Trading. The latter has acquired responsibilities for such problems as the predatory practices of different bus companies. The state has also had to establish executive agencies such as the Vehicle Inspectorate. David Banister also raises the question of how far such forms of contract provision may be employed to provide transportation infrastructure on scales larger than the Channel Tunnel or the Dartford–Thurrock road bridge.

In the policy fields of local consumption-management Malcolm Harrison raises the special example of land-use planning. He points to the fact that land-use planning is one of the few areas where public participation and judicial supervision of executive action have developed because private property is involved.

The private property involved is also of two different kinds. One is that used for the purposes of production and the other is privately-owned accommodation. This produces a divergence of interests in the allocation of new land uses between 'land users' and 'land inhabitants'. The former tend to engage in corporatist forms of negotiation with local planning authorities. The latter have insisted that, as Malcolm Harrison says, planning has become more open to pluralist pressures at the local level. In practice this means that concessions have had to be made by 'land users', sometimes in the form of planning gain, to 'land inhabitants'.

Finally, Roger Duclaud-Williams cites the major example of the way in which the British and French governments adjusted the supply of trained teachers in the 1970s. He reaches the initially surprising conclusion that the centralised French government had much less success in achieving this aim than did the formally less centralised British.

The main reason for this difference was that where, as in the French case, the state 'chose' to provide a public service like education in a bureaucratised and centralised manner, it unintentionally locked itself into constraining institutional forms and created powerful trade union and professional opposition. This made it very difficult to achieve the end of reducing the supply of trained teachers. In the British case where more pluralist interests were involved, the state was able to pick a course between them by selecting allies who would also support its preferred policy solutions.

This last case study also serves to show how unpredictable the nature of pluralist outcomes can be. There is no guarantee that they will necessarily favour the interests of the consumers rather than the providers of services.

That serves as a suitable note on which to end these conclusions. It underlines the overall conclusion of this book. It is that the empirical reality of state action in Western democracies demonstrates considerable variety and that although some interests are undoubtedly favoured more often than others there are many exceptions which prove this rule.

Bibliography

Acheson, D. (1981), *Primary health care in inner London: report of a study group*, London: DHSS.

Aday, L.A., Andersen, R., Fleming, G. (1980), *Health care in the U.S.: equitable for whom?* London: Sage.

Alford, R.R. (1975), *Health care politics: ideological and interest group barriers to reform* Chicago: University of Chicago Press.

Alford, R. and Friedland, R. (1985), *Powers of theory*, Cambridge: Cambridge University Press.

Albu, A. (1980), 'British attitudes towards engineering education', in Pavitt, K. (ed.), *Technical innovation and British economic performance*, London: Macmillan.

Ambrose, P. (1986), 'Whatever happened to planning?', London: Methuen.

Ascher, K. (1987), *The politics of privatisation: contracting out private services*, London: Macmillan.

Ashford, D. (1982), *British dogmatism and French pragmatism, central-local policymaking in the welfare state*, London: Allen and Unwin.

Association of Metropolitan Authorities (1986), *Achievements in council housing*, London: Association of Metropolitan Authorities.

Association of Metropolitan Authorities (1988) *Housing facts*, London: Association of Metropolitan Authorities.

Atkinson, M.M. (1986), 'The bureaucracy and industrial policy', in Blais, A. (ed.), *Industrial policy* (Toronto: University of Toronto Press).

Aubert, V. et al. (1985) *La forteresse enseignante*, Paris: La Fédération de l'Education Nationale, Fayard.

Audit Commission (1986), *Managing the crisis in council housing*, London: HMSO.

Bailey, E.E. (1986) Deregulation: causes and consequences, *Science*, 234, 1211–16.

Ballion, R. (1982), *Les consommateurs d'ecole*, Paris: Stock.

Bassett, K. (1984), 'Labour, socialism and local democracy', in Boddy, M. and Fudge, C. (eds), *Local Socialism?*, London: Macmillan.

Baumol, W.J. (1982) Contestable markets: an uprising in The Theory of industry structure, *American Economic Review*, 72, 1, 1–15.

Bergthold, L. (1984), 'Crabs in a bucket: the politics of health care reform in California', *Journal of Health Policy, Politics and Law*, 9, 2, 203–22.
Bergthold, L. (1987), 'Business and the pushcart vendors in an age of supermarkets', *International Journal of Health Services*, 17, 1, 7–26.
Bergthold, L. (1988), 'Purchasing power business and health policy change in Massachusetts', *Journal of Health Policy, Politics and Law*, 13, 3, 425–52.
Berrill, Sir K. (1986), 'Regulation in a changing city – bureaucrats and practitioners', *Midland Bank Review*, Summer, 14–19.
Birnbaum, P. (1980), 'States, ideologies and collective action in western Europe', in *Social Science Journal*, 32.
Birnbaum, P. (1982), *The heights of power*, Chicago: University of Chicago Press.
Birnbaum, P. (1988), *States and collective action*, Cambridge: Cambridge University Press.
Birnbaum, P. and Badie, B. (1983), *Sociology of the state*, Chicago: University of Chicago Press.
Bishop, A. S. (1971), *The rise of a central authority for education*, Cambridge: Cambridge University Press.
Blais, A. (1986a), 'Industrial policy in advanced capitalist democracies', in Blais, A. (ed.), *Industrial Policy*, Toronto: Toronto University Press.
Blais, A. (1986b), *A political sociology of public aid to industry*, Toronto: Toronto University Press.
Boddy, M. and Fudge, C. (eds) (1984), *Local socialism*. London: Macmillan.
Bodenheimer, T.S. (1989), 'The fruits of empire rot on the vine: US health policy in the austerity era', *Social Science and Medicine*, 28, 6, 531–8.
Booth, P. and Crook, T. (1986), *Law cost home ownership*, Aldershot: Gower.
Boumard, P., Hess, R. and Lapassade, G. (1987), *L'université en transe*, Paris: Syros.
Bowles, S. and Gintis, H. (1976), *Schooling in capitalist America*, London: Routledge and Kegan Paul.
Bowles, S. and Gintis, H. (1986), *Democracy and capitalism*, London: Routledge and Kegan Paul.
Boyd, R. (1987), 'Government–industry relations in Japan: access, communication and competitive collaboration', in Wilks, S. and Wright, M. (eds), *Comparative government–industry relations*, Oxford: Clarendon Press.
Braendgeard, A. (1986), 'Danish industrial policy: liberalism revised or revisited', in Hall, G. (ed.), *European industrial policy*, London: Croom Helm.
Brickman, R., Jasanoff, S. and Ilgen, T. (1985), *Controlling chemicals: the politics of regulation in Europe and the United States*, Ithaca: Cornell University Press.
Brown, P. (1988), 'Recent trends in the political economy of mental health' in Giggs, J. and Smith, C.J. (eds) *Location and stigma: contemporary perspectives on mental health and mental health care*, London: Allen and Unwin.
Brown, P. and Ashton, D. (eds) (1987), *Education, unemployment and labour markets*, Falmer: Falmer Press.
Bulpitt, J. (1983), *Territory and power in the UK*, Manchester: Manchester University Press.

Burnett, John (1978), *A social history of housing 1815–1970*, London: Methuen.
Burns, H. (1974), *The American banking community and new deal banking reforms, 1933–35*, Westport: Greenwood Press, 1974.
Califano, J. (1988), *America's health care revolution*,
Caroli, B. (1987), *First ladies*, New York: Oxford University Press.
Carr-Hill, R. (1988), 'The inequalities in health debate: a critical review of the issues', *Journal of Social Policy*, 18, 509–42.
Carswell, J. (1986), *Government and the universities in Britain*, Cambridge: Cambridge University Press.
Cawson, A. (1982), *Corporatism and welfare*, London: Heineman Educational.
Cawson, A. (1982), *Corporatism and welfare social policy and state intervention in Britain*, London: Heinemann Educational.
Cawson, A. (ed.) (1985), 'Organised interests and the state', London: Sage.
Cawson, A. and Saunders, P. (1983), 'Corporatism, competitive politics and class struggle', in King, R. (ed.), *Capital and politics*, London: Routledge and Kegan Paul.
Cawson, A., Holmes, P. and Stevens, A. (1987), 'The interaction between firms and the state in France: the telecommunications and consumer electronics sectors', in Wilks, S. and Wright, M. (eds) *Comparative government–industry relations*, Oxford: Clarendon Press.
Central Policy Review Staff (1980), *Education, training and industrial performance*, London: HMSO.
Chancellor of the Exchequer (1984), 'Building Societies: a new framework', Cmnd. 9316, HM Treasury, London; HMSO.
Chandler, M.A. (1986), 'The state and industrial decline: a survey', in Blais, A. (ed.), *Industrial policy*, Toronto: Toronto University Press.
City University Housing Research Group (1981), 'Could local authorities be better landlords?', London: The City University Housing Research Group.
Clapham, David (1987), 'The new face of public housing', in Clapham, D and English, J. (eds), *Public housing: current trends and future developments*, London: Croom Helm.
Clapham, David (1989), *Goodbye council housing?* London: Unwin Hyman.
Clark, G.L. (1981), 'Law, the state and the spatial integration of the United States', *Environment and Planning A*, 13, 1197–227.
Clark, G.L. (1984), 'A theory of local autonomy', *Annals of the Association of American Geographers*, 74, 195–208.
Clark, G.L. (1985), *Judges and the cities*, Chicago: University of Chicago Press.
Clark, G.L. and Dear, M.J. (1984), *State apparatus*, Boston, Mass.: George Allen and Unwin.
Cockburn, C. (1977), *The local state*, London: Pluto Press.
Cohen, P. and McRobbie, A. (eds) (1987), *Training without jobs*, London: Macmillan.
Cohen, S.S. and Zysman, J. (1987), *Manufacturing matters: the myth of the post-industrial economy*, New York: Basic Books.
Cohodes, D.R. (1986), 'America: the home of the free, the land of the

uninsured', *Inquiry*, 23, 227–35.

Conlan, T (1988), *New federalism: intergovernmental reform from Nixon to Reagan* Washington: Brookings Institution.

Cooper, W. (1987), 'The financial services trade war', *Institutional Investor*, November, 117–20.

Corrigan, P. (1979), 'The local state', *Marxism Today*, July.

Coulter, P. (1975), *Social mobilization and liberal democracy*, Lexington, Mass. Lexington Books.

Cowan, R. (1985), 'Ill wind in the willows', *Roof*, 10, 5, 11–14.

Cox, G., Lowe, P. and Winter, M. (1987a), 'The state and the farmer: perspectives on industrial policy', in Cox, G. Lowe, P. and Winter, M. (eds), *Agriculture: people and policies*, London: Allen and Unwin.

Cox, G., Lowe, P. and Winter, M. (1987b), 'Agriculture and conservation in Britain: a policy community under siege', in Cox, G. Lowe, P. and Winter, M. (eds) *Agriculture: people and policies*, London: Allen and Unwin.

Craig, P. (1986), 'The house that jerry built? Building societies, the state and the politics of owner-occupation', *Housing Studies*, 1, 2, 87–108.

Craig, P. and Harrison, M.L. (1984), 'Corporatism and housing policy: the best possible political shell?', in Harrison, M.L. (ed.), *Corporatism and the Welfare State*, Aldershot: Gower.

Crookell, H. (1985) 'The impact of government intervention on the major appliance industry in Canada', in McFetridge, D.G. (ed.) *Canadian industrial policy in action*, Toronto: University of Toronto Press.

Crosland, A. (1971), 'Towards a labour housing policy,' Fabian Tract 410, Herbert Morrison Memorial Lecture, London: Fabian Society.

Crozier, M. (1964), *The bureaucratic phenomenon*, London: Tavistock.

Crozier, M. et al. (1974), *Où va l'administration Francaise?* Paris: Les Editions d'Organisation.

Curwen, P.J. (1986), *Public enterprise: a modern approach*, Brighton: Wheatsheaf Books.

Daunton, Martin (ed.) (1984), *Councillors and tenants: local authority housing in English cities, 1919–1939* Leicester: Leicester University Press.

David, S.M. and Kantor, P. (1979), 'Political theory and transformations in urban budgetary arenas: the case of New York city', in Marshall, D.R. (ed.) *Urban policy making* Beverley Hills: Sage.

Davies, C. (1987) 'Things to come: the NHS in the next decade', *Sociology of Health and Illness*, 9, 302–17.

Davis, M. (1984), 'The political economy of later imperial America', *New Left Review*, 143, 8–38.

Dearlove, J. (1979), *The re-organisation of British local government*, London: Cambridge University Press.

De Baecque, F. and Quermonne, J. L. (1981), *Administration et politique sous la 5 ème republique, Janvier 1959–Mai 1981*, Paris: Presses de la Fondation Nationale des Sciences Politiques.

de Kervasdoné J. and Rodwin V.G. (1984), 'Health policy and the expanding role of the state, 1945–80', in de Kervasdoné, J., Kimberly, J.R. and

Rodwin V. (eds), *The end of an illusion: the future of health policy in western industrialized nations*, Berkeley and Los Angeles: University of California Press.

De Maupeou-Abboud, N. (1974), *Ouverture du ghetto etudiant*, Paris: Editions Anthropos.

Department of the environment (1977), *Housing Policy: A Consultative Document* London: HMSO.

Department of the Environment (1980), 'Land for private housebuilding', Circular 9/80, London: HMSO.

Department of the Environment (1984), 'Land for housing', Circular 15/84, London: HMSO.

Department of the Environment (1989), 'The nature and effectiveness of housing management in England; London: HMSO.

Department of Transport (1984), *Airline competition policy*, London: HMSO.

Department of Transport (1978), *Report on the review of highway inquiry procedures*, Cmnd. 7133, London: HMSO.

Department of Transport (1988), *Vehicle inspectorate becomes first executive agency*, Press Notice 383, 25 July.

Department of Transport (1989), *Transport statistics: great Britain 1978–1988, London: HMSO.*

Department of Transport BR Network South East , LRT London Underground Ltd, (1989), *Central London Rail Study*, London: HMSO, January.

De Swaan, A. (1988), *In case of the USA in the modern era*, Cambridge: Polity Press.

Deubner, C. (1984), 'Change and internationalization in industry: toward a sectoral interpretation of West German politics', *International Organization*, 38, 501–35.

Deyo, F, C. (ed.) (1987), *The political economy of the new Asian industrialism*, Ithaca: Cornell University Press.

Dillon, J.F. (1911), *Commentaries on the law of municipal corporations*, Boston, Mass.: Little, Brown.

Donegani, J. M. and Sadoun, M. (1976), 'La réforme de l'enseignement secondaire en France depuis 1945', *Revue Française de Science Politique*, **26**, no. 6.

Downs, A. (1957), *An economic theory of democracy*, New York: Harper and Row.

Dubar, C. (1980), *Formation permanente et contradictions sociales*, Paris: Editions Sociales.

Duchêne, F. and Shepherd, G. (eds) (1987), *Managing industrial change in Western Europe*, Oxford: Martin Robertson.

Duclaud-Williams, R. (1978), *The politics of housing in Britain and France*, London: Heinemann.

Duclaud-Williams, R. (1983), 'Centralization and incremental change in France: the case of the Haby educational reform', *British Journal of Political Science*, **13**.

Duclaud-Williams, R. (1985), 'Local politics in centralized systems: the case of French education', *European Journal of Political Research*, **13**.

Duclaud, Wiliams, R. (1985), 'Teacher unions and educational policy in France', in Lawn, M. *The Politics of Teacher unionism*, London: Croom Helm.

Duclaud-Williams, R. (1988), 'Policy Implementation in the French public bureaucracy: the case of education', *Western European Politics*

Duclaud-Williams, R. (1988), 'Student protest, 1968 and 1986 compared' in Hanley, D. (ed.) *May 1968 twenty years on*, London: Macmillan.

Duncan, S. and Goodwin, M (1988), *The local State and uneven development*, Cambridge: Polity Press.

Duncan, S. and Goodwin, M. (1982b), 'The local state and restructuring social relations', *International Journal of Urban and Regional Research*, 6, 157–86.

Duncan, S. and Goodwin, M. (1982a). 'The local state functionalism, autonomy and class relations in Cockburn and Saunders, *Political Geography Quarterly*, 1, 77–96.

Dunleavy, P. (1979), 'The urban bases of political alignment', *British Journal of Political Science*, 9, 409–43.

Dunleavy, P. (1980a), *Urban political analysis*, London: Macmillan.

Dunleavy, P. (1980b), in Jones, G. (ed.), *Central-Local Relations*, Aldershot: Gower.

Dunleavy, P. (1981), *The politics of mass housing in britain 1945–1975*, Oxford: Clarendon Press.

Dunleavy, P. (1982), 'Quasi-governmental sector professionalism: some implications for public policy-making in Britain', in Bar A: *Quangos in Britain*, London: Macmillan.

Dunleavy, P. (1984), 'The limits to local government', in Boddy, M. and Fudge, C. (eds), *Local Socialism?*, London: Macmillan.

Dunleavy, P. (1986a) 'Explaining the privatization boom: public choice versus radical approaches', *Public Administration*, **64**, 1, 13–34.

Dunleavy, P. (1986b), in Goldsmith, M. (ed.), *Central-Local Relationships*, Aldershot: Gower.

Dunleavy, P. and Duncan, K. (1989), *Understanding the politics of transport*, Paper presented at the ESRC Seminars on Decision-Making Processes in Transport, London, March.

Dunleavy, P. and O'Leary, B. (1987), *Theories of the State*, Cambridge: Polity Press.

Dunleavy, P. and Rhodes, R. (1983), 'Beyond Whitehall', in Drucker H. et al. 106–33.

Dunsire, A. (1982), 'Challenges to public administration in the 1980s', *Public Administration Bulletin*, 39, August, 8–21.

Dyson, K. (1980), *The state tradition in western Europe*, Oxford: Martin Robertson.

Dyson, K. and Wilks, S. (eds) (1983), *Industrial crisis*, Oxford: Martin Robertson.

Dyson, K. and Wilks, S. (1983), 'Conclusions' in Dyson K. and Wilks, S. (eds) *Industrial crisis* Oxford: Martin Robertson.

Eaglesham, E. (1956), *From schoolboard to local authority*, London: Routledge & Kegan Paul.

Elazar, D.J. (1984), *American federalism: a view from the states*, New York: Harper and Row.

East Japan Railways (1987), Restructuring of the Japanese National Railways – Process leading to Privatisation and Division, August.

Elston, M. (1988), *The sociology of professional dominance: medicine in a changing health service*, Paper presented to an ESRC/British Sociological Asociation meeting on *Medical Sociology Problems of the Eighties*, London, December. Revised version forthcoming in Calnan, J. Bury, M. and Gabe, J. (eds) *Medical sociology: problems of the eighties* London: Routledge and Kegan Paul. European Conference of Ministers of Transport (1988), *Regulatory reform in the transport sector*, Paris: ECMT.

European Conference of Ministers of Transport (1988) *Investment in Transport Infrastructures in ECMT Countries*, Paris, OECD.

Feldman, R. (1986), *Japanese financial markets: deficits, dilemmas and deregulation*, Cambridge, Mass.: MIT Press.

S.E. Finer, (ed.) (1975), *Adversary politics and electoral reform*, London: Anthony Wigram.

Flora, P., and Alber, J. (1981), 'Modernization, democratization and the development of welfare states in western Europe', in Flora, P. and Heidenheimes, A.J. (eds), *The development of welfare states in Europe and North America*, New Brunwick: Transaction Books.

Flora, P and Heidenheimer, A.J. (1981), 'The historical core and changing bondaries of the welfare state', in Flora, P. and Heidenheimer, A.J. (eds), *The Development of welfare states in Europe and North America*, New Brunswick: Transaction Books.

Forrest, R. and Murie, A. (1988), *Selling the welfare state*, London: Routledge and Kegan Paul.

Fox, D.M. (1986), *Health policies, health politics: the British and American experience 1911–1965*, Princeton, NJ: Princeton University Press.

Frankel, J. (1984), *The yen/dollar agreement: liberalising Japanese capital markets*, Washington: Institute for International Economics/MIT Press.

Frobel, F., Heinrichs, J. and Kreye, O. (1980), *The new international division of labour*, Cambridge: Cambridge University Press.

Fuchs, R.V. (1986), *The health economy*, Cambridge, Mass.: Harvard University Press.

Gallup (1988) *Council Tenants 30 March–12 April 1988*, London Social Surveys (Gallup Poll) Ltd.

Gamble, A. (1981), *An introduction to modern social and political thought*, London: Macmillan

Gamble A. (1988), *The free economy and the strong state*, Basingstoke: Macmillan.

Ganz, G. (1977), *Government and industry*, Abingdon: Professional Books.

Gillis, R.P. and Roach, T.R. (1986), *Lost initiatives: Canada's forest industries, forest policy and forest conservation*, New York: Greenwood Press.

Gilpin, R, (1987), *The political economy of international relations* Princeton: Princeton University Press.

Gilroy, P. (1982), 'Steppin' out of Babylon – race, class and autonomy', in Centre for Contemporary Cultural Studies, *The empire strikes back*, London: University of Birmingham Hutchinson.

Ginzberg, E. (1986), 'The destabilization of health care', *New England Journal of Medicine*, 315, 757–61.

Gordon, M. (1981), *Government in business*, Montreal: C. D. Howe Institute.

Gough, I. (1979), *The political economy of the welfare state*, London: Macmillan.

Gower, L.C.B. (1982), *Review of investor protection: a discussion document*, London: HMSO.

Gower, L.C.B. (1984), *Review of investor protection: report: part 1*, London: HMSO. Cmnd. 9125,

Grant, J. (1977), *The politics of urban transport planning*, London: Earth Resources Research.

Grant, W. (1982), *The political economy of industrial policy*, London: Butterworth.

Grant, W. (1986), 'Why employer organisation matters', University of Warwick Department of Politics Working Paper.

Grant, W. (ed.) (1987), *Business interests, organizational development and private interest government: an international comparative study of the food processing industry*, Berlin: de Gruyter.

Grant, W. (1989), *Government and industry: a comparison of the US, Canada and the UK*, Upleadon: Edward Elgar.

Grant, W., Paterson, W. and Whitston, C. (1988), *Government and the chemical industry: a comparative study of Britain and West Germany*, Oxford: Clarendon Press.

Graz, A. (1986), 'Where has the urban crisis gone?', in Gottdeiner, M. (ed.), *Cities in Stress*, Beverley Hills: Sage.

Green, D. (1983), 'Strategic management and the state: France', in Dyson, K. and Wilks, S. (eds.) *Industrial crisis*, Oxford; Martin Robertson.

Greenwood, J. and Wilson, D. (1984), *Public administration in Britain*, London Allen and Unwin.

Gremion, P. (1976), *Le pouvoir périphérique*, Paris Seuil.

Griffith, B., Iliff, S. and Baynor, G. (1987) *Banking on Sickness: Commercial Medicine in Britain and the USA*, London, Lawrence and Wishart.

Griffiths, R. (1983) *NHS Management Inquiry Report*, London, DHSS.

Gwilliam, K. (1989), 'Setting the market free: deregulation of the bus industry, *Journal of Transport Economic and Policy*, 23 1, 29–43.

Gyford, J. (1986), *The politics of local socialism*, London: Allen and Unwin.

Hall, P. (1986), *Governing the economy*, Cambridge: Polity Press.

Hall, S. (1985), Authoritarian populism: a reply to Jessop et al.', *New Left Review*, 151, 115–24.

Ham, C. (1985), *Health policy in Britain*, London: Macmillan, 2nd edn.

Hamon, H. and Rotman, P. (1984), *Tant qu'il y aura des profs*, Paris: Seuil.

Hansard (1979), House of commons, Parliamentary Debaters, Session 1978–79, 15 May cols. 79–80.

Harden, I. and Lewis, N. (1986), *The noble lie*, London: Hutchinson.

Harris, L. (1980), 'The state and the economy: some theoretical problems', *Socialist Register*, 17, 243–62.

Harris, N. (1986), *The end of the third world: newly industrializing countries and the decline of an ideology*, Harmondsworth: Penguin.

Harrison, M.L. (ed.) (1984) *Corporatism and the welfare state*, Aldershot: Gower.

Harrison, M. L. (1984) 'The Coming Welfare Corporatism', *New Society*, 67, 1110, 321–3.

Harrison, M. L. (1986), 'Consumption and urban theory: an alternative approach based on the social division of welfare', *International Journal of Urban and Regional Research*, 10, 2, pp. 232–42.

Harrison, M. L. (1987), 'Property rights, philosophies, and the justification of planning control', in Harrison, M. L. and Mordey, R. (eds), *Planning control: philosophies, prospects and practice* London: Croom Helm.

Harvey, D. (1982). *The limits to capital*, Oxford: Blackwell.

Hayward, J.E.S. (1986), *The state and the market economy: industrial patriotism and economic intervention in France*, Brighton: Wheatsheaf.

Hayward, S. and Renate, W. (1989). *Privatizing from within: the NHS under Thatcher, Local Government Studies*, 15, pp. 19–34.

Heald, D. A. (1984), 'Privatisation': analysing its appeal and limitations', *Fiscal Studies*, 5, 1, 36–46.

Heald, D. A. and Thomas D. (1986), 'Privatisation as theology', *Public Policy and Administration*, 1 (1), 49–66.

Heertie, E. (ed.) (1988), *Innovation, technology, and finance*, Oxford: Blackwell.

Helco, H. and Wildavsky, A. (1981, 2nd edn), *The private government of public money*, London: Macmillan.

Henderson, D. (1986), *Innocence and design: the influence of economic ideas on policy*, Oxford: Blackwell.

Hensher, D. A. (1986), 'Privatisation: an interpretative essay', *Australian Economic Papers*, 25 47, 147–74.

Hepworth, N. P. (1988), *What future for local government?* Institute of Economic Affairs, Inquiry Number 4, August.

Heycock, M. (1986), 'The social content of development control: an analysis of planning appeal decisions in relation to housing need', Brunswick Environmental Paper 61, Brunswick School of the Environment, Leeds Polytechnic.

Hiatt, H. M. (1987), *America's health in the balance: choice or chance?* New York: Harper and Row

Hills, John (1987), *The voluntary sector in housing: the role of housing associations*, London: London School of Economics.

Hindess, B. (1987), *Freedom, equality, and the market: arguments on social policy*, London: Tavistock Publications.

Hirsch, F. (1977), 'The Bagehot problem', *The Manchester School*, 241–57.

Hodge, D. and Staeheli, L. (1990), 'Social transformation and changing urban electoral behaviour', in Johnston, R. J., Shelley, F. M. and Taylor, P. J.

(eds) *Developments in electoral geography*, London: Routledge and Kegan Paul.

Hood, C. (1981), 'Axeperson spare that quango', in Hood, C. and Wright, M. (eds), *Big government in hard times*, Oxford: Martin Robertson.

Hood, S. and Young, N. (1984), 'Conclusions: the way ahead', in Hood, N. and Young, S. (eds) *Industry, policy and the Scottish economy*, *Edinburgh: Edinburgh University Press*.

Horne, J. (1985), *Japan's financial markets: conflict and consensus in policymaking*, London: Allen and Unwin.

House of Commons (1985) 2nd *Report from the social services Committee: community care with special reference to adult mentally ill and mentally handicapped people*, London: House of Common.

Ingham, G. (1984) *Capitalism divided? The city and industry in British social development*, Basingstoke: Macmillan, 1984.

Inquiry into British housing (1985), Report of the National Federation of Housing Associations, London.

Institute of housing (1987), *Preparing for Change*, Institute of Housing, London.

Irvine, K. (1987), *The right lines*, London: Adam Smith Institute.

Issel, W. (1985), 'Social change in the United States, 1945–53', London: Macmillan.

Jenkins, K., Oates, G. and Stott, A. (1985), *Making things happen: a report on the implementation of government efficiency scrutinies*, Report to the Prime Minister, London: HMSO.

Jessop, B. Bonnett, K. Bromley, S. and Ling, T. (1984), 'Authoritarian populism, two nations, and Thatcherism', *New Left Review*, 147, 32–60.

Johnson, C. (1984), 'Introduction: the idea of industrial policy', in Johnson, C. (ed.), *The industrial policy debate*, San Francisco: ICS Press.

Johnston, R. J. (1979), *Political, electoral and spatial systems*, Oxford: Oxford University Press.

Johnston, R. J. (1982), *Geography and the state*. London: Macmillan.

Johnston, R. J. (1983), 'Texts and higher managers: judges, bureaucrats and the political organization of space', *Political Geography Quarterly*, 2, 3–20.

Johnston, R. J. (1984a), 'Human geography as a generalising social science: trans-Atlantic contrasts in local government', *The Geographical Journal* 150, 335–41.

Johnston, R. J. (1984b), *Residential segregation, the state and constitutional conflict in American metropolitan areas*, London: Academic Press.

Johnston, R. J. (1984c), 'The political geography of electoral geography', in Taylor, P. J. and House, J. W. (eds), *Political geography: recent advances and future directions*. London: Croom Helm.

Johnston, R. J. (1985), 'Places matter,' *Irish Geography*, 18, 58–63.

Johnston, R. J. (1986a), 'Placing politics', *Political Geography Quarterly*, 6, s63–s78.

Johnston, R. J. (1986b), 'The general good of the community', *Planning Perspectives*, 1, 131–45.

Johnston, R. J. (1986c), 'Individual freedom and the world-economy,' in Johnston, R. J. and Taylor, P. J. (eds), *A world in crisis?*, Oxford: Blackwell.

Johnston, R. J. (1987), 'Dealignment, volatility and electoral geography'. *Studies in Comparative International Development*, 22, 3–25.

Johnston, R. J. and Taylor, P. J. (1987). 'Basic geographical divisions in the modern world,' *Geographical Education* 5, 3, 5–11.

Jones, G. (1980), 'Introduction', *Central–local relations*, Aldershot: Gower.

Judd, D. R. (1979), *The politics of American cities*, Boston, Mass.: Little, Brown.

Karn, Valerie (1985), 'Housing', in Ranson, S. Jones, G. and Walsh, K. (eds), *Between centre and locality* London: Allen and Unwin.

Katzenstein, P. J. (1984), *Corporatism and change: Austria, Switzerland and the politics of industry*, Ithaca: Cornell University Press.

Katzenstein, P. J. (1985), *Small states in world markets: industrial policy in Europe*, Ithaca: Cornell University Press.

Kay, J. A. and Thompson, D. J. (1986), 'Privatisation: a policy in search of a rationale', *Economic Journal*, 96 1, 18–32.

Kellerman, B. (1982), *All the president's kin*, London: Robson.

Kindleberger, C. (1978), *Maniacs, panics and crashes: a history of financial crises*, London: Macmillan.

King, R. (1985), 'Corporatism and the local economy', in Grant, W. (ed.), *The political economy of corporatism*, London: Macmillan.

Kinzer, D. (1988), 'The decline and fall of deregulation', *New England Journal of Medicine*, 318, 2, 112–16.

Klein, R. (1984), 'The politics of ideology versus the reality of politics: the case of Britain's NHS in the 1980s', *Milbank Mem. Fund Q: Hlth. Soc.*, 62 1, 82–109.

Knox, P.L. and Cullen, J. (1981), 'Planners as urban managers', *Environment and Planning A*, 13, 885–9.

Kogan, M. (1971), *The government of education*, London: Macmillan.

Krieger, J. (1986), *Reagan, Thatcher, and the politics of decline*, Cambridge: Polity Press.

Krieger, J. (1987), 'Social policy in the age of Reagan and Thatcher', *Socialist Register*, 177–98.

Laffin, M. (1986), *Professionalism and policy: the role of the professions in the central–local government relationship*, Aldershot: Gower.

Lash, S. and Urry, J. (1987), *The end of organized capitalism*, Cambridge: Polity Press.

Laver, M. (1984), 'The politics of inner space: tragedies of three commons', *European Journal of Political Research*, 12, 59–71.

Laver, M. (1986), 'Public, private and common in outer space', *Political Studies*, 34, 359–73.

Lawton, D. (1980), *The politics of the school curriculum*, London: Routledge and Kegan Paul.

Le Grand, J. (1982), *The strategy of equality*, London: Allen and Unwin.

Le Grand, J. and Robinson, R. (eds.) (1984), *Privatisation and the welfare state*, London: Allen and Unwin.

Le Grand, L. (1982), *Pour un collège démocratique*, Paris: La Documentation Française.

Liebenstein, H. (1966), 'Allocative efficiency and X-efficiency', *American*

Economic Review, 56, 392–415.

Lindblom, C.E. (1977), *Politics and Markets*, New York: Basic Books.

Lowi, T. (1972), 'Four systems of policy, politics and choice', *Public Administration Review*, 32, 298–310.

Lundmark, K. (1983), 'Welfare state and employment policy: Sweden', in Dyson, K. and Wilke, S. (eds), *Industrial Crisis*, Oxford: Martin Robertson.

Luft, H.S. (1985), 'Competition and regulation', *Medical Care*, 23 5, 383–400.

McFetridge, D.G. (1985), 'The economics of industrial policy', in McFetridge, D.G. (ed.), *Canadian industrial policy in action*, Toronto: University of Toronto Press.

Macpherson, C. (1966), *The real world of democracy*, Oxford: Clarendon Press.

Malpass, P. and Murie, A. (1987), *Housing policy and practice*, London: Macmillan.

Mann, M. (1984), 'The autonomous power of the state: its origins, mechanisms and results'. *European Journal of Sociology*, 25, 185–213.

Mann, M. (1986), *The sources of social power. Volume 1*. Cambridge: Cambridge University Press.

Market and Opinion Research International (1988), *Council tenants' attitudes towards housing*, London: MORI.

Marmor, T.R. and Morone, J. (1983), *Political analysis and American health care*,

Marsh, N. (ed.) (1987), *Public access to government-held information* London: Stevens.

Massey, D. (1984), *Spatial divisions of labour*, London: Macmillan.

Maurice, M. Sellier, F. and Silvestre, J.-J. (1986), *Politiques d'education et organisation industrielle en France et en Allemagne*, Cambridge, Mass: MIT Press.

Mawson, J. and Miller, D. (1986), 'Interventionist approaches in local employment and economic development', in Hausner, V. (ed.), *Critical issues in urban economic development. Volume I*, Oxford: Clarendon Press.

Maynard, A (1974), *Health care in the European community*, London: Croom Helm.

Mény, Y. (1984), 'Decentralisation in socialist France', *Western European Politics*, 7, 1.

Mény, Y. and Wright, V. (1987a), 'State and steel in western Europe', in Mény, and Wright, V. (eds) *The politics of steel: western Europe and the steel industry in the crisis years*, Berlin: de Gruyter.

Mény, Y. and Wright, V. (eds) (1987b), *The politics of steel: western Europe and the steel industry in the crisis years*, Berlin: de Gruyter.

Merrett, Stephen (1979), *State housing in Britain*, London: Routledge and Kegan Paul.

Middlemas, K. (1979), *Politics in industrial society*, London: Deutsch.

Miller, G.J. (1981), *Cities by contract*, Cambridge, Mass.: MIT Press.

Miller, S. (1985), 'Self-regulation of the securities markets: a critical examination', *Washington and Lee Law Review*, 42, 853–7.

Mills, L. and Young, K. (1986), 'Local authorities and economic development: a preliminary analysis', in Hausner, V. (ed.), *Critical issues in urban economic development. Volume I*, Oxford: Clarendon Press.

Minister without Portfolio (1985), *'Lifting the burden'*, Cmnd. 9571, London: HMSO.

Mohan, J.F. (1989), 'Commercialisation and centralisation: towards a new geography of health care' in Mohan, J.F (ed.) *The political geography of contemporary Britain*, London: Macmillan.

Moran, M. (1981), 'Monetary policy and the machinery of government', *Public Administration*, 59, 47–61.

Moran, M. (1986), *The politics of banking*, 2nd edn, London: Macmillan.

Mordey, R. (1987), 'Development control, public participation and the need for planning aid', in Harrison, M.L. and Mordey, R. (eds), *Planning Control: Philosophies, Prospects and Practice*, London: Croom Helm.

Morichi, S. (1987), 'Financial resources for railway construction', *Journal of the Japanese Society of Civil Engineers*, 72, 10, 43–8 (translation from the Japanese).

Morris, R. (1987), 'Rethinking welfare in the United States: the welfare state in transition' in Friedmann, R.R., Gilbert, N. and Sherer, M. (eds), *Modern Welfare States: a Comparative View of Trends and Prospects*, Brighton, Wheatsheaf.

Murie, Alan (1985), 'The nationalization of housing policy', in Loughlin, M. Gelford, M.D. and Young, K. (eds), *Half a century of municipal decline 1935–1985*, London: Allen and Unwin.

Myrdal, G., (1944), *An American Dilemma*, New York: Harper and Brothers.

National Audit Office (1987), *Department of Trade and Industry: assistance to industry under section 8 of the Industrial Development Act 1982*, London: HMSO.

National Audit Office (1988), *Road planning*, Report by the comptroller and Auditor general, No. 688 (October) London: HMSO.

National Audit Office (1989), *Coronary Heart Disease*, House of Commons Paper HC-208, London: HMSO.

Navarro, V. (1978), *Class struggle, the state, and medicine*, London: Martin Robertson.

Navarro, V. (1986), *Crisis, health and medicine: a social critique*, London: Tavistock.

Newton, K. and Karran, T. (1985), *The politics of local expenditure*, London: Macmillan.

O'Connor, J. (1971), *The fiscal crisis of the state*, New York: St. Martin's Press.

Oda, H. and Grice, R.G., (eds), (1988), *Japanese banking, securities and anti-monopoly law*, London: Butterworths.

OECD (1983), *Positive Adjustment Policies* Paris: Organisation for Economic Cooperation and Development.

OECD (1987), *Financing and delivering health care: a comparative analysis of OECD countries*, Paris: OECD.

OECD, *International trade in services: securities* Paris: OECD.

Offe, C. (1984), *Contradictions of the welfare state*, London: Hutchinson.

Offe, C. (1985), *Disorganized capitalism contemporary transformations of work and politics*, Cambridge: Polity Press.

Ohta, K. (1989), 'The development of Japanese transportation policies in the context of regional development', *Transportation Research*, 23A, 1, 91–101.

O'Leary, B. (1987), 'Why was the GLC abolished?' *International Journal of Urban and Regional Research*, 11, 193–217.

Orbach, Laurence (1977), *Homes for heroes*, London: Seeley Services.

Osei-Kwame, P. and Taylor, P.J. (1984), 'A politics of failure', *Annals of the Association of American Geographers*, 74, 574–89.

Pahl, R.E. (1975), *Whose City?*, London: Longman.

Palmer, I. (1985), 'State theory and statutory bodies', *Sociology*, **19**, 4, 523–40.

Palmer, J.L. and Sawhill, J.V. (eds) (1984), *The Reagan record: an assessment of America's changing domestic priorities*, Cambridge, Mass.: Ballinger.

Panitch, L. (1980), 'Recent theorisations of corporatism', *British Journal of Sociology*, 31, 159–87.

Pater, J. (1981), *The making of the National Health Service*, London: King's Fund.

Patten, John (1987), 'Rented sector has failed says Patten', *Housing association weekly*, 13 March.

Peet R. (ed.) (1987), *International capitalism and industrial restructuring*, Boston Mass.: George Allen and Unwin.

Périé, R. (1987), *Education nationale à l'heure de la décentralisation*, Paris: La Documentation Française.

Pestoff, V. (1987), 'The effect of state institutions on associative action in the food processing sector', in Grant W., (ed.), *Business interests, organizational development and private interest government*, Berlin: de Gruyter.

Petchey, R. (1986), 'The Griffiths reorganisation of the NHS: Fowlerism by stealth?', *Critical Social Policy*, 17, 87–101.

Plant, R. (1983), 'The resurgence of ideology', in Drucker, H. (ed.), *Developments in British politics*, London: Macmillan.

Pliatzky Report (1980), *Report on non-departmental public bodies*, Cmmd. 7797, London: HMSO.

Pollitt, C. (1980), 'Performance measurement in the public services: some political implications', *Parliamentary Affairs*, **39**, 3, 315–29.

Power, Anne (1984), *Local Housing Management: a priority estates project survey*, London: Department of the Environment.

Power, Anne (1987), *The crisis in council housing: is public housing manageable?* London: HMSO.

President's Commission on Industrial Competitiveness (1985), *Volume 1: global competition: the new reality* Washington, DC: Government Printing Office.

Prost, A. (1968), *Histoire de l'enseignement en France de 1800 à 1967*, Paris: Armand Colin.

Raine, J. (1981), *in defence of local government*, Birmingham: University of Birmingham, INLOGOV.

Ranade, W. and Haywood, S. (1989),'Privatizing from within: the NHS under Thatcher', *Local Government Studies*, 15, 19–34.

Ranson, S. and Tomlinson J. (eds) (1986), *The changing government of education*, London: Allen & Unwin.

Reade, E. (1984), 'Town and county planning', in Harrison, M.L. (ed.), *Corporatism and the Welfare State*, Aldershot: Gower.

Remond, R. Coutrot, A. and Boussard, I. (1982), *Quarante ans de cabinets ministériels*, Paris: Presses de la Fondation Nationale de Sciences Politiques.
Rees, R. (1986), 'Is there an economic case for privatisation?' *Public Money* 5, 4, 19–26.
Reid, M. (1982), *The secondary banking crisis, 1973–75*, London: Macmillan.
Reid, M. (1988), *All-change in the city: the revolution in Britain's financial sector*, London: Macmillan.
Renaud, M. (1975), 'On the structural contraints to state intervention in health', *International Journal of Health Services*, 5,559–71.
Rex, J., (1986), *Race and ethnicity*, Milton Keynes: Open University Press.
Rex, J. and Mason, D. (eds) (1986), *Theories of race and ethnic relations*, Cambridge: Cambridge University Press.
Rhodes, R. (1981), *Control and power in central–local relations*, Aldershot: Gower.
Rhodes, R. (1985), *The national works of local government*, London: Allen and Unwin.
Rhodes, R. (1986a), in Goldsmith, M. (ed.), *Central–local relationships*, Aldershot: Gower.
Rhodes, R. (1986b), 'The changing relationships of the national community of local government, 1970–83', in Goldsmith, M. (ed.) *Central–local relations*, Aldershot: Gower.
Richardson, J. and Jordan, G. (1985), *Governing under pressure*, Oxford: Blackwell.
Rickard, J. (1986a), 'Privatisation in the transport sector, in Ramanadhan, V.V. (ed.), *Privatisation in the UK*, London: Rantledge and Kegan Paul.
Rickard, J. (1988b), *Private sector finance in transport*, Paper Presented at the PTRC Annual Conference.
Rivett, G (1986) *The development of the London hospital system, 1823–1982*, London: King Edwards Hospital Fund.
Richardson, J. and Jordan, G. (1979), *Governing under pressure*, Oxford: Blackwell.
Ringen, S. (1987), *The possibility of politics: a study in the political economy of the welfare state*, Oxford: Oxford University Press.
Ringer, F. (1979), *Education and society in modern Europe*, Bloomington: Indiana University Press.
Rokkan, S. and Urwin, D. (1983), *Economy, territory and identity: politics of west European peripheries*, London: Sage.
Rose, R. (1974), *The problem of party government*, London: Macmillan.
Rose, R. (1980), *Do parties make a difference?*, London: Macmillan.
Rostow, W.W. (1960), *Stages of economic growth*, Cambridge: The University Press.
Rydin, Y. (1984), 'The struggle for housing land: a case of confused interests', *Policy and Politics*, 12, 4, 431–46.
Rydin, Y. (1986), *Housing land policy*, Aldershot: Gower.
Sakita, M. (1989), 'Restructuring of the Japanese national railways: review and analysis', *Transportation Quarterly*, 43, 1, 29–45.
Salter, B. and Tapper, T. (1985), *Power and policy in education – the case of the independent schools*, Falmer: Falmer Press.

Sardell, A. (1988), *The V.S. experiment in social medicine: the community health center program 1965–86*, Pittsburg: University of Pittsburg Press.

Saunders, C. (ed.) (1981), *The political economy of new and old industrial countries*, London: Butterworths.

Saunders, P. (1979), *Urban politics*. London: Hutchinson.

Saunders, P. (1980), 'Local government and the state', *New Society*, 51, 550–1.

Saunders, P. (1984), 'Rethinking local politics', in Boddy, M. and Fudge, C. (eds), *Local socialism?*, London: Macmillan.

Saunders, P. (1985), 'Corporatism and urban service provision', in Grant, W. (ed.) *The political economy of corporatism*, London: Macmillan.

Saunders, P. (1986), *Social theory and the urban question*, London: Hutchinson, 2nd edn.

Savary, A. (1985), *En toute liberté*, Paris: Hachette.

Schaffer, B. and Lamb, G. (1981), *Can equity be organized?* Aldershot: Gower and Paris: UNESCO.

Scharpf, F.W. (1988), 'The joint-decision trap: lessons from German federalism and European integration', *Public Administration*, 66, 3, 239–78.

Scheingold, S. (1974), *The politics of rights*, New Haven: Yale University Press.

Schinn, T. (1980), *L'ecole polytechnique*, Paris: Presses de la Fondation Nationale des Sciences Politiques.

Schmandt, H.J. and Wendel, G.D. (1983), 'Health care in America: a political perspective in Greer, S. and Greer, A.L. (eds), *Cities and sickness health care in urban America* (Urban Affairs Annual Reviews, vol. 25) New York and London: Sage.

Schmitter, P. and Lehmbruch, G. (1979), *Trends towards corporatist intermediation*, New York and London: Sage.

Schmitter, P.C. (1974) 'Still the century of corporalism?' *Review of Politics*, 36, 85–131.

Schuller, T. (1986), *Age, capital and democracy: member participation in pension scheme management*, Aldershot: Gower.

Schultz, R. and Alexandroff, A. (1985), *Economic regulation and the financial system*, Toronto: University of Toronto Press.

Secretaries of State for the Environment and Wales (1977), *Housing policy: a consultative document*, Cmnd, 6851, London: HMSO.

Seligman, J. (1982), *The transformation of Wall Street*, Boston: Houghton Mifflin.

Sharpe, L.J. and Newton, K. (1984), *Does politics matter?*, Oxford: Oxford University Press.

Short, J., Fleming, S. and Witt, S. (1986), *Housebuilding, planning and community action*, London: Routledge and Kegan Paul.

Sidenius, N.C. (1983), 'Danish industrial policy: persistent liberalism', *Journal of Public Policy*, 3, 9–61.

Simmie, J. (1986), 'Structure plans, housing and political choice in the south east', *Catalyst*, 2, 2, 71–83.

Simpson, I. (1987), 'Planning gain: an aid to positive planning?', in Harrison, M.L. and Mordey, R. (eds), *Planning control: philosophies, prospects and practice*, London: Croom Helm.

Smith, D. (1983), in Held, D. et al. (eds) *States and societies*, Oxford: Martin Robertson.
Smith, D. (1987), 'Knowing your place', in Thrift, N. and Williams, P. (eds), *Class and space*, London: Routledge and Kegan Paul.
Smith, N. (1984), *Uneven Development*, Oxford: Blackwell.
Smith, A. and Jacobson B. (eds) (1988), *The nation's health: a strategy for the 1990s* A report from an Independent Multidisciplinary Committee chaired by Professor Alwyn Smith, London: King Edward's Hospital Fund.
Soisson, J. P. et al. (1986), *Enjeu de la formation professionnelle*, Paris: Fayard.
Sonnenblum, S., Kirlin, J. and Rees, J. (1977), *How cities provide services: an evaluation of alternative delivery systems*, Cambridge, Mass: Ballinger.
Sack, R.D. (1983), 'Human territoriality: a theory', *Annals of the Association of American Geographers*, 3, 55–74.
Sack, R.D. (1986), *Human territoriality*, Cambridge: Cambridge University Press.
Starkie, D.N.M. (1982), *The motorway age*, Oxford: Pergamon.
Starkie, D.N.M. (1984), 'BR: Privatisation without tears', *Economic Affairs* 5, 1, 16–19.
Starr, P. (1982), *The social transformation of American medicine*, New York: Basic Books.
Starr, R. (1987), *Richard Hatfield: the seventeen year saga*, Halifax, NS: Formac.
Stevens, B. (1988), 'Blurring the boundaries: how the federal government has influenced welfare benefits in the private sector', in Weir, M. et al. (eds) *The politics of social policy in the United States*, Princeton, NJ: Princeton University Press.
Stevens, R. (1986), 'The future of the medical profession', in Ginzberg, E (ed.), *From physician shortage to patient shortage*, Boulder Col: Westview Press.
Stevenson, G. (1982), *Unfulfilled union: Canadian federalism and national unity*, Toronto: Gage.
Strange, S. (1986), *Casino capitalism*, Oxford: Blackwell.
Strange, S. (1988), *States and markets: an introduction to international political economy*, London: Pinter.
Streeck, W. (1983), 'Beyond pluralism and corporatism: German business associations and the state', *Journal of Public Policy*, 3, 265–84.
Stretzer, D.F. (1975), *Special districts in Cook County*, Research Paper 169, Chicago: Department of Geography, University of Chicago.
Suleiman, E. (1974), *Power and bureaucracy in France, the administrative elite*, Princeton, NJ: Princeton University Press.
Suleiman, E. (1977), 'Higher education in France: a two-track system', in *Western European Politics*, 1, 3.
Suzuki, Y. (1987), *The Japanese financial system*, Oxford: Clarendon Press.
Swenarton, Mark (1981), *Homes fit for heroes* London: Heinemann.
Tabb, W.K. and Sawers, L. (eds) (1984), *Marxism and the metropolis*, New York: Oxford University Press.
Taebel D.A. and Cornehls, J.V. (1986), 'Ideological and policy perspectives

of urban transportation', in De Boer, E. (ed.), *The sociology of transport*, Oxford: Pergamon.

Taylor, P. (1984), *Smoke ring: the politics of tobacco*, London: Bodley Head.

Taylor, P.J. (1985), *Political geography: world-economy, nation-state and locality*, London: Longman.

Taylor, P.J. (1986), 'An exploration into world-systems analysis of political parties', *Political Geography Quarterly*, 5, S5–S16.

Taylor, P.J. (1988), 'The myth of developmentalism', in D. Gregory,   and Walford, R. (eds), *New models in geography*, London: Macmillan.

Taylor, R.C.R. (1984), 'State intervention in postwar western European health care: the case of prevention in Britain and Italy', in Bornstein, S., Held, D. and Krieger, J. (eds), *The state in capitalist Europe*, London: Allen and Urwin.

Teaford, J.C. (1979), *City and suburb*, Baltimore: Johns Hopkins University Press.

Therborn, G. and Roebroek, J. (1986), 'The irrevesible welfare state: its recent maturation, its encounter with the economic crisis, and its future prospects', *International Journal of Health Services* **16**, 3, 319–78.

Thompson, D. (1988), 'Privatisation: introducing competition, opportunities and constraints', in Ramanadham, V.V. (ed.), *Privatisation in the UK* London: Routledge and Kegan Paul.

Thompson, F.J. (1987), 'New federalism and health care policy: states and the old questions', *Journal of Health Policy, Politics and Law*, **11**, 4, 647–70.

Tiebout, C.M. (1956), 'A pure theory of local expenditures', *Journal of Political Economy*, 64, 516–35.

Townsend, P. and Davidson, N. (1982), *Inequalities in health: the Black report*, Harmondsworth: Penguin.

Trebilcock, M. (1986), *The political economy of economic adjustment: The case of declining sectors*, Toronto: University of Toronto Press.

Tullock, G. (1965), *The politics of bureaucracy*, Washington DC: Public Affairs Press.

Tupper, A. (1986), 'Federalism and the politics of industrial policy', in Blais, A. (ed.) *Industrial policy* Toronto: University of Toronto Press.

Tyson, W.J. (1988), *A review of the first year of bus deregulation*, Report to the Association of Metropolitan Authorities and Passenger Transport Executive Group, August.

United States' Congress (1986), *Restructuring financial markets: report*, Committee on Energy and Commerce, US House of Representatives, 99th Congress, 2nd Session, Print 99 – DD.

Urry, J. (1981), *The anatomy of capitalist societies: The economy, civil society and the state*, Basingstoke: Macmillan.

Usher, D. (1987), *Housing Privatisation: The Sale of Council Estates*, Working Paper 67, Bristol: School for Advanced Urban Studies, University of Bristol.

Vaudiaux, J. (1974), *La formation permanente – enjeu politique*, Paris Armand Colin.

Veljanovski, C. (1987), *Selling the state: privatisation in Britain*, London: Weidenfeld and Nicholson.

Vickers, J. and Yarrow, G. (1988), *Privatization: an economic analysis*, London: MIT Press.

Vincent, G. (1987), *Sciences-Po: Histoire d'une réussite*, Paris: Olivier Orban.

Vogel, D. (1986), *National styles of regulation*, Ithaca: Cornell University Press.

Wakiyama, T. (1987), 'The implementation and effectiveness of MITI's administrative guidance', in Wilks, S. and Wright M. (eds), *Comparative government–industry relations*, Oxford: Clarendon Press.

Waldegrave, William (1987), *Some reflections on housing policy*, London: Conservative Party News Service.

Walford, G. (1984), *British public schools: policy and practice*, Falmer: Falmer Press.

Weir, M., Orloff, A.S. and Skocpol, T. (1988), 'Understanding American social policies', in Weir, M. et al. (eds), *The politics of social policy in the United States*, Princeton, NJ: Princeton University Press.

Wetherley, P. (1988), 'Class struggle and the welfare state: some theoretical problems considered', *Critical Social Policy*, 22, 24–40.

Whitehead, C.M.E. (1983), 'Housing under the conservatives: a policy assessment', *Public Money*, 3, 1, June.

Whitehead, C. and Kleinman, M. (1986), *Private rented housing in the 1980s and 1990s*, Cambridge: Department of Land Economy, University of Cambridge.

Whitener, M. (1988a), 'The steady erosion of Japan's 'Glass-Steagall'', *International Financial Law Review*, May, 11–14.

Whitener, M. (1988b), 'Japan tackles insider trading', *International Financial Law Review*, June 15–18.

Whitt, J.A. (1982), *Urban elites and mass transportation: the dialectics of power*, Princeton, NJ: Princeton University Press.

Wilks, S. and Wright, V. (eds) (1987), *Comparative government–industry relations*, Oxford: Clarendon Press.

Williams, N.J., Sewel, J.B. and Twine, F.E. (1987), 'Council house sales and the electorate: voting behaviour and ideological implications', *Housing Studies*, 2, 4, 274–82.

Williamson, O.E. (1975), *Markets and hierarchies: analysis and antitrust implications*, New York: The Free Press.

Willis, D. and Grant, W. (1987), 'The United Kingdom: still a company state?', in van Schendelen, M.P.C.M. and Jackson, R.J. (eds), *The politicisation of business in western Europe*, London: Croom Helm.

Wilson, Sir H. (1980), *Report of the Committee to Review the Functioning of Financial Institutions*, Cmnd. 7937, London: HMSO.

Wooley, J. (1984), *Monetary politics: the federal reserve and the politics of monetary policy*, Cambridge: Cambridge University Press.

Young, S. and Hood, N. (1984), 'Industrial policy and the Scottish economy', in Hood, N. and Young, S. (eds), *Industry, policy and the Scottish economy* Edinburgh: Edinburgh University Press.

Zysman, J. (1983), *Governments, markets and growth*, Ithaca: Cornell University Press.

Zysman, J. (1983), *Governments, markets and growth: financial systems and the politics of industrial change*, Oxford: Martin Robertson.

Name Index

Subject Index